AN IRISHMAN IN THE IRON BRIGADE

Mr. and Mrs. Robert A. Sullivan (John Ehlers)

Pvt. James P. Sullivan in his Iron Brigade frock in late 1862, while he was in Wisconsin before his second enlistment.

AN IRISHMAN IN THE IRON BRIGADE

The Civil War Memoirs of JAMES P. SULLIVAN, Sergt., Company K, 6th Wisconsin Volunteers

by

WILLIAM J. K. BEAUDOT

and

LANCE J. HERDEGEN

FORDHAM UNIVERSITY PRESS
New York

Copyright © 1993 by Fordham University Press
All rights reserved
LC 93–12574
ISBN 0–8232–1500–8 (hardcover)
ISBN 0–8232–1501–6 (paperback)
ISSN 1044–5315
Irish in the Civil War, No. 3
Reprinted 2001

Library of Congress Cataloging-in-Publication Data

Beaudot, William J. K.
    An Irishman in the Iron Brigade : the Civil War memoirs of
James P. Sullivan, Sergt., Company K, 6th Wisconsin volunteers /
William J. K. Beaudot, Lance J. Herdegen.
        p.   cm.—(Irish in the Civil War, ISSN 1044–5315 ; no. 3)
    Includes bibliographical references and index.
    ISBN 0-8232-1500-8
    1. Sullivan, James P., Sgt.   2. Wisconsin—History—Civil War,
1861–1865—Personal narratives.   3. United States. Army. Wisconsin
Infantry Regiment, 6th (1861–1865)   4. United States—History—Civil
War, 1861–1865—Personal narratives.   5. Wisconsin—History—Civil
War, 1861–1865—Participation, Irish American.   6. United States—
History—Civil War, 1861–1865—Participation, Irish American.
7. Irish Americans—Wisconsin—Biography.   I. Herdegen, Lance J.
II. Title.   III. Series.
E537.5 6th.B4   1993
973.7′475—dc20   93-12574
                                                            CIP

Printed in the United States of America

CONTENTS

Photographs following page 48

SERIES EDITOR'S PREFACE

The Irish experience in the American Civil War assumed many guises. Probably the best known Irish soldiers were those who served in all-Irish units, under green Irish flags, and accompanied by Catholic chaplains. Such units preserved and strengthened the separate cultural identity of Irish-Americans. On the Union side the Irish Brigade, Corcoran's Legion, and several other green-flag Irish regiments became focal points for Irish interest, both in America and in the old country, in the Civil War. For many, the experience of such ethnic units became synonymous with the Irish experience in the Northern armies.

Yet the great majority of the more than 150,000 Irish-Americans who fought for the Union did not serve in ethnic regiments. Most were sprinkled in smaller groups throughout the 2,000 regiments raised in the North during the war. In many ways, then, the experience of James "Mickey" Sullivan, who served four eventful years with the 6th Wisconsin Volunteer Infantry, was perhaps more typical of the Irish Civil War experience than was that of the Irish-American soldier who served in an ethnic unit alongside his own countrymen. The 6th Wisconsin was a typical regiment from the upper midwest, composed primarily of native-born Protestant farmers, but also containing a diverse group of Germans, Irishmen, and Scandinavians. But its wartime history was anything but typical.

In 1861 the 6th Wisconsin became part of what would become the "Iron Brigade," a collection of midwestern regiments that earned its nickname for the tenacity it showed on the rugged slopes of South Mountain during the Antietam campaign. Famous for their black hats as well as their fighting spirit, the men of this unit went on to compile a battle record unsurpassed by any brigade in the Union army. From their first significant action at Brawner Farm in northern Virginia in 1862 to their desperate struggle in the "Bloody Railroad Cut" at Gettysburg, they slashed their way into Civil War history. Virtually destroyed at Gettysburg, they lost more men in battle than any similar Union unit in the war.

All the while, "Mickey" Sullivan, with his Irish courage and contagious good humor, fought and joked his way through the war. Fortunately for us, in later years he took the time to preserve the memories of his Iron Brigade exploits in the columns of some local Wisconsin newspapers. From his comical but dangerous confrontation with General Burnside to his spectacular view of Pickett's charge at the battle of Gettysburg, these memories were well worth preserving. Personal, opinionated, picturesque, and hilarious, these reminiscences reveal a unique Irish voice from America's Civil War. We are all indebted to William J. K. Beaudot and Lance J. Herdegen for letting Sullivan speak to a new generation about what he experienced in his years with the 6th Wisconsin Volunteer Infantry.

LAWRENCE FREDERICK KOHL

ACKNOWLEDGMENTS

There are many who have provided kind assistance and offered suggestions and encouragement in the process of producing this book. At the very top of that list are Pat Sullivan
of La Crosse, Wisconsin, and James F. Sullivan of New Port
Richey, Florida. Pat's husband, Bob, is a great-grandson of
"Mickey" Sullivan and she has accepted the task of assem-
bling the Sullivan lore. James F., of course, is Sullivan's son,
and a soldier-poet of some reputation himself. They helped
find and define the elusive "Mickey, of Company K."

Also high on the list is Tom Tomczak, general materials
coordinator for the Milwaukee Public Library, who so gra-
ciously permitted access to files of the *Milwaukee Sunday
Telegraph*. As well, the staff and collections of that library
were invaluable, as was the staff at the Carroll College Library where the W. Norman FitzGerald Civil War Collection
is housed. Our special thanks go also to Dr. Lawrence F. Kohl
of the University of Alabama. His suggestions were thought-
ful and showed his fine scholarship.

We must, too, acknowledge the support and enthusiasm of
our families and friends.

WILLIAM J. K. BEAUDOT
LANCE J. HERDEGEN
Milwaukee, 1993

FOREWORD

It wasn't the brains at the top, but the guts at the bottom that made the Civil War an everlasting monument to the heart and stamina of the common "foot-slogger," soldier, "dog-face"—the "G. I. Joe."

No stone or bronze statue of a sword-brandishing general will ever take the place of the monument forever nestled in the hearts of those who read of their unassuming bravery, their patient acceptance of hardships undreamed of by those never experiencing them.

The common Civil War infantryman's intuition concerning the leadership abilities of those above, his utter contempt for the brainless posturing of those who led them into the "jaws of Hell" and shed their blood on the woods and fields of countless mismanaged conflicts was a tribute to the stock from whence they came, and even though their "book-larning" might have been sadly lacking, their common sense and rural "know-how" gave them an intelligence far greater than credited them.

We Americans, North and South, should never forget that even during some of the bitterest fights of the Civil War, the soldiers of both sides shared their coffee and hardtack whenever possible.

May a loving God, in His infinite wisdom, give them the peace they so richly deserve.

JAMES F. SULLIVAN,
proud son of "Mickey" of Co. K
May 1992

Old Company K
By Mickey of Company K

There are hats[1] in the closets, old, ugly to view,
Of very slight value they may be to you.
But the wealth of the Astors should not buy them to-day,
With letters of honor, old Company "K."

Bright eyes have looked calmly their broad brims beneath,
On the work of the reaper, grim harvester death.
And never once faltered or turned the wrong way,
When with cheers into battle rushed Company "K."

When with noble appearance, and line straight and true,
And lithe springing step, they passed in review,
Their soldierly bearing forced the Generals to say,
They march better than regulars, grand Company "K."

'Twas at the South Mountain,[2] in that terrible pass,
Where soldiers were falling, as a mower cuts grass.
Blood crossing the road caused McClellan to say,
"They are men made of iron, brave Company 'K.' "

When our lines they were broken, and backward did lag,[3]
And old "Daddy Wadsworth" rushed up to Bragg,
Saying the Rebs are triumphant, you must save the day,
Then charged like a whirlwind, old Company "K."

And where are the comrades, so kind and so brave,
Who proudly left Mauston, the Union to save?
The death-roll, so lengthy, does mournfully say,
How foremost in battle was Company "K."

But the Heavenly Commander has said, we have heard,
That duty, well done, shall have its reward.
When the long roll is sounded, the great muster day,
May we all meet in Heaven—brave Company "K."

Notes

1. [These footnotes to the poem were written by Sullivan.] The Iron Brigade wore the U.S. Army regulation big hats, and it was a common remark with the rebel prisoners that their officers used to say, "It's no use to fight that Big Hat Brigade, we will only get cut to pieces."

2. At South Mountain the blood of the killed ran down the side of the mountain and across the turnpike in a large stream.

3. At Fitz Hugh's Crossing, where we charged across the Rappahannock in pontoon boats in the face of their batteries on the heights and the infantry in breastworks on the opposite bank, and drove them away, opening a passage for the army to cross.

AN IRISHMAN IN THE IRON BRIGADE

INTRODUCTION

No soldier went off to the Civil War in 1861 with lighter step than James Patrick Sullivan. A hired man in Juneau County, Wisconsin, when the war started, the farmer boy was among the first to answer President Lincoln's call for volunteers. "I wanted to do what I could for my country," he said. Sullivan went on to serve his four years, give or take a few weeks, in the most celebrated organization in the Army of the Potomac—the "Iron Brigade of the West." He fought in a score of major battles. The Johnnies shot off a toe at South Mountain, left him shell-shocked at Second Bull Run, wounded him in the shoulder at Gettysburg, and knocked him cold with an artillery burst at Weldon Rail Road. But the most unlikely injury of his war days came at the hands of a 7th Wisconsin soldier in his own brigade: a whack from a musket ramrod accidentally fired during a ceremonial volley of blanks. "Nothing discouraged," his company commander wrote later, Sullivan bore all with reckless Irish courage and good humor. He was the only man in his regiment to formally enlist on three separate occasions.[1]

In his volunteer days Sullivan was remembered as "full of mischief," with a sharp glint in his friendly blue eyes—what in the camps was called "a thorough-going soldier." A photograph from 1862 (frontispiece) shows him in a knee-length, blue wool army frock coat, his dark hair carefully combed, the young face full of resolve, and shoulders squared so he might appear taller for the camera. One old comrade recalled the boy soldier of 1861–65 "never lost a fight, never neglected a duty." Sullivan was decidedly "Western" in outlook, with a brash Gaelic manner and the frontier conviction that he was as good as any man, with shoulder straps or without. It was not surprising to discover, in reading the records of his regiment, a notation that "Private James P. Sullivan," while on sentry duty, was caught "conversing with Rebel Pickets and attempting to cross over the river." He was fined $13—a month's pay.[2] His first captain, Rufus Dawes, who always took a more sober view of life, recalled Sullivan's "unconquerable good humor and genuine wit," and said: "For genuine sallies of humor at unexpected times, I never saw his equal. Such men are of priceless value in an army." Another comrade left a stronger assessment: "A hundred men wore the star of generals who did not dare or do as much in the war as J. P. Sullivan."[3]

In 1865 Sullivan returned to civilian life with a new wife (met in Philadelphia while recovering from his Gettysburg wound) and an infant son. The ex-soldier had seen much and done more, and nothing was ever quite the same. Like many Wisconsin veterans, he took his new family to the Dakota Territory to look for opportunity, but the dry Plains country was so unlike the green, rolling river bluffs of his boyhood that he was soon home. By 1880 he had moved to south central Wisconsin and again was farming. It was dull work for a fellow who had seen Second Bull Run, South Mountain, Gettysburg, and Appomattox Court House, but there were fields to plow, a family to raise, and a crop to tend—enough to keep a man busy. The years passed—not all easily—and it was a long time before he again recalled his days with "Old Company K" of the 6th Wisconsin Volunteers in the "Iron Brigade." The memories stirred him to seek out the old comrades and read the newspapers carrying the "soldier news" of reunions and veteran camp-fires. In time, Sullivan began to write his own stories of his war days, and in those delightful yarns he was "Mickey of Company K" or "the true Irishman himself"—a plucky "greenhorn patriot" the bigger fellows told to go home "to feather out" as he was too small for tossing rebels over his shoulder with a bayonet.

Like so many of the ex-soldiers, James P. Sullivan came to regard his four years in Union blue as one of the most important times in his life. Certainly that recognition was voiced by many of the old veterans as they talked of days long ago when they were "marching along" on young, tireless legs and looking with bright, clear eyes on "a hundred circling camps." One of Sullivan's old comrades from the 6th Wisconsin, Milwaukee newspaperman Jerome A. Watrous,[4] tried to explain it in print:

> How true it is that for a dozen or fifteen years after the war ended, the soldiers seemed to shun their experience. Their three or four years of hard service, in a terrible war, was more than they anticipated, and it proved a well rounded up load, mentally and physically. But now, almost twenty years after returning to civil life, they look back to the stirring times from '61 to '65, and recall the experiences and incidents with the keenest pleasure. The ties of friendship and affection which bind the veterans together are very powerful. That of no fraternal or secret society compares with it. We may account in part for the readiness of comrades to talk about the war from the fact that all who participated in the great struggle are more proud of that service than anything they have done in the whole course of their lives. Is it not something to be proud of?[5]

Certainly that was the case with James Sullivan. He began writing of his soldier days in the 1880s, complaining that the accomplishments of his famous brigade were being overlooked and forgotten. "It may be owing to the fact that our men were not of the hymn-singing, testament-carrying kind who spent their time in camp in writing home letters of the 'Just Before The Battle Mother' variety," Sullivan said, "but they were always ready for march or battle, and when that was over they were more interested in a stag dance or penny ante than what the newspapers were saying about them. . . ."[6] He would try to set the record straight.

Life for Sullivan in the 1880s lacked the drama of his war years. Graying now, and suffering twinges of pain—reminders of old battle hurts, including a splinter of a rebel shell carried in the base of his skull—the soldier-turned-farmer was angry for himself and for comrades who were attempting to secure some government recompense for years of hard service. In one of his stories, written in 1883, Sullivan complained of his current life working "a worthless forty acres of land" in Forest Township, a Vernon County community of less than 900.[7] He railed against men of the "coffee cooling brigade" who, during the war, "could make money out of the blood of the soldier," and were now raising impediments to pensions. In the winter of 1884 he wrote again, taking issue with pension examining boards which accused wounded veterans, such as himself, of malingering—of their failure "to do a full day's work in a harvest field." He fumed at the "red tape, spies and disgraceful methods" which sought to portray "every soldier to be a perjured, lying rascal. . . ."

When Sullivan himself attempted to secure homestead acreage in Wisconsin after the war, the U.S. Land Department wanted proof that his father was naturalized before he could obtain a patent. The government, Sullivan pointed out, required no proof of citizenship in 1863 when his older brother, John, enrolled for the draft. John Sullivan, in fact, served in the famous 8th Wisconsin Infantry until 1865. Left unsaid, of course, was that J. P. Sullivan, himself an immigrant, apparently needed no proof of naturalization when he volunteered in 1861, or when, after being wounded at South Mountain and discharged for disability, he re-enlisted a second time.[8] It was all troubling. He was doing his best to maintain a meager farm with a wife, Angeline, met and married during the war; a 20-year-old son, George, born in 1865, and three growing youngsters—Anna, 11, John, 10, and James, 7 (not James F., born to J. P.'s second marriage and still living at this writing). The nation seemed to be drifting into an era that Sullivan, and many like him, could not understand. The Republican Party, a source of postwar veteran strength, had split in 1884, the liberal wing bolting for Democrat Grover Cleveland. Even the conquered South was once again on the rise with former rebel generals and officials ascendant and regaining control; they seemed to be winning politically what they had lost militarily.[9]

On a visit to Madison, Sullivan was further disturbed to discover that his own state had no record of what he and his comrades of the old brigade had achieved two decades earlier on the battlefields of Virginia, Maryland, and Pennsylvania. Wisconsin annually appropriated thousands of dollars "wrung from poor and often needy farmers" to pay university professors, educate lawyers, or support state fairs, he wrote with anger in 1883, while there were not even a few dollars to "prepare a record of the patriotism of those who gave health, wealth, life and limb, for the honor of our state."[10]

Like many old soldiers those days, the Wisconsin veteran was also struggling emotionally to put the great experience of his youth in perspective, to stamp his life with some semblance of validity, and to leave a record for posterity. After all, the former general and president, Ulysses S. Grant, was setting down memoirs during his last diseased days of life.[11] And many Eastern writers, whom Sullivan readily took to task, were confecting recollections and war histories. Even traitorous former Confederate President Jefferson Davis, a man Sullivan held partly responsible for sundering the Union, just three years before published his massive apologia for the Confederacy.

Writing as "Mickey, of Company K," Sullivan did not seek to glorify or mythologize what he and his old comrades in the 6th Wisconsin had accomplished. He told his story in straight-ahead Western fashion: quick to disparage incompetent generals who failed the men, "patriotic speculators" who fleeced the volunteers of their pay, and an army that carelessly tossed out the used-up soldier. And he was sarcastically critical of the "great and good" national government whose mismanagement made life more miserable for the men in ranks.[12] Sullivan was not systematic in his writings; he wrote only of things that interested him, not of every battle and camp. His first piece, for example, published in 1883, was an account of Gettysburg. It was not until 1886 that he wrote of the raising of his company in the early days of the war; only in 1888 did he describe his wounding at South Mountain.

In mid-September of 1883 he journeyed to the nearby Mississippi River town of La Crosse to attend the reunion of the Iron Brigade Association, an organization formed by the former soldiers who had served in the old brigade—the 2nd, 6th, and 7th Wisconsin, 19th Indiana, 24th Michigan, and Battery B of the 4th U.S. Artillery. Established in 1880, it provided an occasion each year for the old comrades to gather, renew friendships, and talk about those days of youth when they had stood the test of battle and saved the Union. Sullivan, in fact, was the first enlisted man to address the gathering, having been invited by his former regimental and brigade commander, Edward S. Bragg—at the time a Wisconsin congressman.[13]

At La Crosse he renewed acquaintance with Jerome A. Watrous, who was running a small feature and society weekly newspaper in Milwaukee. In his dispatch on the "camp-fire," Watrous briefly mentioned Sullivan and called him "a man of note." But the man of 1883, Watrous also observed, was "not the smooth-faced boy of '61"—Sullivan's "side whiskers and whitening hair tell of twenty-two years flown."[14] The talk itself was a great success; "Mickey, of Company K," a great camp favorite of those days long ago, told of his regiment's role in a Rappahannock River crossing under fire during the Chancellorsville campaign in 1863.[15]

The meeting led to a contributor-editor relationship. Watrous had taken the editor's chair at *The Milwaukee Sunday Telegraph* in 1879 and quickly tapped into the rising tide of the veterans' movement. He wrote and solicited recollections and "letters" from the old soldiers, and Sullivan was a contributor the next six years. Using his war journals, diaries, and letters to refresh his memories, Sullivan wrote of the soldier-in-ranks and told of Second Bull Run, South Mountain, Gettysburg, and of army pets and camp tricks. The "boys" asked for more, and for a brief, shining time Sullivan was again famous as "Mickey, of Company K"—the "soldier-poet" of the old 6th Wisconsin Volunteers.

But the moment was fleeting. The years crowded in and soon took a toll on the veterans, old war injuries keeping more and more close to home and calling others to "the final muster." Then the Spanish-American War claimed the nation's attention and energy; Sullivan himself volunteered for duty as a recruiting officer. By the turn of the century, *The Telegraph* had closed its doors and was already being forgotten—one of dozens of failed newspapers. Sullivan himself died in 1906, and a year later his old war diaries, journals, and letters were swept away in a flood at his old home town. By then, just a handful of people remembered "Mickey, of Company K," and his stories of the Civil War.

More than a century would pass before Sullivan's writings were again printed, and it was all by chance that they were rediscovered. In 1987 the authors were given a copy of a newspaper clipping of his Gettysburg story by former Milwaukee postal official Merton G. Eberlein, then retired and living at Mauston, where he was active with local history groups. He found the account pasted in a scrapbook preserved by the Van Wie family, whose kinsmen served with such distinction in the 6th Wisconsin. There was no indication of publication or date, but Sullivan's story of Gettysburg gave rise to the thought of a possible book on the forgotten charge of the 6th Wisconsin at Gettysburg—a goal accomplished in 1990.[16] It was while researching the action at the railroad cut that other Sullivan stories were found in the dusty, bound volumes of *The Telegraph* preserved at the Milwaukee Public Library.

J. P. "Mickey" Sullivan himself proved to be more elusive. There were a few brief mentions of Sullivan in Rufus R. Dawes' classic war memoir of his regiment, *Service with the Sixth Wisconsin Volunteers,* and only a little more in the state's war records. Ultimately, the search resulted in a telephone call to Mrs. Robert A. Sullivan of La Crosse, who had done some genealogical research at the Hillsboro Public Library. After a brief introduction, she was asked: "Do you know anything about a James P. Sullivan, who was a soldier in the Civil War?" "Of course I do," she replied with a laugh. "You're talking about 'J. P.' He was my husband Bob's great-grandfather." She then revealed an even more astounding fact: that a son of the old soldier—James F. Sullivan, born in 1901—was alive and well and living in retirement in Florida. They added details to the story of J. P. Sullivan.

All that was fortunate because Sullivan's collection of stories did not amount to a war memoir in the traditional sense; he had directed his efforts at entertaining the former soldiers, especially the "old braves of the Iron Brigade." "Mickey" always felt he was writing not so much for his family or history, but for the men who were never more than high privates in back ranks, such as his messmates of those days— the "ragtag and bobtail of Company K." His stories were delightful accounts of the rough-hewn "Western" soldiers in an Eastern army and what he saw and did and felt during his days as a volunteer. The Gettysburg story, for example, was one of the best recollections of that epic battle by a soldier in the ranks. In it, Sullivan detailed the charge of his 6th Wisconsin at the railroad cut, told of his hours as a wounded soldier behind Confederate lines, and wrote how he climbed the cupola of the town's railroad station to watch the final great charge of Lee's Army of Northern Virginia.

He may have been but a common soldier during the Civil War, but Sullivan was an intelligent and perceptive man. He may have missed the finer points of grammar, but he possessed a flare for a finely tuned phrase; he displayed an alliterative bent and a sense of cadence and rhythm in what he wrote. He also used his diaries, letters, and journals to set the record straight on certain events that had come under his observation during 1861–65. It should be noted that his regiment, the 6th Wisconsin, was a stalwart one in the most famous brigade in the Army of the Potomac, making him an eyewitness to some of the war's most significant events. He also left a private's view of some of the Union's major soldiers—George McClellan, Irvin McDowell, John Pope, and Ambrose Burnside (whom he challenged with a cocked rifle-musket) as well as unheralded heroes such as circus-boy George Chamberlain, little Hugh Talty, Tommy Flynn, Erastus Smith, and the fallen hero of Company K, Capt. John Ticknor.

In one of his Civil War stories, Sullivan left a fond recollection of the forgotten Wisconsin volunteers who long ago stood in defense of the Union. Those "greenhorn patriots" were "hardy lumbermen, rugged farmer boys and sturdy mechanics," Sullivan said; "gay, brave, fun-loving boys" who faced hardship and death in a "cool and unconcerned manner."

One of them was "Mickey, of Company K."

NOTES

1. U.S. Pension Office, James P. Sullivan Pension File, affidavit of April 18, 1891. His first enlistment came in 1861 as his company was mustered into Federal service, the second when Sullivan decided to return to the

regiment following his wound and subsequent disability discharge after South Mountain, and, finally, as the 6th Wisconsin "veteranized" in late 1863.

2. General Order No. 26, 6th Wisconsin Volunteer Infantry, May 17, 1863, Order Book, 6th Wisconsin Infantry, U.S. National Archives and Records Service. The fine was levied by Lt. Col. Rufus R. Dawes.

3. Rufus R. Dawes, *Service with the Sixth Wisconsin Volunteers* (Marietta, Ohio, 1890), pp. 47, 314; Jerome A. Watrous, *Milwaukee Sunday Telegraph,* September 27, 1885.

4. Watrous, born in New York State, migrated to Wisconsin and grew to manhood in Appleton. At the war's outset, he enlisted as a private soldier in Edward S. Bragg's company of volunteers. He rose through the ranks to become adjutant of the Iron Brigade late in the war, and his bravery at the Battle of Gravelly Run in March 1865 won him a commendation. *Wisconsin Soldiers' and Sailors' Reunion Roster* (Fond du Lac, Wisc., 1880), p. 26; [Frank A. Flower], *History of Milwaukee, Wisconsin* (Chicago, 1881), pp. 632–33.

5. [Jerome A. Watrous], "Talking Over the Old Times," *Milwaukee Sunday Telegraph,* November 25, 1883.

6. James P. Sullivan, "The Charge of the Iron Brigade at Gettysburg," *Milwaukee Sunday Telegraph,* November 11, 1884.

7. The area, part of the state's western upland, featured low, grassy hills and valleys with fields marked by clumps of oak and limestone outcrops. The rolling countryside, where the diminutive Civil War veteran worked his land, crowded down toward the Mississippi River some 40 miles to the west. James P. Sullivan, *Milwaukee Sunday Telegraph,* February 13, 1883; *The Blue Book of the State of Wisconsin* (Madison, 1895), p. 239; Lawrence Martin, *The Physical Geography of Wisconsin* (Madison, 1965), pp. 41–50.

8. Sullivan, *Milwaukee Sunday Telegraph,* February 13, 1883; *Roster of Wisconsin Volunteers, War of the Rebellion, 1861–65* (Madison, 1886), Vol. I, p. 599.

9. Gordon Carruth, ed., *The Encyclopedia of American Facts and Dates* (New York, 1979), p. 332; U.S. Census, Wisconsin, 1880.

10. James P. Sullivan, *Milwaukee Sunday Telegraph,* September 30, 1883.

11. Grant, with the support of Samuel Clemens (Mark Twain), finished his two-volume memories while dying of cancer. His *Personal Memoirs* were published after his death, and secured a measure of financial security for his family. Grant died July 23, 1885. See Richard Goldhurst, *Many Are the Hearts: The Agony and the Triumph of Ulysses S. Grant* (New York, 1975); *Dictionary of American Biography* (New York, 1946). Vol. VII, pp. 500–501.

12. Sullivan, *Telegraph,* September 30, 1883.

13. Bragg, like several regimental officers, was born in New York State. As a 23-year-old he migrated to Wisconsin in 1850 to practice law. A "War Democrat," he raised a company called "Bragg's Rifles" in 1861. He rose through officer ranks to full colonel, and commanded the Iron Brigade in June 1864. A capable officer, he was promoted to brigadier general of volunteers. After the war, he returned to law and politics and was elected to Congress. He later served in ministerial posts. When the Iron Brigade Association was formed at Milwaukee in 1880, Bragg served as first vice

president and de facto leader of the organization. He died in 1912. *Dictionary of Wisconsin Biography,* p. 46; *Dictionary of American Biography,* Vol. II, pp. 587–88; *Biographical Directory of the United States Congress, 1774–1989* (Washington, D.C., 1989), p. 659.

14. Jerome A. Watrous, *Milwaukee Sunday Telegraph,* September 30, 1883.

15. *La Crosse Republican,* September 22, 1883.

16. Lance J. Herdegen and William J. K. Beaudot, *In the Bloody Railroad Cut at Gettysburg* (Dayton, Ohio, 1990).

Chapter I

GAY, BRAVE, FUN-LOVING BOYS

[James P. Sullivan's beginnings were simple. His parents, Dennis and Catharine (*née* Flynn), immigrated from Ireland to the Wisconsin Territory sometime between 1842 and 1845 with three children—a daughter and two sons. James Patrick had been born June 21, 1843, although sometimes during the war years Sullivan claimed his birthday was in 1841 to appear older. The Sullivan family was like thousands of others from Ireland moving to the new territory. By 1850 the Irish were the largest component of English-speaking immigrants, numbering 21,043; by 1860 they had more than doubled to 49,961, or 6.4% of the state's population.[1] Most settled in the lead-mining regions of the southwest part of the territory or in Milwaukee, the largest city. Wheat was then the most important crop in the territory; potato acreage was also extensive. Regardless of their economic condition, the Sullivan family enlarged: another son and a daughter were born during the 1840s and four more children the following decade. Wisconsin was granted statehood in 1848, and newcomers and natives totaled 305,391 by 1850—a 900% increase in just 10 years. The Sullivan family finally migrated to southwestern Wisconsin into Bad Ax (later Vernon) County, which was formed in 1851. That county, too, was experiencing a population boom, more than doubling from 4,800 in 1855 to 11,000 in 1860; but Irish immigrants were few, accounting for less than 2%. This was so-called coulee country, where most land sold for $1.25 an acre. The Sullivans were one of less than two dozen Irish immigrant families in Greenwood Township.[2]

Young James grew to manhood beside his father and brothers in the fields of western Wisconsin. He was a slight, fresh-faced youngster of 5' 5½" (as with his age, Sullivan often stretched his height to 5' 7½"), light complexion, with brown hair and intent blue eyes. The extent of his education is not known, but he likely attended common school through the sixth or seventh grade, and he picked up, formally or otherwise, a sharp and bright writing style that was to characterize him in his middle years. Sometime prior to the

Federal census of 1860, young Sullivan left home to work as a hired man on a farm near Wonewoc in neighboring Juneau County. He was counted among its 477 residents.[3]

James Sullivan—known as J. P. or "Pat" to family and friends—began the recollection of recruit days with a rambling, curious prologue, cast in Old Testament prose, in which he reviled the progenitors of secession, those "pestilential fellows" whom he scathingly denounced as breeders of dis-Union. He castigated Confederate President Jefferson Davis as the "son of Belial." By 1886, when the piece was composed, the Reconstruction period had been closed for 10 years, and Southern Democrats, including many Confederate veterans, were again ascendant and in control of the former slave states. Sullivan and many other Union veterans may have felt that the war, won militarily at great cost—personal and national—was being lost politically. From his farm in Wisconsin he fired a verbal salvo. Sullivan's story of the raising of Company K, 6th Wisconsin Infantry, was printed in *The Telegraph* in two parts May 9 and 16, 1886.]

OLD COMPANY "K"

An Old Favorite Tells the Story of a Volunteer Company.

"Mickey," of Company K, Chronicles Facts and Incidents in an Entertaining Manner

By Mickey of Company K
CHAP. I—PREFATORY

Now it came to pass in the days of Abraham [Lincoln] the good that a certain son of Belial named Jeff Davis, went out and he drew a third part of the people after him; then the people who dwelt in South Carolina, Georgia, North Carolina, Alabama, Mississippi, Louisiana, Texas, Tennessee, Virginia, Florida, Arkansas. And certain pestilential fellows who considered themselves the elders and leaders of the people came together in council and hailed the aforementioned son of Belial, even Jeff Davis, to sit over them and they said one to another, who is this Abraham that he should rule over us? Is he not of the Mudsills,[4] and did he not split rails with his own hands, and guide a flat boat over our rivers, and is he not of the despised abolitionists? and now he fain could sit in the seat of Washington and rule over us; and make our slaves free; educate the poor white trash, making them equals to our sons and daughters; when we shall no more be allowed to sit in high places and have the people bow down and venerate us.

Now, therefore: let us make unto ourselves a country and a ruler; and grow cotton, which all Nations must have of us, and traders from the uttermost parts of the earth shall come to buy of us; and our slaves shall do all the labor. Neither shall any of our men or women be forced to work any more; and we shall grow and wax great, and Nations shall bow down and serve us. And one [Leonidas] Polk[5] was high priest of those parts and he came before them to urge them on, saying the Lord do thus and so to me if what I say is not to come to pass; for the Lord has surely raised us up to establish a new Kingdom; therefore haste ye and heed the word of the Lord; for He has surely said that the sons of Ham shall be bondmen unto all Nations and if any shall raise the sword against ye, I myself will smite him. And when they had spoken to the people with many words of lying import the people raised a great shout and said: Nay, but we will that Jeff Davis shall rule us, for as for this Abraham we know him not.

But Abraham sent a message saying: Men and brothers, what would ye do? Know ye not that the people have chosen me as your fathers chose Washington and all the others who have been before me, and that I can do nothing against the will of the people? Are we not one race and blood? Did not our fathers together fight to make this Nation? Are not the graves of the patriots strewn over the length and breadth of the land? and though passion may strain, it must not break the tie which binds us together as a people. And certain wise men who had the good of the people at heart, spoke, saying: Take heed what ye do; have ye not the same laws, rights and rulers as the others have; take heed that ye bring not war and pestilence upon yourselves and your homes; cause your young men to be slain with the sword; your slaves set free and your land trampled under foot by armies and chariots of war, but the people only grew more turbulent and cried: The Yankees will not fight, (and they would have slain the wise men but they were conveyed away secretly), and they clamored to Jeff Davis to lead them against the strong places belonging to the people which stayed with Abraham.

Now there was in South Carolina a certain city called Charleston, which had been noted for its turbulence and sedition, and in which had assembled traitors and sedition-makers from all parts of the South. And the rulers before Abraham had built a strong place to protect it from the inroads of a certain beef-eating Philistine, named John Bull,[6] who was a turbulent fellow much given to quarrelling with his neighbors; and in that strong place was a captain of hundreds named Anderson[7] who held the place for Abraham with a stout heart. And Jeff Davis and the men of Beelzebub with him had gathered a host and one Beauregard,[8] a man of mighty work, who fancied himself a great warrior, was appointed captain over it; and encompassed the strong place round about and digged ditches and made embankments against it and planted of engines of war a great number to destroy it. And he sent a message to the captain of the stronghold saying: what are you that defy our armies and the will of our people. Now if, when the sun rise again[,] you and your company remain, I will destroy you and the stronghold together; but Anderson, not daunted by his big words, made answer: I hold this place for my country, and our flag floats over it and shall not be lowered until Abraham who is chief captain of our host and ruler over both those and thy people directs; have a care that thou bring not the vengeance of the North about thy head for they will surely rise and destroy this city if thou firest upon our flag.

But Beauregard heeded not the warning, for he and they were with him were made with their folly and the rising of the sun he caused his engines to rain a shower of deadly missiles of war into the stronghold and from the rising of the sun until the going down of the same did continue to assail it and when fire had placed Anderson and his men in the sorest straits and there was no longer food for his men, he gave up the stronghold and departed with the honors of war.

And Beauregard and his host were wild with delight, and feasted and drank and played on cymbals and cornets and shouted, "this day a new Nation is born; let us rejoice and give thanks to our God who has given us the victory." But when the tidings reached the men of the North, they rose as one man, saying, "are we dogs, that this thing shall be?" and they pressed forward to Abraham by the hundreds and thousands, and hundreds of thousands, (such a mighty host as had never before been seen), saying, appoint thou captains over us and succor us with food that we faint not by the way; for we will hew a way across that rebellious land from North to South and from East to West, and no longer shalt the cry of the slaves arise to disturb the land, and the flag which was trailed in the dust at Sumter shall again wave victorious therefrom, and throughout the length and breadth of the land, and thou shall govern every city, town and hamlet, even as Washington, Jefferson and Jackson did before thee, and grass shall grow in the streets of Charleston which did first incite this rebellion.

And Jeff Davis ruled the South land with a rod of iron; and justice and liberty fled and dwelt no longer within its borders, and forced all to serve him in his armies, and he gathered a mighty host (how be it, Jeff fought not himself), and there was a war in the land for a time, and times and part of a time, and the wail of the widow and cry of the orphan was heard all through the land, and blood flowed as water, for brother slew brother, the sire the son, the son the father, and desolation was all through the south land for the men of the North had kept their oath which they had sworn and had hewed a pathway through the length and breadth of the South land and many strong places were taken and smitten with fire and sword. And Polk, the high priest, and thousands of young of valor were slain. Now, Lee, who was a mighty man of valor and great in war or council, was captain of the Southern host and Grant was chief captain of Abraham's host, Sheridan was captain of the horse and Meade[9] captain of the war chariots and footmen, and they compassed Lee round about, and he

and all his host were taken. And when the tidings was
brought[,] Jeff Davis, that son of Belial gathered all the silver
and gold he had taken from the people and fled, hoping to
reach a strange land; but he was overtaken by swift horsemen.
Now, when Jeff was in power and urging his friends and
neighbors and the people to shed their blood and give their
treasures for his benefit, he made much ado that he would die
in the last ditch of the South ere he would submit to be taken,
or yield to the "hated hireling" of Abraham; but when Abraham's horsemen discovered his hiding place, he called to his
wife: Give now, I pray thee, thine hoop skirt and thine hood
and cloak, and dress me therein and get the water vessels
that I may go draw from the well, peradventure the Yankees
may take me to be thine aged mother, doing the chores, and I
may thus escape falling into their cowardly hands. Now Jeff
had feet like a fair damsel from Chicago, and wore No. 13
"calf skins" and a Chicago man who was present, seeing the
feet, supposed it was one of his city maidens, and advanced to
greet her, and discovered Jeff's evil face; he cried with a loud
voice, "here he is, here he is;" and the arch traitor was taken.[10]
Jeff was confined in a strong place for a time, but at length
was turned out that he might live and be shunned and
excreted by all honest men as the man who caused the death
of more of his friends and made more widows and orphans
and brought more destruction, desolation and misery on the
land to satisfy his vanity and ambition, than any man known
to history.

CHAP. II—THE GATHERING

The rumbling of war storm had been heard for more than
two years; threats had been freely made by demagogues of
the South to secede, if their "rights" were not granted, though
what those rights were they were not careful to mention,
while at the North other demagogues who were ever ready to
pop up like corks to the top of any turmoil that would likely
benefit them, were urging people to resist the laws of the
United States; and our own state legislature by joint resolu-

tion, denounced the United States' supreme court, and declared that the United States was not the exclusive or final judge of its powers, and claimed that the several states which formed the constitution were sovereign and independent, and held the right to judge of its infraction, and also that a positive defiance on the part of the states was the rightful remedy. Some very ardent patriots (who remained at home holding office when the war came) were very vituperative against Chief Justice [Roger] Taney on account of the Dred Scott decision. He had always been opposed to slavery, and had liberated his own slaves, which is probably more than ardent patriots would have done, and did all in their power to precipitate a quarrel between the sections. In such a state of affairs it is no wonder that law-abiding citizens who would have all the expenses to pay and bear the burden of the fighting, looked on aghast and sighed for a Jackson or a Clay to guide the country through the impending storm.

The election of President Lincoln afforded a pretext to the Southern demagogues (though they planned to bring about that event,) to fire the Southern heart with cries that he would free the slaves; that he would deprive the Southern people of their rights under the constitution; prevent Southern men from acquiring lands in the territories; yet again they were very careful not to say how he could do it, whilst the feeling among the mass of the farming community at the North (so far as my knowledge extends) was that Mr. Lincoln would do nothing unlawful and if any just rights of the Southerners were in danger, congress should at once secure them to them; and until Sumter was fired on[11] they were in hopes the storm would blow over; that event at once changed the current of feeling, and "we must lick 'em." "Southern rights be damned." "No Southern or any other right has a right to fire on our flag." "Charleston must be destroyed." "Jeff Davis should be hung," etc., etc., were the expressions used by even the most conservative men, while war, war, war, was the theme of every fireside and gathering; the people felt that the secessionists had forfeited all their right under the constitution by treasonably making war against our government.

Immediately after the fall of Fort Sumter Capt. [Rufus R.] Dawes[12] had begun organizing a company for three months' service, and was very much disappointed when the authorities at Washington refused to accept more than one regiment from this state [Wisconsin], but owing to the expostulations of Governor [Alexander] Randall, who called the attention of the war department that Illinois, with scarcely double our population, had been called on to furnish six regiments, the government as a special favor to him, agreed to accept another regiment. I might write pages on the want of foresight and stupidity of the war department all through the war, but as it does not concern what I am trying to write about, I shall leave it to such correct historians as "Carleton"[13] and others who make any kind of history to order; then came the call for three hundred thousand men for three years during the war.

A war meeting was held in Mauston[14] May 4th, 1861, at which the leading men of the place delivered addresses and prominent citizens came forward and pledged themselves to care for the families of those who should enlist for three years, and the company by acclamation, unanimously declared to change their enlistment to three years during the war. The breaking out of the war found me like Cincinnatus and "Old Pat," following the plow, and to use the words of Tacitus, "I am aware there is a great distance between myself and those illustrious characters," yet I think the motive in my case was the same, to do what I could for the country. The war meeting was held on Saturday, May 4th, and on the following Wednesday, May 8th, 1861, "Reck [Rescun W.] Davis," "Jim Barney" and myself went over to "Bill" Stewards, the adjoining farm, where John St. Clair[15] was acting in the dual capacity of "hired man" and "beau" for "Sal," "old Bill's" buxom daughter. John had been elected corporal and had an enlistment roll on which I entered my name and I became for the first time a 'cruit. *East Lynne*[16] was then running as a serial in the *Mauston Star,* and interest in the household was about evenly divided between it and the "war news," the female portion taking sides with Madame Vine [sic],[17] and we preferring the latest news from the seat of war; and at night when the "chores" were finished and the big lamp lighted, one would read aloud to the others, who listened and commented on the foolishness and vice of Barbara Hare, Madame Vine; or Beauregard or Jeff Davis.

OLD COMPANY "K"

"Mickey" Has a Hard Time to Enlist, But Lt. Crane Helps Him Through.

The Drilling at Mauston —Called to Madison —The Reception Speeches

The Lay of the Land at Camp Randall —Take Breakfast at the Mess house —The Men of Company "K"

By Mickey of Company "K."

The war meeting was attended and we enlisted. The company was authorized to rendezvous at Mauston, begin instructions and await orders. Our squad was the first to arrive then the party from New Lisbon, then the "Yellow River crowd,"[18] and at last the company was formed with the name of "Lemonweir Minute Men," and the following roster:

Captain, Rufus R. Dawes.

1st Lieut., John A. Kellogg.

2d Lieut., John Crane.

Sergeants, David L. Quaw, Linneus Westcott, John Ticknor, Harrison H. Edwards, Eugene P. Rose.

Corporals, John Holden, Franklin Wilcox, John St. Clair, William N. Remington, William S. Campbell, Oliver Fletcher, Eugene L. Anderson, William H. Van Wie.

Privates, Alonzo L. Andress, Chas. A. Alton, Daniel D. Alton, A. [Charles A.] Abbott, Ira Butterfield, Frederick E.

Boynton, James L. Barney, Joseph A. Chase, John Carsley, Thos. J. Cleaveland [Cleveland], Ephriam Cornish, Chas. A. Crawford, John A. Crawford, Thos. Conway, George W. Covey, Geo. E. Chamberlaln, Bucum W. Davies [Rescum W. Davis], Volney DeJean, Williard [Willard] Dutton, Roswell G. Emmons, Enos [Erastus] E. Emmons, Thos. J. Ellsworth, Dennis M. Fuller, Thos. Flynn, Abraham Fletcher, Andrew Gallup, Henry Gallup, William W. Garland, Cassius M. Griggs, Samuel F. Gordon, Levi S. Gardner, Jacob H. Garthwalth [Garthwait], Reuben Hunley [Huntley], William D. Hancock, William P. Harrison, Cyrus Hendricks [Hendrick], Edward B. Hendricks [Hendrick], Israel W. Henrdicks [Hendrick], Thos. Hills [Hill], Llewellyn B. Hills [Hill], Volney Holmes, Peter W. Helmer, Barney McCuin, Emory Mitchell, Daniel J. Miller, Andrew J. Nott, Alex J. Noble, Lorenzo Pratt, William Patterson, James H. Rogers, Joel W. Ranney [Waitsell J. Ranney], Ira Randall, Chas. A. Renolds [Charles H. Reynolds], Edward S. Symons [Simmons], James M. Scoville, Erastus Smith, Cyrus Spooner, William Stevens, James P. Sullivan, Hugh Talty, Andrew R. Thompson, Chas. M. Taylor, John R. Towle, Silas W. Temple, Albert E. Tarbox, Hoel W. Trumble, Lyman B. Upham, William Valleau, Chas. West, Chauncey Wilcox, Samuel O. Woods, Arland F. Winsor, Stephen J. Whitcher [Whicher], Aaron Yates.[19]

Commissioned, 3, non-commissioned, 13, privates, 75; total, 91.

The following joined the company in Camp Randall by transfer, (I think from company E.) Fifer, Alvah J. Atwell, drummer, E. [Elias] G. Jackson.

Recruits, William Anderson, joined in Camp Randall.

Recruits joined at Arlington Heights [Virginia], 1862: Albert H. Rolfe, William Holloway, Henry Revels, William J. Revels, George W. Downing, Daniel Cummings, Wallace B. Hancock, Ralph M. Brown, Peter A. Everson.

Joined at Fredericksburg, 1862: Richard Upham, Jared Williams, Luther Butterfield.

Joined at Warrenton, 1862: Erastus M. [N.] Emmons.

Joined at Fredericksburg, 1863: David C. Van Wie.

Joined while on veteran furlough: William W. Hall, James

H. Rodes [Rhoades], John Kennedy, Amasa Davies [Davis], Samuel Longyear, Thos. W. Mitchell, James J. [I.] Taylor, Edward W. Trumble, George Price, Sylvester O. Stittson [Stillson], Julian [John J.] Simpson, Edward Coppernell [Cuppernell], James H. Thompson, Laban Garner, Chas. M. Gile.

Drafted men joined in front of Petersburg, 1864: Henry Althouge [Aulthaus], Alex Adams, Henry Bronson [Benson], Conrad Bates, George Betner [Bettner], Frederick Brewer, Samuel Carlson, George Carter, James A. Collins, Asa B. Daniels, Henry Eichstein [Eckstein], George H. C. Evers, Frederick Geiger, John W. Gile, Anthony Frembegn [Frembgen], Clark Hickox [Hickcox], Peter Hamm, Theodore Hugo, Nicholas Huhn [Hahn], George Huhn [Hahn], Christian Ille, John Kneprast [Knapprath], Edwin Kreamer, Oliver Kreamer, Gottlieb C. Lohman, John Law, Jacob Meythaler [Maydollar], Porter [John P.] Munger, Emory [Emery] Newkirk, George B. Priestly, Stephen Prouty, James M. Pigg, Elijah Pickering, Nicholas Schwiesthal, Stephen Smyser, John Scott, Peter W. Schumacker, William Seitzer, John Thielman [Tillman], Stephen Thomas, August Wallschlaeger, James P. Williams.

Drafted men and substitutes who joined at Arlington Heights, June, 1865, after the return from Richmond: William Barren [Barrand], Nella [Nele] Davis, Frederick Fenz, Charles Fenz, Tusten Godden [Tostensen Godnen], Henry M. Jones, James Knowles, William Leach, William McAuliff [McCauliff], George Marr, Patrick Rogers, John Biesinger, George F. School [Schall], Henry Suhr, John M. Steiner, Chas. Selling, Chas. T. Schydes [Schydeaty], William Shutt [Schutt], Andrew Shissler [Schussler], William Tinge [Teng], Andry Thumagle [Thurnagle], Joseph Vandyke, Almon D. Wadsworth, Joseph Wheeler, Mark Williams, William Kinkleman, Julius Winters, John Young, Casper Zimmerman [Caspar Zimmermann], John Zeiroth [Zeirath], August Zeisdorf [Zuhldorf], Frederick Zergebel, Liebredth [Liebrecht] Zahn. Total, 198.[20]

CHAP. III—THE TRANSFORMATION

There were many ludicrous and laughable scenes in our attempts to become "Grenadiers of the Guard," by the first intention. With the exception of Corporal Holden,[21] who had been an Ordnance Sergeant so long that he had forgotten all drill and tactics except the "salute," not a man of the company had seen a company drill; "right flank," "left flank," "front," "wheel," etc., were conundrums which the ablest of us were unable to master and the way we went "endways," "sideways," in one row and two rows would puzzle Col. [Rufus] King[22] or any other "maitre de arms" in the country. Our maneuvering was done in the public square at Mauston to the great edification of school children, fathers, mothers, sisters, friends and girls we had not yet left behind us, and if they judged by the loudness of the tones of command and our ability to charge the school house or church, they must have felt the rebellion would soon be a thing of the past. [John] Ticknor,[23] who afterwards became a beau ideal soldier, but who then seemed to look on the thing as a huge joke, had charge of the "squab" to which I belonged, and one time when he had us going endways in good shape, there became imminent danger of a collision between the "squab" and one of the out-houses and not remembering what Scott[24] had prescribed for such occasions, he shouted, "break ranks, boys, and fall in on the other side of the back-house."

A number of the company objected to me on account of my youth and small size, and professed to be afraid that I would disgrace the company by not being able to pitch rebels over my shoulder with a bayonet, or keep up on a march, and would remark "what good would Mickey be in a charge 'bagnets,'" and old Ira Butterfield[25] and several others would look complacently down from their six feet four altitude and good naturedly advise me to go home to mother and wait till I was feathered out and at length it seemed as if the captain would reject me, but Lieut. [John] Crane,[26] whose ancestor, like my own, was some of the "rale ould kind," and who was aware of the proclivity of our race to engage in a "ruction" of any kind, and their staying qualities in any undertaking, took my part and brought me before the justice of the peace in Mauston, who appointed himself my guardian, granted consent to enlist, and swore me into the state service in one time and three motions, and so I became a full fledged member of the company, and that is why my enlistment is dated June 21st on the original muster roll of the company, instead of May 8th, the day of my enlistment.[27]

Somehow, it seemed as if Dawes and the adjutant general's office could never make connection, as we were waiting for orders to report to Camp Randal [Randall], and the office was waiting for us to report there. Thrice we bid farewell to every one in Mauston, and twice we were escorted to the depot but each time no cars were provided, nor had the railroad any instruction to furnish transportation and at length we began to fear that the state would have no use for us; but one night, just before midnight, station agent Fish notified us that cars were attached to the coming train, and with no time for good byes nor any escort, we hustled to the depot and took the train which carried many of the boys away never to see Mauston again. We changed cars at Milton, and Sunday evening, July 7th, 1861 we entered the east gate of Camp Randall. The Fifth regiment was then encamped in the historic old camp and the other companies of the 6th were there waiting for us to complete the regiment. The company was received by Col. [Lysander] Cutler[28] who spoke a few words of welcome, and by Lieut. Col. [Julius P.] Atwood,[29] who welcomed us in quite a speech; but it was the major [Benjamin J.] (Sweet)[30] who embraced the opportunity to spread himself (as [Tom] Flynn ironically termed it) all over the American Eagle. He had been a state senator, and being restricted by the rules of the senate from talking them into insanity, he had loaded himself for our arrival and at once proceeded to fire off his "dictionary words" at me. I don't remember any of his eloquence but one sentence, and that "stuck in my crop" until he left the regiment, which was, "you call yourselves 'Lemonweir Minute Men,' but we had begun to think you were 'Lemonweir Hour Men,'" which implied that it was our fault for not reaching camp sooner; an implication which was wholly undeserved and unnecessary, for we had been (to again quote Flynn) "Pepperin for fear we'd miss a chance to be kilt." I never liked the man afterwards, and frequently thought, after he left us that if company K were hour men getting into camp they were also hour men in staying in the war, and that one of the hour men who was only a lieutenant[31] when Sweet was a major, attained a position of honor which in my estimation was equal to any in the army, the command of the Iron Brigade.

> It's early nixt mornin' to dhrill I was sint,
> 'Twas thin my poor heart began to repint,
> Ora Sergint Machree can't you lave me alone,
> Don't you see I have good hands and arrums av me own.
>
> —*Old Song*

To those who fancy that a soldier's life in camp is one of ease, I wish to say that no greater mistake can be made than to think so, and to show that I know whereof I speak, I will describe a day's duties in camp as it was in Camp Randall in June, 1861, and when I describe one it covers all: Daylight reveille and roll call; and immediately one hour's company drill; then fifteen minutes for preparation, then fall in and march to breakfast; "sick call," "fatigue call," which meant clean up the company quarters and street. "Guard mount," which of course took only those detailed; then two and a half hour's company and squad drill; dinner. At one o'clock fall in and have three hours' battalion drill; supper; dress parade. Tattoo and roll call at 9 o'clock, taps fifteen minutes later. Then the poor greenhorn patriot, tired as an ox after a day's hard logging, was at liberty to lay down on the soft side of a board and dream, if he slept at all, of glory and the grave.

The first week of our life in Camp Randall we spent in wooden quarters built on the east side and north of the gate. When tents were furnished they were pitched on the west side in the northwest corner of the camp. Company D of our regiment[32] occupied barracks about where the present gate is at the terminus of the street railway, and company A[33] were also in barracks where the windmill towers stood at the late reunion.[34] The 5th [Wisconsin] regiment[35] were in tents in a light depression of the ground, just north of what we called headquarters, on the hill and our glorious brass band was in tents between the 5th regiment and ours, and at any time their discordant tootings would have brought a deserved shower of defunct eggs, but at that time we were willing to endure anything to whip secession.[36] The mess room for the two regiments was on the north side of the camp and east of the present gate. A man called Dutcher had the contract for "grubbing" us, and some of the boys grumbled immensely over the hash, which Jim Barney called "cononderfun;" but I think that afterwards many of us would be glad to have a dish of Dutcher's hash. Each company had a long pine table sufficient to accommodate officers and men, and at meal times the company formed and marched in (a rank on each side of the table) when Dawes would command, "Lemonweir Minute Men" (and after muster into service of the U.S.), "company K," "Inward face," "uncover," "seats," when all took seats and Dawes who always did things decently and in order, offered grace before meal, while Flynn, [Erastus] Smith, Billy Campbell, [Samuel] Gordon, Tommy Ellsworth, myself, and all the little fellows on the left, whom Smith called the rag-tag and bobtail of company K, and Flynn the "little imp" of the 6th regiment, would cross our hands, assume a Sunday-go-to-meeting expression of countenance and begin:

> Now I sit me in my seat,
> And pray for something fit to eat.
> If this damn stuff my stomach brake,
> I pray that God my soul will take.
> or
> Oh, thou who blessed the loaves and fishes,
> Look down upon these old tin dishes;
> By thy great power those dishes smash,
> Bless each of us and damn this hash.

Gay, brave, fun-loving boys, many of them met death just as cool and unconcerned as they then ridiculed Dawes' attempts at ready-made piety.

CHAP. IV—GOING TO THE FRONT

Several days after our arrival in camp the company marched up to "headquarters" on the hill and were rigidly examined by the medical officers, the company being chiefly hardy lumbermen, rugged farmer boys and sturdy mechanics, none failed to pass, and on July 16th, we were directed to prepare for muster into the service of the U. S. Flynn, as usual, commented by saying, "we'll be mustered now and salt and peppered afterwards," and after events showed that he was no false prophet. I will describe the mustering process and many of your readers understand all about the salting and peppering. Muster into service of the U. S., in our case, consisted of forming in company line, opening order to the rear, when several officers pass along in front of each rank, the company close order and the first or orderly sergeant calls each man's name who steps out and passes the mustering officer, saluting him in passing. Various writers have been describing the salting and peppering process in *THE SUNDAY TELEGRAPH* for the last six or seven years, so I will say nothing about it here.

After being mustered in, the state furnished uniforms and we at length felt that we were soldiers in every sense of the word. The uniform was a short gray jacket reaching to the hips, faced with black at the ends of the collar, on the upper side of the cuff, on the shoulders and straps on the sides to hold up the waist belt, gray pants with a black welt in the outside seam, a fatigue suit of pepper and salt gray cotton, (i.e., a sack coat and trowsers with red welt in outside seam,) two heavy dark blue woolen shirts, two pairs of drawers, two pairs socks, a pair of cowhide shoes, a linen and glazed cloth cap cover, cap, etc. every article received from the state was of excellent quality, except the dress caps, and that was something wonderfully and fearfully made. What a carpenter would call the carcass was made of hair cloth, the frame and studding of wire and whalebone, and the siding of gray cloth; the inside finish of black alpaca and the cornice base board, and outside trimmings of patent leather, a front vizor or porch square with front elevation and projecting on a level; a rear vizor or piazza extending downwards at one-third pitch, and the whole heavily and strongly put together according to specification. The caps afforded the boys an unlimited opportunity to exercize their powers of sarcasm, and they were universally named after a useful chamber utensil, and many were the theories advanced and overthrown in regard to the use of the hind vizor or tail piece; but Hugh Talty[37] finally solved the vexed question by asserting in an indisputable manner "that whin we were fi'tin', the inemy couldn't tell whin we were advancin' or retratin'," which was accepted as the only correct and reasonable hypothesis. The caps furnished the boys an excellent substitute for footballs and considerable exercise in "hop, step and a jump," the jump generally ending on top of somebody's cap, but the caps like Banquo's ghost,[38] would not [stay] down but Antlers-like sprang up refreshed after every disaster, the hair cloth acting as an indestructible spring to restore them to the original shape after the pressure was withdrawn, and it was not till they were remodeled by taking out the hair cloth and cutting off the rear vizor that the boys took to them kindly and generally. The size of the shoes, also, furnished much harmless mirth and jokes; and "gunboats," "flatboats," "schooners," "ferryboats," "mudscows," etc. were mild terms applied to those worn by such as Ira Butterfield, [Chauncey] Winsor, [Joseph A.] Chase and others of the No. 13s, while [Tommy] Flynn said that the writer could go through all the facings without moving the toes of his shoes from the front. When we afterward "drew" from the U.S., we realized very forcibly the difference of quality in favor of our state uniform.[39]

At length came that July day when the Nation held its breath over the tidings from Bull Run,[40] and at last when the truth was reluctantly made known we realized for the first time we were to have a chance [to fight], and telegrams were at once received directing the 5th and 6th to be sent on to Washington. Thanks to the prudence of such men as Governors [Alexander] Randall [of Wisconsin], [Richard] Yates [of Illinois], [Samuel J.] Kirkwood [of Iowa], [Andrew G.] Curtin [of Pennsylvania] and others the blundering war department, as at many times during the war was saved from the direct consequences of its folly, and a stream of men who afterwards formed the bone and sinew of our armies was hurried forward to again save the capital. Col. Cutler being a Milwaukee man, and having two Milwaukee companies in his regiment, (company D, which had been made famous through the Lady Elgin disaster,[41] and Company F, the "Turners"),[42] it was decided our regiment would go via Milwaukee, and July 8th, 1861, we started for the city of beer and pale bricks. The citizens had made elaborate preparations for our welcome, and a feast was spread, at which everything likely to tempt the appetite was furnished, and to which our boys after their tiresome march through the streets, did ample justice, but what impressed us most favorably was the kindness of many beautiful ladies who seemed to think they could not do enough for us. That trip through Milwaukee sustained many a poor fellow afterward on a tiresome march, in the privation of soldier life, or in the fury of battle by reminding him that at home in the center of wealth, talent and beauty of the state he had many strong and warm friends, and nerving him with the thought that come what would, they should have no cause to be ashamed of him.[43]

We arrived at Harrisburg, Pa., two days afterwards, and were dumped like a train load of stock, outside the city and found quarters for the night in a pasture field, and next morning for the first time we partook of the bounty of our great and good government. The policy of the great and good at the time I speak of seemed to be that anything was good enough for persons willing to risk their lives to preserve that same great and good, and in fact, it seemed all through the war as if the remark of [Wisconsin] Governor Randall, "that when a man enlisted the authorities seemed to think he forfeited all rights that they were bound to respect," governed all those connected with the war department. Jeff Davis, if in citiman's clothes, could travel the length and breadth of Washington or any city in the North, while a Union soldier who had maybe spilled his blood to prevent Jeff Davis from taking the aforesaid city would be arrested at every corner or public place, if he appeared there without a pass. But to return to the bounty of our "great and good" government.

Next morning after reaching Harrisburg we drew rations, but although we were a little short of those necessities previously, we did not eat those drawn, immediately, for the reason that most of us had been in the habit of using such things as coffee, pork, flour, etc., after having undergone a cooking process. But the brainy part of the "great and good" running things in the commissary department at Harrisburg considered cooking entirely superfluous, or like the old Scotchman who rebuked his grandson for effeminacy, because he made himself a snow pillow, or a sign of democracy, and was determined so far as in his power to prevent any such unnecessary luxuries where he had control, and consequently issued us damaged hard tack of the consistency and nutritiousness of sole leather, green coffee, rusty bacon, sugar, vinegar, (if you had anything to get it in), and the everlasting bean. Inasmuch as there was not a coffee mill, coffee pot, skillet or kettle in company K, one may imagine how sumptuously we fared on the above menu. Those who had the money ran the guard, an easy proceeding, as all the weapon he had was "halt," and being obliged to remain on his beat, his halt was not very effective at long range, and in a very short time company K was without a quorum, and bakers, piedealers, hotel-keepers and others in Harrisburg experienced a boom in their particular lines of trade.

In due course of time we reached Washington and took our share of the reviews, fort building, inspections, and above all, the senseless knapsack drills. In November we crossed the river into Virginia and camped on Arlington Heights, the property of General Lee,[44] to which we did our share to confiscate. I will never forget that awful winter. The Potomac froze and during the January thaw we were compelled to split puncheons and plank our street in order to be able to go from one end to the other, while the blood-thirsty editors at home were asking "why don't the army move?" When the army did move company K went with it and took part in, and left its dead on every battle-field, until the end came at Appomattox.

I have prepared from incomplete notes made during the war, the following list of killed and wounded:

Killed at Second Bull Run, Levi S. Gardner.

South Mountain, George E. Chamberlain, Reuben Huntley.

Antietam, William P. Harrison, Chas. A. Abbott, Daniel Cummings.

Fitzhughs Crossing, Hod [Hoel] W. Trumble.

Gettysburg, John Ticknor, Abraham Fletcher, James M. Scoville, Thomas Conway, Albert Tarbox.

Wilderness, Julian [John J.] Simpson.

Laurel Hill, Aaron Yates.

Petersburg, Linneus [Linnaeus] Westcott, Edward C. Cuppernell, Wallace B. Hancock.

Weldon R. R., William J. Revels.

Hatchers Run, James H. Thompson, James P. Williams, Israel W. Hendricks, John Scott, Nicholas Huhn [Hahn], John W. Gile, Henry Eichstein [Eckstein].

Five Forks, Anthony Frembeyn [Frembgen]. In rebel prison by guards, Oliver Fletcher, William D. Hancock.[45]

Died of disease, Harrison H. Edwards of a broken heart, at Arlington, Roswell G. Emmons, at Yellow House, of diarrhea, George Hahnn [Hahn], Volney DeJean, Casius M. Griggs.

Deserted, Jacob H. Garthwaith [Garthwait], Volney Holmes, Neeba [Nele] Davis, drafted man, at Jeffersonville, Ind., June, '65, Barney McCuin.[46]

Wounded: William N. Remington, Daniel J. Miller, Albert H. Rolfe, Andrew R. Thompson, James P. Sullivan, Hugh Talty, James H. Rhodes, James W. Knapp, William H. Van Wie, William W. Garland, Frederick Brewer, George Carter, Amasa A. Davis, George W. Downing, Samuel Longyear, Emory [Emery] Newkirk, George B. Priestly, James M. Pigg, Henry Revels, Edward S. Simons [Simmons], Edward W. Trimble [Trumble], John St. Clair, Franklin Wilcox, Eugene L. Anderson, John Crawford, Joel W. Ranny [Waitsell J. Ranney], James L. Barney, Daniel D. Alton, Ephraim Cornish, Peter A. Everson, Thomas Flynn, Lorenzo Pratt, Eugene P. Rose, John M. [R.] Towle, Silas W. Temple, Chauncy [Chauncey] Wilcox, Samuel O. Woods, Thomas L. Ellsworth, Andrew Gallup, Erastus M. [N.] Emmons, Erastus Smith, Llewellen B. Hills [Llewellyn B. Hill], William Anderson, Rolf [Ralph] M. Brown.[47]

The above list is not complete but only those of which I had personal knowledge and many of the killed had been previously wounded.

July 14th, 1865, company K was mustered out of the United States service, and July 30th were paid off and discharged. The members are now scattered all over the country from Washington Territory to Texas. A number still reside at and near Mauston, and five or six in my neighborhood, but the casualties of war and other infirmities have put an end to their soldiering days. But most of them like myself have active young patriots growing up who will be able to take our places should it ever be necessary to do as General [Lucius] Fairchild[48] said in 1865, when he welcomed home the remnant of the consolidated 6th and 2nd.[49] "Should our country be again in danger we'll raise another 2nd, 6th and 7th, and Indiana will furnish another 19th and we'll send to Michigan for a 24th and we'll have another Iron Brigade."

NOTES

1. The Sullivans were among the pre-1845 potato famine immigrants attracted to America for opportunity. Wisconsin was a destination for many immigrants in the mid-1840s. It was actively agitating for statehood during this period, and immigrant aide societies were extolling its virtues abroad. And the state was accessible by two important waterways, the Mississippi River and, as in the case of the Sullivans who traveled from Canada, the Great Lakes. Grace McDonald, *The History of the Irish in Wisconsin in the Nineteenth Century* (New York, 1976), pp. 8–9.

2. U.S. Census, Wisconsin, 1850; Wisconsin State Census, 1855; U.S. Census, Wisconsin, 1860. Greenwood Township had 442 residents in 1860.

3. *Juneau County, The First 100 Years* (Friendship, Wisc., 1988), p. 52.

4. A "mudsill," in the parlance of the day, was a member of the laboring class. The term was first applied in 1858 by South Carolina Sen. James H. Hammond, and by 1878, in Southern political circles, it meant a white laborer. It was also applied by Southerners to all Northerners. Mitford M. Mathews, *A Dictionary of Americanisms on Historical Principles* (Chicago, 1951), p. 1097.

5. Polk attained prominence during the Civil War and Reconstruction periods, first as a member of the state legislature, later in military service and in the postwar constitutional convention. *Dictionary of American Biography*, Vol. XV, pp. 40–41.

6. A reference to England.

7. Son of a Revolutionary War soldier, Robert Anderson was born in 1805 and graduated from West Point in 1825. He fought in the Mexican War. When secession became imminent, he was sent to command the Federal garrison at Charleston, South Carolina. He spiked the guns at Fort

Moultrie and shifted his base to Fort Sumter. In April 1861 he defended the fort against rebel bombardment for 34 hours before he was compelled to surrender. On April 14, 1865, he was returned to Charleston to again raise the national flag over Sumter. Anderson died in 1871. *Ibid.,* Vol I, pp. 274–75.

8. Pierre Gustave Toutaint Beauregard, born in New Orleans in 1818, graduated from West Point when he was 20. He served as an engineer for Gen. Winfield Scott during the Mexican War, winning a promotion for gallantry. Beauregard became a brigadier general in the Confederacy, and ordered the bombardment of Fort Sumter that began the Civil War. He fought at First Bull Run and was then sent to the Western Theater, succeeding to command when Joseph E. Johnston was fatally wounded at Shiloh. He was later charged with the defense of Petersburg in 1864. He died in 1893. *Ibid.,* Vol. II, pp. 111–12.

9. George G. Meade, born in 1815, graduated from West Point in 1835. He left the army to pursue a career in civil engineering, but in 1842 was reinstated. With the exception of the Mexican War, Meade's' service involved military engineering. Shortly after the outbreak of the war, he was made brigadier general of volunteers and given command of a Pennsylvania brigade. Meade was wounded during the Peninsula Campaign, but served at Second Bull Run, South Mountain, Antietam, and Fredericksburg. After Chancellorsville, Meade was named to command the Army of the Potomac and won a victory at Gettysburg. When Grant came East as lieutenant general, Meade became little more than titular head of the Army of the Potomac. After the war, he was placed in charge of the military division of the Atlantic, based in Philadelphia. He died in 1872 of pneumonia. *Dictionary of American Biography* (New York, 1946), Vol. XXI, pp. 474–76; Ezra J. Warner, *Generals in Blue* (Baton Rouge, La., 1964), pp. 315–17.

10. Davis escaped from Richmond, Virginia, on April 3, 1865, and after learning of Lee's surrender at Appomattox Court House he fled south. Following Gen. Joseph Johnston's surrender, Davis hoped to escape the country, but was captured near Irwindale, Georgia, May 19, 1865. A popular but untrue story circulated at the time said that Davis donned his wife's clothing in his unsuccessful effort to escape capture. Davis survived until he was 81, dying in 1889. *Ibid.,* Vol. V, p. 130.

11. Fort Sumter was bombarded at 4:30 A.M. on April 12, 1861 and surrendered the afternoon of the next day.

12. A descendant of Revolutionary War ancestors, Dawes was born in southeast Ohio July 4, 1838. With his father, Henry, he traveled to Wisconsin in 1855, purchasing land near Mauston in Juneau County. Rufus attended the University of Wisconsin at Madison and traveled back and forth from Wisconsin to Ohio. He completed his college studies in Marietta, Ohio, in 1860, then returned to Wisconsin, helping his father campaign for minor county offices. When Fort Sumter fell, Dawes began recruiting a company of volunteers. He was elected captain in May 1861. *Dawes-Gates Ancestral Lines,* comp. by Mary Walton Ferris (privately printed, Chicago, 1943), p. 3; Dawes, *Service,* pp. 6–8.

13. The pseudonym for Charles Carleton Coffin. A native of New Hampshire, he was a war correspondent for the *Boston Journal.* After the war and until his death, he traveled and wrote more than a dozen books, many for

children. Some of his Civil War histories were serialized in *The National Tribune,* a soldier newspaper published in Washington, D.C. He died in 1896. *Dictionary of American Biography,* Vol. IV, pp. 265–66.

14. Mauston, the county seat of Juneau County, is nestled in the verdant rolling west central part of the state on the Lemonweir River. Wisconsin attained statehood in 1848 and its population in 1860 was just under 776,000. Mauston numbered 487, while the entire county listed 8,770. *The Blue Book of the State of Wisconsin* (Madison, 1885) p. 404; U.S. Census, Wisconsin, 1860.

15. Davis, of White Creek, advanced to corporal and re-enlisted in 1864 for three years; he served until the regiment mustered from service in July 1865. Barney, also of White Creek, was wounded in September 1862, and again in the Wilderness, in May 1864; he was discharged because of wounds in October 1864. St. Clair, of Summit, moved into noncommissioned officer ranks, and was taken prisoner near Petersburg in 1864. He was mustered from service June 15, 1865. *Roster of Wisconsin Volunteers,* Vol. I, pp. 533, 534, 536.

16. *East Lynne* was a popular melodramatic novel by English writer Mrs. Henry (Ellen) Wood; published in 1861, it sold over a million copies in cheap editions and was widely serialized in newspapers, as was the custom of the day. Max J. Herzberg, *The Reader's Encyclopedia of American Literature* (New York, 1962), p. 295; David Daiches, ed., *The Penguin Companion to English Literature* (New York, 1971), p. 559.

17. "Lady Isabel Vane" and "Barbara Hare" were the novel's lead characters. *Ibid.*

18. Yellow River was an area north of Mauston on the Wisconsin River where lumberman and mill hands worked. The community was named "Necedah," the Indian word for Yellow River. In 1851, several men who would later join the "Lemonweir Minute Men" arrived to work on a mill, among them Erastus N. Emmons, Emory Mitchell, and Reuben Huntley; the latter two brought their families to the community that summer. The following year, John Carsley and Columbus Dawes, a kinsman of Rufus Dawes, arrived; and in 1853, Robert Dawes began working. On April 5, 1853, the town of Necedah was organized, and elections for officers held. Among those gaining office were: Robert Dawes, chairman; Charles Dawes, overseer of highways; and Reuben Huntley, one of the constables. John T. Kingston, "Early Exploration and Settlement of Juneau County," *Collections of the State Historical Society of Wisconsin* (Madison, 1879), Vol. VIII, pp. 403–405.

19. In 1907, Earl M. Rogers claimed that from the Town of Forest, where Sullivan would reside after the war, two enlistees were from a "settlement of colored people," who were "always recognized as good citizens." The men, unnamed, served in Company K ". . . and they were faithful soldiers, each of them receiving wounds in battle." Earl M. Rogers, ed., *Memoirs of Vernon County* (Madison, 1907), p. 201.

20. Spelling corrections were taken from the *Roster of Wisconsin Volunteers,* Vol. I, pp. 533–36.

21. Holden, a Mexican War veteran, walked 16 miles from Wonewoc to Mauston to enlist. But his service was short. Unable to stand the rigors of military life, he was discharged for disability December 13, 1861. *Ibid.,* p. 534.

22. Born in New York in 1814, and a graduate of West Point in 1833, King migrated to Milwaukee in 1845 and became, successively, editor and publisher of *The Milwaukee Sentinel,* a Whig newspaper. In 1861, he volunteered and was commissioned brigadier general of U.S. Volunteers. He was placed in command of the unit which later evolved into the Iron Brigade. With the appointment of John Gibbon in May 1862 to brigade command, King was placed in command of a division. He resigned from the army in 1863, and was appointed minister to the Papal States. He died in 1876 in New York. *Dictionary of Wisconsin Biography* (Madison, 1961), p. 207.

23. Ticknor, a sawmill hand living in Mauston at the outbreak of the war, quickly rose to the ranks of sergeant and became captain of Company K. He was killed July 1, 1863, at Gettysburg. U.S. Census, Wisconsin, 1860; *Roster of Wisconsin Volunteers,* Vol. I, p. 533; Dawes, *Service,* p. 17.

24. A reference to Gen. Winfield Scott's *Infantry Tactics, or Rules for the Exercise and Maneuvers of the United States Infantry,* a three-volume work issued in 1835 and republished in 1847. During the Civil War, it was universally called *Scott's Tactics.*

25. Butterfield, of Lemonweir, was discharged for disability March 7, 1863. His brother, Luther, joined the 6th Wisconsin in February 1862, but was also discharged for disability in May 1862. Both spent their last years at the National Soldier's Home in Milwaukee and were buried at Wood National Cemetery next to one another. *Roster of Wisconsin Volunteers,* Vol. I, p. 533.

26. Crane, of Lindina, was the 2nd lieutenant of Company K. He was one of several immigrant Irish officers purged from the regiment's ranks by Col. Lysander Cutler and others; he resigned October 30, 1861. *Ibid.,* p. 33; Herdegen and Beaudot, *Railroad Cut,* pp. 120, 124. Three months after his resignation, John Crane enlisted in the 17th Wisconsin as 1st lieutenant of Company A. He was promoted to regimental adjutant November 25, 1862, and served until his term expired on March 28, 1865. Patrick McCauley, another Irish officer who resigned from the 6th Wisconsin, enlisted in the 17th on December 30, 1861; he became the regiment's major in September 1864 and served until the end of the war. *Roster of Wisconsin Volunteers,* Vol. II, pp. 49, 50.

27. Sullivan left conflicting evidence, but it is most probable that he was born June 21, 1843. Thus, the impetuous young man was only 17 in May of 1861—not old enough to take the Federal oath. He turned 18 on June 21 and was then of age.

28. Cutler, the regiment's crusty first commander, was born in Massachusetts in 1808. He migrated to Milwaukee in 1856. He earned the sobriquet "Grey Wolf" while staking mining claims in upper Michigan before the war. He rose to command the Western brigade and, later, a division in the Army of the Potomac. He was wounded at the 6th Wisconsin's first action at Gainesville, Virginia, in August 1862, as well as at Fredericksburg and Weldon Railroad. He resigned in July 1865, his health broken, and he died in Milwaukee July 31, 1866. *Dictionary of Wisconsin Biography,* p. 92; [Flower], *History of Milwaukee,* pp. 789–92.

29. Atwood, a Madison attorney before the war, was the regiment's first lieutenant colonel. He resigned in September 1861. *Roster of Wisconsin Volunteers,* Vol. I, p. 494.

30. Sweet, like many of the other early officers of the regiment, was born in New York. He settled in Wisconsin to pursue political aspirations, and was admitted to the Wisconsin Bar in 1857. He was elected to the state legislature. At war's outbreak, he helped recruit a company of volunteers, and was appointed major of the 6th Wisconsin. He quickly ran afoul of New Englander Lysander Cutler, the regiment's colonel, and although Sweet was promoted to lieutenant colonel, the antipathy between the two officers resulted in Sweet's resignation. He became colonel of the 21st Wisconsin and was wounded in the battle of Perryville in Kentucky in September 1862. His active field service ended, he became commander of the Federal prison at Camp Douglas in Chicago and became embroiled in the infamous effort to root out Copperheads among the city's Democrats in 1864. He later joined the federal bureaucracy, and died January 1, 1874. Michael J. Fitch, *Echoes of the Civil War as I Hear Them* (New York, 1905), pp. 60, 67–71; Frank L. Klement, *Dark Lanterns* (Baton Rouge, La., 1984), pp. 191–217; *The Blackhat, Occasional Newsletter of the 6th Wisconsin Volunteers,* Nos. 25 and 26.

31. Sullivan referred to John Kellogg, who resigned as Juneau County attorney at the start of the war and enlisted despite a wife and family. He was elected Company K's 1st lieutenant and became captain of Company I, and ultimately colonel of the regiment. Kellogg was wounded and captured in the Wilderness in May 1864. He escaped and returned to the war, commanding what was left of the Iron Brigade in the final months of the war. He died in 1883. Dawes, *Service,* p. 6; *Roster of Wisconsin Volunteers,* Vol. I, p. 494; John A. Kellogg, *Capture and Escape* (Madison, 1908).

32. The "Montgomery Guards," recruited from the Milwaukee Irish community.

33. The "Sauk County Riflemen" were recruited from the area north of the Wisconsin River near Baraboo in the central part of the state.

34. A reference to the 1885 Iron Brigade Association reunion in Madison.

35. The 5th Wisconsin, which was transported East a week before the 6th, was briefly brigaded with the 6th Wisconsin. The 5th was replaced by the 7th Wisconsin.

36. The 6th Wisconsin brass band was inarguably the worst musical aggregation in the Army of the Potomac. Company C's Loyd G. Harris wrote frequently about the band in postwar years. *Milwaukee Sunday Telegraph,* November 12, 1882; November 26, 1882; August 16, 1885.

37. Talty, whose name is often misspelled in the regiment's records as "Tolty," veteranized and mustered out July 14, 1865. At 5-foot-3, he was the smallest man in his company and the source of constant amusement. Even Dawes, writing a quarter century after, noted that "Tall T," as he was called by his messmates, was a "marvel," often carrying an extra knapsack for the "little fellows." Because he was shorter than the uniform regulations allowed, Dawes paid particular attention to the little man, and when Talty was asked, "Who is your tailor?" he would call back, "The Captain, be gob!" Talty was 26 when he enlisted from Lisbon, Juneau County, and listed his occupation as railroader. An Irish immigrant, Talty was light complexioned, with sandy hair and blue eyes. He died sometime before 1885. Wisconsin Adjutant General's Office, Regimental Descriptive Rolls, 6th Wisconsin Infantry, Company K; U.S. Census, Wisconsin, 1860; Dawes, *Service,* p. 47; *Roster of Wisconsin Volunteers,* Vol. I, p. 536.

38. In Shakespeare's *Macbeth,* Banquo was a Scottish general and noble-man who, having been killed by Macbeth, came back to haunt the main character during a banquet.

39. A complete description of the state gray issue and later uniforms of the 6th Wisconsin was written by H. Michael Madaus; it is Appendix III, Herdegen and Beaudot, *Railroad Cut,* pp. 301–67.

40. The first battle of Bull Run, or "Bull's Run" as it was initially called by the Wisconsin boys, was the first major confrontation between Union and Confederate armies. It was fought July 21, 1861, and Federal Gen. Irvin McDowell's force was sharply defeated. The 2nd Wisconsin, soon to be brigaded with the 6th, fought at Bull Run. Alan D. Gaff, *If This Is War* (Dayton, Ohio, 1991).

41. Sullivan was in error. It was the "Union Guard," an Irish prewar militia company and not the "Montgomery Guard," that was involved in the fundraising excursion that ended in the sinking of the Lake Michigan vessel. The tragedy stemmed from a controversy between Wisconsin Gov. Alexander Randall and Garrett Barry, the captain of the militia company. Randall openly defied the Fugitive Slave Law, propounding that he would not enforce it. Captain Barry, however, said his militia men were obliged to enforce national law. The governor disarmed the Union Guard and dis-banded the unit. In September 1860 the Lake Michigan excursion side-wheeler *Lady Elgin* was chartered to raise money to rearm the Irish militiamen and to convey people to hear Democratic speakers in Chicago. On the return trip to Milwaukee, September 6, the streamer was struck by a schooner and sank. Some 300 lives were lost and almost every Irish family in Milwaukee was touched by the tragedy. Bayrd Still, *Milwaukee, The History of a City* (Madison, 1948), p. 153; Richard N. Current, *The History of Wisconsin, the Civil War Era, 1848–1873* (Madison, 1976), pp. 271, 277–81.

42. The all-German "Citizens Corps" was sometimes called the Turners after the German gymnastic societies called "Turnverein," which were numerous in cities such as Milwaukee, Cincinnati, and others with large immigrant populations. Company C of the 5th Wisconsin was known as the "Milwaukee Turners;" its members were composed of the city's German immigrants. [Flower], *History of Milwaukee,* p. 708.

43. When the 6th Wisconsin departed from Milwaukee after being fêted by the city July 24, 1861, one enterprising private used the occasion to coax a kiss from a comely young woman. Leaning from the railroad car window, the gray-clad soldier asked, "Say, Miss, won't you kiss me for my mother." Perhaps to his surprise, she reached up and with tears streaming down her cheeks, she clutched him with both arms and kissed him, to the hoots of his comrades. The unidentified private never forgot the emotional incident of that hot July day. *Milwaukee Sunday Telegraph,* April 8, 1883.

44. Robert E. Lee's prewar home was at Arlington Heights near Washington, D.C. It was inherited by Lee and his wife, Mary Custis, in 1857. The couple had been married there in 1831, and were to spend 30 years of their lives in the Greek Revival mansion. Lee, in 1861, wrote his letter of resignation from the U.S. Army in the home. When Federal forces crossed the Potomac River in the spring of 1861, one of the initial positions occupied was the Lee mansion because of its strategic location. Mrs. Lee fled the

home. The building, a stuccoed brick structure, featured eight heavy Doric columns supporting a massive pediment. In 1864 the title of the estate passed to the U.S. government and Union soldiers were buried on the grounds. In 1934 its care passed to the National Park Service, and today it serves as the central office for Arlington Cemetery. *Washington: City and Capital* (Washington, D.C., 1937), pp. 440–41.

45. Fletcher was one of a hand-picked 10-man detail which, in June 1864, was sent to destroy the Danville, Virginia, railroad. All were captured and Fletcher was listed as missing in action. Hancock was on the same detail. He was captured and later shot by a rebel guard while imprisoned at Salisbury, North Carolina. *Roster of Wisconsin Volunteers,* Vol. I, p. 534; Dawes, *Service,* p. 294–95.

46. Garthwait, of White Creek, deserted June 22, 1862; Holmes, of Fountain, was wounded at South Mountain, and deserted May 7, 1864, during the Battle of the Wilderness; and Davis, of Woodland, deserted June 27, 1865, just three months after being drafted. McCuin's name is not recorded, however. *Ibid.,* p. 534, 535.

47. Corrections from *Roster of Wisconsin Volunteers,* Vol. I, pp. 533–36.

48. Fairchild commanded the 2nd Wisconsin at Gettysburg during the fierce morning action in McPherson's Woods July 18, 1863. He returned home a hero and in 1864 rode the wave of Republican Party patriotism to become Secretary of State. In 1866 he was elected governor, and served two terms. He thereafter was appointed to various foreign ministerial posts; upon his return to Wisconsin, he became active in veterans' organizations. He died in 1896. *Dictionary of Wisconsin Biography,* p. 125.

49. Those members of the 2nd Wisconsin who re-enlisted in 1864 were temporarily designated the Wisconsin Independent Battalion; the unit served as provost guard for the division. On November 27, 1864, the battalion was officially folded into the 6th Wisconsin as Companies G and H. *Roster of Wisconsin Volunteers,* Vol. I, pp. 379–81; Dawes, *Service,* p. 311.

Chapter II

GIVING 'EM WISCONSIN HELL

[One of the early articles by J. P. Sullivan appeared in the fall of 1883. He had likely written it earlier in response to an "Entreaty" by Jerome A. Watrous, whose soldier newspaper was growing in circulation and influence among the state's veterans. Like some of his other writings, the piece, describing an incident which occurred in the summer of 1862 before the 6th Wisconsin was to experience its first battle, is laced with humor and iconoclasm.

The farmers, piney boys and mechanics under crusty Col. Lysander Cutler, had arrived in the sprawling Washington camps nearly a year before the incident. They were eventually brigaded with the 2nd Wisconsin, 7th Wisconsin, and the 19th Indiana. The four regiments were initially commanded by Milwaukee's Rufus King, but in May 1862, West Pointer John Gibbon, a stiff-backed regular army artillery officer, was given leadership of the Western unit.[1]

Even before Gibbon assumed command, superficial changes had taken place that would come to mark the unit as something special. The state-issued gray uniforms that Mickey had so much fun in describing were discarded. In their place was prescribed the regular army nine-button dark blue frock coat. And some units—all four regiments would eventually follow—had already been issued the tall black-felt hat of the U.S. Regulars which, in not many months, would stamp the Westerners as a vaunted fighting unit to friend and foe.

Gibbon, with the assistance of Madison's Frank A. Haskell, one of several transplanted New Englanders who joined the 6th Wisconsin, helped shape and hone the four regiments through months of tedious drill and preparation. Private Sullivan had also sustained his first wound in that pre-battle period. At a Washington's birthday ceremony at Arlington Heights in February of 1862, he had been struck in the back by a steel musket ramrod; some damned fool in the 7th Wisconsin, it seemed, failed to withdraw the rod after loading for a ceremonial volley of blanks, and Mickey had been knocked to his knees. That put the testy young Irishman off his feet for a few days, but he soon returned to the back rank with the other "ragtag and bobtail" of Company K.[2]

Sullivan's attitude toward freed slaves, several of whom served as cooks and wallopers in the 6th Wisconsin, may seem racist or, at least, condescending in the late twentieth century, but there was little meanness in what he wrote. Like a majority of Union soldiers, he was not motivated to fight for the abolition of slavery. Perhaps only one in ten soldiers enlisted to free the slaves, and many denied emancipation was a war aim; they would feel betrayed by the government's change in policy. Sullivan's attitude toward emancipation was lukewarm at best, and in other of his Civil War writings he reinforced this view. Many blue-coated soldiers from urban areas, especially in the Middle West, actually feared the competition for jobs as freed blacks swarmed to Northern cities. Many objected also to the ignorance of former slaves who, they felt, were not ready for the requirements of freedom and citizenship.[3] Sullivan was a young man of rural America who was rarely exposed to blacks. Late in life, Sullivan's views would change, and he acknowledged the necessity of eradicating slavery. The episode was printed in *The Milwaukee Sunday Telegraph* on October 21, 1883.]

HOW WE LOST OUR COOK
An Incident of Rappahannock Station
By Mickey, of Co. "K."

Some time in June, 1862, a gentleman, a brunette, curly hair and prominent lips, who had concluded to "lay down de shubbel and de hoe," and seek independence and affluence, came into our regiment at Fredericksburg, and scraped up an acquaintance with "Nigger Jack," who had accompanied company E, from Fond du Lac and who was as well known through the brigade as was General [John] Gibbon. The aforesaid handsome gentleman was afraid of being returned to labor and poverty, as [Gen. Irvin] McDowell was known to be one of the "kid glove policy" generals, whose affinity for the "man and brother" was only equalled by that of Lieut. [David L.] Quaw.[4] [Capt. Rufus R.] Dawes assembled the united wisdom of the company and explained, in glowing terms, the advantages which would result from an alliance, offensive and defensive, between company K and the person Ben Butler disrespectfully classed as contraband of war,[5] and informed them that if the company would raise half the pay he would contribute the other half and the contraband could do double duty as company cook and what was ignominiously termed captain's "Dog robber," and William was duly elected and installed in charge of the company kitchen, which consisted of all out doors and a hole in the ground for the fire.

The alliance proved satisfactory to all the contracting parties. William was always "on deck" and the meals ready in proper season, and the coffee had not lost its blackness nor when the beans or rice burnt or scorched any oftener than before, and Dawes' boots and sword shone like a new chromo, and at night William would relate to an attentive audience stories of his former slave life in de cotton and de cane and terbacker fiel's of de souf. Things went along swimmingly until the skirmish at Rappahannock station,[6] where Lee sent his compliments in the shape of a few Whitworth solid shot, and our fellows, who had never heard a rebel cannon before, but had been kept well posted about the "black flags" and "railroad" iron of the rebels by the warlike editors at home, and thinking that nothing else could make such unearthly screams, they said the "greybacks were slinging railroad iron." Their battery finally got the range of our regiment, which was drawn up in double column by division, and a shot ricochetted through the regiment, doing no damage, however, except destroying Colonel Cutler's mess chest, and the old greybeard, who had been an indifferent spectator hitherto, ordered the regiment to "fall in" and he marched it about a length to one side, out of the line of fire. William, who had previously located the hole in the ground part of the kitchen at some convenient place in the rear, and had got dinner ready, was now bringing it forward to serve up, and was coming up with a camp kettle of coffee in each hand and a mess pan of fried pork gracefully balanced on his head. He reached the ground where the regiment had been laying, and at that moment a shot with a more fiendish shriek than any which had yet come over, went screaming through the air. William hesitated a moment and then his knees began to lower until he dropped the camp kettles, and shooting out from under the mess pan, he started for the rear at a rate that Maud S. never dreampt of.[7] The boys encouraged him all in their power by cheers and yells and such exclamations as "go it William." "We'll bet on the bob tail nag." "They are coming, William." "They'll catch you, William." "You are the one, William," etc., until he was out of sight and it was generally supposed while the regiment was in the service that William was retreating, and in fact I heard a comrade assert at the late reunion in La Crosse [September 1883], that William was still running.

The incident afforded an infinite fund of amusement to the regiment, and the inquiry was frequently made if "Dawes had heard anything about his nigger," or "when was company K going to 'dine;' " but although it was fun for them and us, too, we were the only sufferers, as we had no dinner or supper nor in fact any meal until our culinary department was re-organized by forming the company into messes of four men each, and we had no more company cooks.[8]

[Within a few days after the humorous incident of the Company K cook, the 6th Wisconsin and other regiments were tested in battle for the first time near Gainesville, Virginia. The engagement, sometimes called Brawner Farm, occurred on a late August day and was part of the opening of the Second Bull Run campaign. It was at Gainesville that the 6th Wisconsin, along with the 2nd and 7th Wisconsin and 19th Indiana, were confronted by a considerably larger force of rebels. Like the 6th Wisconsin's charge on the railroad cut at Gettysburg, the baptismal fight of the brigade at Gainesville was later overshadowed by larger events. It was also overlooked by later historians, and not until Alan T. Nolan's study, *The Iron Brigade*, was published in 1961 was the signal achievement of the Westerners brought to light. At Gainesville the four regiments exhibited stern Western mettle that would serve them well on future bloody fields and earn for them a reputation as one of the hardest fighting units in the Federal armies.[9]

Sullivan, as was his wont, castigated what he considered incompetent army commanders—this time Gen. John Pope, whom he called "Hindquarters in the saddle." When Sullivan wrote of these events, he had become enmeshed in the bureaucracy of the pension system, having made several attempts to secure what he felt was a rightful monthly allotment of a few dollars for his war service and battle scars. But he was having difficulty convincing examining boards that he was unable to carry out a full day's labor on his farm fields. The graying veteran already appeared older than his years— he had turned 40 the summer before the Gainesville piece was published—and it was difficult for him to coax more than a meager living from the western Wisconsin soil. The parade of veterans, meanwhile, filled the state's governor's chair and most other offices, elected by their old comrades who "voted as they shot." Sullivan, perhaps emboldened by the reception of his recollections of Gettysburg, scoured his war diary and other sources to produce his story of Gainesville. Sullivan's article was published in *The Milwaukee Sunday Telegraph* on November 4, 1883.]

"BOYS, AIM LOW—FIRE."
So Said General Cutler at Gainesville
—What a man in the "Blue Line"
Says About the Fight

THE BATTLE OF GAINESVILLE
By Mickey, of Co. "K."

About the first of July, 1862, General [John] Pope who had captured the rebels that the gunboats had dislodged from Island No. 10 and New Madrid,[10] (and in consequence fancied himself the greatest general of the age), took command of all the troops in the vicinity of Washington not belonging to McClellan's army proper, and styled them the "Army of Virginia." He issued his first order dated "Headquarters in the saddle," and the soldiers, with their usual aptitude to ridicule all attempts at self-glorification on the part of generals, said that he must have his brains where most persons have their hindquarters, and immediately dubbed him "Hindquarters in the saddle Pope,"[11] and after events fully justified their judgment. After a series of the most silly and bombastic orders which very much resembled the legislation of this state in so far as one countermanded, modified or explained the preceding one, his literary display was finally interrupted by "Stonewall" Jackson, who having performed his part in turning the flank of McClellan's army on the Peninsula, turned his attention to the direction of the Shenandoah Valley, where the rich harvest was ripe and awaiting shipment to Richmond. On the 9th of August, "Stonewall" ran into Bank's corps at Cedar Mountain,[12] and a hot fight ensued in which, "On both sides stores of blood was lost, nor much success could either boast," although Banks held the ground and claimed a victory.[13] Our brigade was then at Fredericksburg and we got orders to immediately march towards Culpeper, and [Gen. Franz] Sigel's corps, which was in the Valley of the Shenandoah, and [Gen. William] Rickett's division of our corps, at Catlett's Station and in the vicinity of Manassas Junction, were also ordered forward to support Banks. As reconnaissance developed the fact that "Stonewall" had fallen back behind the Rapidan [River] and Pope immediately reported him in full retreat towards Richmond, completely demoralized, and, after compelling his army to remain encamped more than a week during the hottest part of the year, on the battle field, subject to the overpowering stench of decaying horses and half buried bodies, when fifteen minutes' march would have placed them in an adjoining grove of timber where they would have shelter from the sun and have plenty of good water, and be removed from the filth and unwholesomeness of a battle field, he was startled by the news that instead of being in a demoralized retreat towards Richmond[,] "Stonewall" was crossing the Rappahannock on his right flank and rear. Our whole force immediately started in pursuit and all the talk was (which we understood originated at headquarters) "that Stonewall Jackson had got into a bag and General Pope was going to tie the string and keep him there." But the next news was that "Stonewall" had taken the army train[14] and Pope's headquarters train at Catlett Station and had sent Pope's uniform to Richmond where it was displayed in a show window labeled "This belongs to the man who never saw anything but the backs of enemies;" and the next news was that "Stonewall" had captured Bristow Station[15] and had telegraphed to Washington for and received supplies and an entire new outfit for his army. Our men had lost all confidence in Pope's abilities and it was openly remarked in the ranks that [Gen. Irvin] McDowell was a traitor,[16] and Banks' inefficiency was so well known that it was a current saying that when his pickets were attacked he would burn all the government stores and wagon trains and fall back to Washington. Siegel [sic] was the only corps commander that had the confidence and respect of the men, for they believed he would fight. Our men were on the shortest possible allowance of rations, while at the same time thousands of rations were being burned daily instead of being issued to the men, and finally our brigade "rallied" on the commissary department while passing through Warrenton and General Gibbon made room on the caissons and limbers of battery B[17] for the hard tack boxes and bacon we "gobbled."[18]

Now [Gen. Joseph] Hooker, who had arrived from the army of the Peninsula, interrupted "Stonewall" at Bristow before he [Jackson] had got all his new harness and things issued and gave him a sound threshing, driving him back towards Pope, and on the afternoon of Aug. 28th, which will long be remembered in many a Wisconsin and Indiana home, our brigade met him at Gainesville.

Between 6 and 7 P.M., of that day [Thursday], our brigade (Gibbon's brigade, King's division, and McDowell's corps,) were leisurely marching along on the Warrenton "Pike," towards Manassas Junction, chatting, joking and laughing in their usual manner when a rebel battery opened on them from a clump of woods on their left. We halted and lay down along the side of the road and General Gibbon ordered the 2d [Wisconsin] regiment forward to take the battery. Forward they went, with lusty cheers, only to find that the battery was heavily supported by infantry, and although the 2d stood a murderous fire, unflinchingly, they were unable to advance, and another regiment [19th Indiana] went forward to support them, only to find they were in turn overlapped and in danger of being outflanked. Another regiment [7th Wisconsin] went forward to support them and finally our colonel [Cutler] who was watching the fight from the top of the fence ordered our regiment, the 6th, to fall in[,] remarking that "we could not let our comrades be slaughtered in that manner," and at the same time orders came for us to advance. We climbed over a fence and went forward in line of battle with full regimental front and step, and "guide left," as regular as if on parade. It was about 80 rods across the field to a strip of woods, and when about half way across I looked back and saw our colonel, Cutler, sitting on his big black horse as straight as a rod. We had never been engaged at close quarters before, and the experience was new to all of us. I don't know how the others felt, but I am free to confess that I felt a queer choking sensation about the throat, but some one in the rear rank awkwardly stepped on my heel and I instantly forgot all about the choking feeling and turned to him, angerly, to demand if there was not room for him to march without skinning my heel; and we were jawing and fussing until the colonel shouted halt, and there, about six or eight rods in front of us was a heavy column, marching by the flank, which I supposed was part of our division and had no idea they were rebels on their way to out-flank the 19th Indiana. The colonel gave the command: "Sixth Regiment, ready! aim—aim low, fire!" and our regiment delivered one of the volleys by regiment for which it was noted. Every gun cracked at once, and the line in front, which had faced us at the command "ready," melted away, and instead of the heavy line of battle that was there before our volley, they presented the appearance of a skirmish line that had rallied by fours, there being only groups left, here and there, but another line moved up and took their place, and we stood there, firing at each other, at short range, until our men fired away twenty rounds of cartridges and the rebels fell back and another line took their place, and we engaged them. Many of our men fired forty rounds of ammunition without stirring out of their tracks and in fact, we stood there until midnight, without moving a rod either way. From prisoners taken it was learned that Jackson's famous "Stonewall division" and another division under [Gen Richard] Ewell were in that woods, and both divisions fought our brigade. In vain General Gibbon went to division headquarters for aid, and although the rest of our division lay there in sight and hearing, not a shot was fired nor a man sent forward to our assistance. Our brigade could not advance and the rebels could not drive us one foot, and it was a straight stand up and take it between the two rebel divisions, and our brigade, in which the advantage of numbers more than three to one, was on the side of Jackson and also that he had the cover of the timber while our men were in the open field. The rebels finally drew off, but not until Ewell had lost a leg[19] and their divisions had been cut up pretty badly, and prisoners told us that the rebel officers had said "it was no use to fight them damn fools; they did now know enough to know when they were whipped," and their ammunition had run out, while our fellows, who carried twenty extra rounds in their pockets were pretty well supplied. About midnight General [Rufus] King, who had just learned that his division was attacked, sent orders for us to resume the march for Manassas Junction, which we reached shortly after daylight at the same time that Fitz John Porter's corps, of McClellan's army did, which marched side and side with us for some distance.

I hardly knew our brigade, it was so reduced in size and the men looked so dirty and powder-stained that I could scarcely tell my own tentmates, and it seemed as if their dispositions changed with their appearance.

The intensest feelings of anger were manifested against the commander who allowed one brigade alone and unaided to fight the best divisions in the rebel army. The remainder of the division had the excuse that they had no orders, and did not know that we were so hard pressed, but we thought they were pleased to see "them western galoots" get fits. Our men halted and made coffee, and "Little Johnny Gibbon" won the affection of the brigade for all time by his manly sympathy for his men. The brigade had lost almost a thousand men, and amongst them all the colonels of the different regiments were killed or wounded. Col. Edgar O'Connor, of the 2d Wisconsin, (who had been promoted from the regular army to command the 2d, after the first Bull Run, at the special request of that grand old patriot, Governor Randall,) was killed. Col. Cutler, of our regiment, was shot in the thigh, but kept the field until the pains overcame him, and the giant Sol. Meredith, colonel of the 19th Indiana, whose great size made him incur the risks of two ordinary men, was also wounded, and I believe injured by his horse falling dead under him.[20] The killed and wounded were left on the field and abandoned by both armies, as Stonewall left the ground next morning for Bull Run, and it was not until more than a year afterwards that General Cutler, who was then in command of the brigade during the Mine Run campaign, made a detail from the brigade to bury the dead who lay in rows where they had fallen, and whose bones were bleaching in the hot, southern sun. With the exception of Gettysburg, our brigade never sustained so severe a loss, and yet reports, in speaking of it, only say that King's division had a severe skirmish on the 28th, whereas, outside of our four regiments and battery B, 4th U.S. artillery, which belonged to our brigade, I have no knowledge of a shot being fired by any of King's division. It may seem strange that our brigade was allowed to be cut to pieces without getting help, but that seemed to be the way with Pope's army. "Every one for himself and the devil take the hindmost."

[Sullivan was, of course, in error. Two regiments of Gen. Abner Doubleday's Brigade—the 56th Pennsylvania and 76th New York— fought to the left of the 6th Wisconsin during the battle. And that error prompted a rebuttal in the following week's issue of *The Milwaukee Sunday Telegraph*. It appeared November 11, 1883, and was by-lined "Orderly," who was likely Charles King, the son of Division Commander Rufus King. Young King served as his father's orderly at the battle.][21]

Mickey on Gainesville.

A very interesting paper was that with which our K company poet soldier favored the soldiers' column last Sunday, and nobody who saw the grand old Iron Brigade the night of Gainesville—or afterwards—would ever say a word to detract one atom from its well-won glory. But it is a poor rule that won't work both ways, and it is hardly fair to Mickey to run down other fellows who were doing their best to help him that night. So well-known is the valor of that Wisconsin-Indiana brigade of King's old division that it need never have to resort to the questionable practice of lifting itself by pulling down some other, and this is what Mickey had unquestionably done.

Now the writer of this has heard of Mickey, and believes him to have been a thorough-going soldier. Starting in with this idea it is further assumed that Mickey was so busy loading and firing (with occasional intermissions, perhaps, to damn that luckless rear-guard man who barked his heel) he absolutely did not know what was going on further to his left. Believing therefore that he is as generous a soldier as he was a brave one, it is conjectured that Mickey will be glad to do honor where honor is due, when he has been informed of his mistake.

Mickey says that except Gibbon's brigade and Battery B, he has "no knowledge of a shot being fired by any of King's division." More than that he says "although the rest of the division lay there in sight and hearing, not a shot was fired nor a man sent forward to our assistance." Here Mickey is in error. When the fight began[,] [Gen. John Porter] Hatch's brigade was sent out of sight a mile ahead. [Gen. Marsena R.] Patrick's brigade was over a mile behind. [Gen. Abner] Doubleday's was the only one close at hand, and that Doubleday's brigade was speedily ordered in to support Gibbon, and that the 56th Pennsylvania and the 76th New York pushed right forward on the same line with the 6th Wisconsin wherein Mickey was blazing away for all he was worth, is attested by the reports of General Doubleday and Colonels [J. William Hofmann] Hofman and [Charles B.] Wainwright, and by the fact that right there on that line the 56th lost their colonel, four captains, two lieutenants and 55 enlisted men, shot down and the 76th 10 killed, 72 wounded (including five officers) and 18 missing. The 95th was sent to the right in support of old Battery B, and did not get into the heavy fire. Mickey is hardly to blame for his lack of information on this point as it was quite the custom to speak of it as Gibbon's fight as though no other brigade was engaged.

In saying, too, that not until midnight was General King aware that his division was attacked, and that that officer allowed our brigade to fight alone and unaided, Mickey does grave injustice to a man who yielded to none in his love and admiration for the Iron Brigade. It was General King who sent orders to Patrick to push in to Gibbon's support, to Hatch

Alan T. Nolan

Charles Keeler of the 6th Wisconsin in the distinctive uniform
of the Iron Brigade. Keeler was wounded in the legs at Gettysburg.

Edward Bragg, the second commander of the 6th Wisconsin.

H. Michael Madaus

Lysander Cutler was the first colonel of the 6th Wisconsin.

Charles L. Foster

John Gibbon, the second commander of the Iron Brigade.

*From John A. Ehlers, SERVICE WITH THE SIXTH
WISCONSIN VOLUNTEERS*

Rufus R. Dawes, the first captain of Company K, who as
lieutenant colonel led the 6th Wisconsin's charge on the Railroad Cut at Gettysburg.

Jerome A. Watrous, 6th Wisconsin veteran and newspaperman who published Sullivan's writings.

James P. Sullivan with his second wife, Bessie, and their son,
James Fitz.

James P. Sullivan gravesite at Ontario, Wisconsin. At left, original military stone; right, marker placed by son George.

to hasten back, and to Doubleday to hurry forward, and though it was barely dark by the time Hatch and his men did return and though Patrick's orders failed to reach him in time, it was no fault of General King. More than this, at nine o'clock at night King wrote to [Gen. William] Ricketts, telling him to come to his support as Jackson was there in full force, and that hour, 9 o'clock, Hatch, Gibbon and Doubleday were there with King talking over the situation and "Little Johnny Gibbon," as Mickey affectionately calls him, was vehemently urging General King to fall back and push for Manassas—the very move that resulted in their wounded being left on the field.

You were a good fighter, Mickey, they all say that, and you must know that "fair play is a jewel." You cannot tell us too much of the splendid service of the Iron Brigade. We will endorse you right straight through; but when you level your accusations at General King you strike at its organizer and first commander, you aim a blow at soldiers whose honor and reputation are as dear to them as your own is to you, and— such a thing should never be done—where the facts are not as you state them.

—ORDERLY

[It was four months after his piece on Gainesville was published that Sullivan pulled together his recollections of Second Bull Run, which occurred August 29–30, 1862. While Sullivan's regiment was not heavily engaged in the latter battle, his recollections were enriched by his dark humor and eye for evocative detail—for example, a frightened rabbit taking refuge under a fallen soldier. He could almost casually toss off an observation of a comrade being killed and in the same sentence describe a laughable incident of another soldier who somersaulted when an enemy bullet struck the man's belt and rubber blanket. This seeming indifference toward the death of comrades may have been a way to heal the psychological scars left by the loss.

Sullivan, himself an immigrant, was not above poking fun at a German officer's manner of speech in the heat of battle. And, as in nearly all his writings, he once again heaped invective upon the incompetent army leaders—here, Gen. John Pope, who, the Irishman wrote, had "no talent to direct the men," displayed "ignorance and self conceit," and was naught save an "ignominious failure." The piece was published in *The Milwaukee Sunday Telegraph* May 16, 1884.]

SAVE MINE PATTERY
A Man in The Ranks Writes an
Interesting Chapter About a Great Battle

THE IRON BRIGADE AT BULL RUN
By Mickey, of Co. K

The morning of the 29th of August our brigade reached Manassas Junction. Bleeding, angry, hungry, tired, sleepy, foot-sore and cut to pieces, those who had coffee made and drank it and those who did not have it borrowed from the others. [Tommy] Flynn, of company K, who hailed from Knightstown, Indiana,[22] went over to the 19th [Indiana] to learn how his friends fared last night, after Gainesville, and brought back a supply of pork and sugar that some of them let him have, and our mess dined in high pomp as the result of his efforts. It was a notable fact, all through the war, there existed the strongest feelings of friendship amongst the different regiments of the brigade for one another. If any one wanted to get into what Nick Whiffles would call a "pijen difficulty," all that was necessary for him to do was to get into the 19th and say a word against the "Wisconsin boys," and the same held good in any of our regiments about them. After drinking our coffee and resting for an hour or two, we drew sixty rounds of ammunition and "fell in" and took up the line of march towards Bull Run, where the sudden boom of cannon indicated that the enemy had made a stand. We reached the battle field early in the afternoon and then we learned that [Gen. Franz] Sigel and [Gen. Jesse] Reno had fallen in with "Stonewall" Jackson and that [Gen. Joseph] Hooker and [Gen. Phil] Kearney were driving back the advance guard of Lee's army. We moved into an open field and the 2d Wisconsin recognized the ground on which they had fought at the first

Bull [Run] a year before.[23] A hot battle broke out about sundown and lasted until 8 or 9 o'clock, and the left of our line advanced some distance to a piece of woods. Before midnight the firing ceased and we understood that Lee had been beaten and to-morrow would finish the job, and that the much dreaded "Stonewall" was gobbled with his army, but the next day brought a very different story. Skirmishing began on the left at daylight, and it sounded to me like a dozen of carpenters shingling a roof. I went out on the battle field of yesterday in search of hard tack,[24] as my haversack was empty and I told Flynn that a fellow might as well be shot to death as die of hunger, and he promised to look after my gun and traps if the company moved before I returned. I entered a strip of woods where Sigel's men had fought two days before and found two or three haversacks with some hard tack in them, and when I was about to return a fellow called to me for help. Following his calls I came to a North Carolina rebel that had his ankle broke and had laid there for two days. He had his back against a small tree and being unable to shift himself, he was smeared and daubed with filth and blood in a dreadful manner. The poor fellow wanted water and having no canteen I went farther into the woods in search of one, the rebel skirmishers fired several shots at me, but I showed them that I was tending one of their wounded and they did not fire any more. I found a dead rebel and he had a little round keg half filled with water and I cut it off and brought it to the wounded man and gave him a hard tack or two and helped him to shift himself into a more comfortable position and promised to send out help to him when I went back, which I did, and a couple of stretcher bearers went out and brought him in. There was a ridge of ground where we lay and a heavy line of artillery was posted along the crest, 24 or 30 pieces, and they were wishing for the rebels to come out of the woods so they would "warm 'em," as they expressed it, but the rebels did not come. General [Irvin] McDowell and several other officers rode along the line and McDowell had on the oddest looking hat I ever saw, and our fellows said he wore that so the rebels could distinguish him, and not direct their fire in his direction. The rebels did not come out to us and we got orders to go to them.

We advanced in line of battle to the edge of the woods and halted and lay down. Things were pretty hot on our left and after a bit the second platoon of company K got orders to advance as skirmishers and ascertain if there were any Johnnies in the woods.[25] We advanced over the ground I had been on that morning and had not gone far when we got a volley from the rebel skirmishers, killing Levi Gardner dead in his tracks; Hod [Hoel W.] Trumbull had his rubber blanket folded up very narrow (about 3 or 4 inches wide) and it was around his waist under his waist belt. He was running forward when a bullet hit him on the waist belt and rubber blanket and he turned the completest somersault I ever saw, and some of us laughed heartier at it than at the antics of a circus clown. All the injuries he received was to have the wind knocked out for a second or two.[26] We chased the skirmishers out of the woods to the other side, and a line of battle rose up from behind a rail-road embankment and gave us a volley that made things hum. Lieut. [John] Ticknor, having complied with orders and found plenty of Rebs there, gave orders for the skirmishers to fall back, but I did not hear them in the uproar, and taking shelter behind a small tree I began to peg away at the Rebs until I exhausted the 20 rounds that was in the top compartment of my cartridge box, and when I stopped to refill it I saw I was alone and I dug out of there in a hurry. The regiment had advanced further into the woods and moved to the left and I finally found them laying down and the Rebs were trying to shell them with shell and case shot, and the tree tops and limbs were falling in all directions. I was very angry at Ticknor, thinking that he had carelessly left me there alone and not yet having arrived at the dignity of using what Hotspur calls "a good mouth filling oath," but still clung to the "cuss" words of my boyhood, I asked him with an indignant "dog gone" him why he left me there to fight the whole rebel army alone. Lt. Colonel [Edward S.] Bragg ordered me to lay down, and all the satisfaction I got from Ticknor, was, "Lay down, Mickey, you damfool, before you get killed," and I lay down and transferred my cartridges to the upper part of my cartridge box.[27] The rebel skirmishers kept up a brisk fire and hit several of our men whose patience was sorely tried lying there without being allowed to fire a shot, and finally we were ordered to fall back as the rebels had driven the left of the line, and we were in danger of being outflanked. We fell back slowly before the rebel skirmishers and under fire of their artillery. In crossing the field we passed through a small orchard and the color bearer was shot, or the colors caught in the trees, causing a temporary halt in the center of the line. That prince of good soldiers, Frank A. Haskell,[28] who had been our adjutant and was now brigadier adjutant general on Gibbon's staff, sprang forward exclaiming, "By Heavens, these colors must never go down before the enemy," but the flags were already up and facing the regiment and marking time with his sword he called, "Left, left, right, left," as he had done many times at Arlington Heights on drill; the regiment straightened up and marched as well as it ever did on review. We fell back behind the guns and lay down to support them and they opened fire and the Rebs did not advance beyond the edge of the woods. Their artillery was opening a close and destructive fire on the guns in front of us and canister and case shot were flying in all directions. A canister or grape shot[29] hit Ed. Symon's [Simmons] haversack as it lay on his thigh and scattered his stock of hardtack and coffee in all directions, and he mourned more over the loss of his "grub," as he called it, than if it had been an arm.[30] With the exception of the cannonade before the rebels made the final charge on Cemetery Hill at Gettysburg, I have never seen such a heavy fire. All who were there will not forget when the tail was shot off from one of battery B's horses and fell, still shaking and quivering several feet away. Nor the rabbit that was so much scared by the tremendous noise that it ran and took shelter under one of our men who was laying down, or the man whose leg was shot off and was making such good time for the rear by the aid of his musket. The rebels were driving our left back and we could see the battle flag of [Gen. William] Rickett's division go forward only to fall back in turn when the charge of the enemy met it. The 5th New York zouaves, which belonged to [Gen. Gouverneur K.] Warren's brigade of Fitz John Porter's corps, and was conspicuous by their uniform,[31] stood their ground well and fell back slowly, but some of the troops on their right broke and left them alone and they were forced to give way. There was a Massachusetts regiment supporting a battery on our left, and before the rebel wave struck them they broke and ran (uncovering the battery) and took shelter in a ditch (that had been used as a rear [privy pit] by all hands while we had been on the field) much to our indignation and disgust. Flynn voiced the feelings of our fellows when he said "there is not divils enough in the confederacy to make me put my head in that ditch." The battery left unsupported was in imminent danger of being captured, and the commander, a brave German officer, galloped up to Lt. Col. Bragg crying worse than a whipped schoolboy, "Mine pattery vas gone, mine pattery vas gone." Bragg, who was watching events in his usual cool, indifferent way, with one eye shut and the other not open, said, "we'll take care of your battery," and the satisfied and delighted officer rode back and directed the fire of his men. The 2d Wisconsin, which had lost all of its field officers and been terribly cut up at Gainesville, was temporarily consolidated with the 7th [Wisconsin], and they were ordered forward and took position, one on each side of the battery and just behind the brow of the ridge, and the rebels, who were sure of the battery, came rushing forward with exultant yells. The 2d and 7th waited until they were very close and then rose and gave them a volley that halted them right there and the order to fix bayonets and charge caused them to conclude that they did not want that battery, and they scampered back for the woods as fast as they could go, under a withering fire of all the guns that could bear on them. We understood when we were placed on that ridge that it was the key of the battle field, and if keys of battle fields are of any use to win battles, I fail to see why we did not win that, as I am very sure we held that key and were not driven an inch by the rebels, nor did our pieces have to "limber to the rear" until we were finally marched off the field. After dark[,] orders were given to fall back and cover the road to Centerville, and we lay down on the field which was lit up by the flash of an occasional gun, and we could hear the boom of cannon on the right where the "One armed devil," Phil Kearny,[32] was holding his position like a bull dog; and Sigel and Reno, who had not lost any ground, still held the field. About midnight we had orders to march, and leisurely fell back all night, crossing Cub Run next morning, where we halted and formed lines across the road to stop the pursuing rebels, but they did not choose to attack, and we continued our march to Centerville, and Sumner's corps, which had come up to support Pope, came forward and relieved us and after marching, starving and fighting a week, without a night's rest, we lay down in the mud and rain and slept as only the tired soldier can when he has a chance.[33]

A recent writer narrating how his company, after a fatiguing march (in dust so thick that one was unable to see the length of the company,) was turned out and worked all night constructing a bridge only to get orders as the last plank was laid at daylight, to destroy it, described that campaign as "blunder," and that is the only word that does justice to Pope's Bull Run campaign. It was said, but I did not see it, that Pope, McDowell and Sigel quarrelled on the battle-field, and that Sigel drew his pistol to shoot Pope, calling him a cowardly ignoramus, who was not qualified to hold the rank of corporal. Be that as it may, I know that our part of the army had no idea that we were defeated, and I think, had he been an energetic commander, with two fresh corps coming up to his support, and his centre and right wing intact, there was no occasion for Pope to retreat from Bull Run, leaving his dead and wounded uncared for; many of the latter of whom died for want of care before the ambulance corps and citizens of Washington went out and brought most of them in. During the sixty days that Pope was in command the army had one uninterrupted series of disasters, and although they fought well and lost heavily, there was no talent to direct the men. Pope blames Fitz John Porter,[34] but the enlisted men of the army thought that he should blame his own ignorance and self conceit, for, if he had handled his army half as well as Porter's men fought at Bull Run, the result would have been different. I have seen it stated on authority that Pope claimed he had only 35,000 men in that campaign, which is as false as his charges against Porter. Pope had Bank's corps, seven or eight thousand strong (but they took no part in the battles after Cedar Mountain, but they did Pope good service, though, destroying his trains and supplies); Sigel's corps, twelve or fifteen thousand strong, McDowell's corps, twenty-five or thirty thousand; Burnside's army, under Reno, ten or twelve thousand; Hooker and Kearney's divisions of [Gen. Samuel P.] Heinzelman's corps, Keye's corps, and Fitz John Porter's corps, of McClellan's army, took part in the second Bull Run, while Sumner's and [Gen. William B.] Franklin's corps, of the same army, were within supporting distance, at Centerville, in all, to say nothing of Sumner and Franklin about 80,000 men; but Pope, who had come there to show the "Army of the Potomac" how to fight, had to have some excuse for his ignominious failure. I don't wish to be understood as being unfair and prejudiced against Pope any more than against any of the other military failures of the war; but when Pope took command he made such a braying of trumpets in his own praise as to render him particularly conspicuous.

It is a mystery to the men who served in the late war why McDowell, who never won a battle, and Pope, who was continually defeated from the time the enemy appeared in his front until he took shelter in the defences of Washington, should hold high commands at this day, while Warren, who served all through with distinction and never lost a fight, should have to spend his means and life in trying to vindicate himself from a charge that the men who served under him never knew what the offence was he had committed.[35]

[Sullivan did not write about the battle of South Mountain, the next major action for the 6th Wisconsin and Western Brigade, until May 13, 1888—and it was the final Sullivan piece published by Jerome Watrous in *The Milwaukee Sunday Telegraph*. The Irishman's life was on the threshold of turmoil as he produced these latter memoirs. His days as a farmer in Vernon County were coming to a close; chasing a plow, rooting out potatoes, or milking cows never suited Mickey. He would, within a year after writing his last articles, become a townie in Ontario in Forest Township, where wrenching life changes would characterize his later years.

At the conclusion of the Second Bull Run campaign, Robert E. Lee determined to raid the North, moving his army into Maryland. The Army of the Potomac, again under Gen. George B. McClellan, moved to intercept the rebel columns. The Black Hat Brigade, after marching into Maryland, was ordered to make a diversion against Turner's Gap on September 14, then being held by elements of the Confederate army. It was again near dark when the four regiments pushed up the National Road toward the South Mountain pass to give battle, and there earned the celebrated name "The Iron Brigade."

In his telling of the action, Sullivan again evinced an almost casual indifference to the death of his comrades. George Chamberlain, his mess-mate and comrade for more than a year, was killed, but Sullivan passed over the tragedy. He wrote as well of a confrontation with Gen. Ambrose Burnside, in which the slight private, who had recently celebrated his 19th birthday, gained the upper hand on the fearsome-whiskered officer. And, again, Sullivan scourged army generals for their incompetence and the War Department for its long-range meddling. Finally, Sullivan provided an arresting portrait of his return to Wisconsin as a disabled veteran, his impatience with the citizens back home, and of his decision to re-enlist. The piece appeared May 13, 1888.]

A PRIVATE'S STORY
OF THE MEMORABLE BATTLE
OF SOUTH MOUNTAIN.

"Mickey, of Company K,"
Gives an Entertaining Chapter
—How He Drove Off
a Corps Commander With a Single Gun
—How the Fight at South Mountain Commenced
—Return to the Army.

By "Mickey" of Company K.

After the battle of Chantilly[36] the army fell back inside the defenses of Washington defeated, disgusted, dispirited, but not despairing. Gallant little Hugh Talty put the whole thing in a nutshell when he said, "Arrah, if the big ginerals wus wurth a cint, we'd show thim rebels what dilgant hands we were at fightin," and the feeling was due to lack of skill in our commander and the meddling interference of the war department in keeping several different armies to protect Washington, neither of which was strong enough for any purpose but that of defeat. Orders were received placing McClellan [in command] of all the troops in the defense of Washington, and most of our men were jubilant in consequence but [Erastus] Smith[37] and myself, who had no inclination to throw up our hats for anybody unless he had done something to deserve it. We reserved our cheers for future use.[38] But we felt that whatever might happen, the blunders of the past month would not be repeated, and we might at least expect good common sense at headquarters. Pope, McDowell and several more of that ilk were relieved from command, and "Fightin Joe" Hooker took command of our corps. Our brigade camped at Upton's Hill and once more received enough to eat.[39]

The situation was threatening and then came the news that Lee had crossed the Potomac to liberate Maryland, and carry the war to the North. About dark we received orders to march, and crossing the Long Bridge[40] we moved into Washington city and lay around in the streets and on the sidewalks and doorsteps expecting every minute to march, until daylight began to show itself in the east, and then we set out at a tremendous pace, via Tennallytown, for Rockton [Rockville], Maryland. The day was very warm, and the clouds of dust nearly suffocating, and we marched all day with only the shortest possible halts and no stoppage for coffee, and in the afternoon the men, who were completely worn out, began to straggle and fell out in squads. I marched until after 3 o'clock, and seeing no prospect of coffee or any let up in the pace we were going, I assumed command of myself and gave orders to halt and lay down, which I did, and using my knapsack for a pillow I tried to get a little rest. General Burnside,[41] who was in command of his own army under [Gen. Jesse] Reno and [Gen. Jacob D.] Cox's Kanawha division of Ohio men, came along, riding in a powerful black horse and he was forcing the stragglers along by attempting to ride over those who were laying down, and he ordered me to get up and go on; and I paid no attention to it, as I considered I did not belong to his command and he was not my "boss," and with an exclamation that he'd make me leave there, he spurred his horse towards me.

All the fighting blood of my race from "Shan Dhu" down to Yankee rose up at the thought of being ridden over like a dog, and I sprang to my feet and cocking my gun, which had been loaded the day before on picket, brought it to a ready, determined, let the result be what it would, to kill him right there. Whether he was struck with the shame at the thought of riding down a tired and worn out boy, or that he saw death in my eyes I don't know, but he stopped and asked to what regiment I belonged, and when I told him he said, "You're one of the western men," and an officer that had followed him up remarked that that was General Gibbon's command, and Burnside said something which I understood to be to hurry along as soon as I could, and he rode off and I laid down and was not disturbed again. After laying for an hour or two I moved on and went into a farm house and bought a canteen of fresh milk and a batch of biscuits and afterwards moved on until I overtook several of company K, and we went along, gaining addition to our number and apples, potatoes, chickens and other additions to the larder, and at dusk we took possession of a small grove and had coffee with milk in it and biscuits, roast potatoes, apples and burned chicken to our hearts' content. Early next morning, refreshed and vigorous, we started and soon overtook the command bivouacked in a field close to the road, where it had halted for the simple reason that there was no longer any one there to march. And two days later when camped at a little village called Triadelphia,[42] I was directed to report to Lieutenant Colonel Bragg, and after asking me some questions he said: "You behaved pretty well at Bull Run and I'll let you off this time," and I escaped the $1 and $2 "blind"[43] that he inflicted on [Oliver] Fletcher, Flynn and several more of my potato squad.

The army advanced by easy marches and on the night of the [September] 13th we camped at Monocacy Bridge, and we understood that Lee had discovered the fact that "My Maryland" did not care about being "liberated," and he was retreating towards Harper's Ferry, which the indefatigable

"Stonewall" was besieging, and that Lee would hold the passes of the mountains until "Stonewall" succeeded in his efforts.[44] Early the next morning the pursuit was commenced and after passing through Frederick City and Middletown, we reached the foot of South Mountain where our brigade was destined to become famous. About 3 P.M. of Sunday, September 14th, we marched along the base of the mountain towards the right, and after going some distance countermarched and returned to the foot of the gap and then we learned that our brigade had been assigned the difficult task of carrying what was known as Turner's or Bolivar Gap. We halted some time to allow the remainder of our division now under the command of General [John] Hatch, to get their positions on the side of the mountain, and when all was ready our brigade was ordered forward and the famous action was commenced. Company K, of the 6th, and Company B, 2d, were ordered forward and employed as skirmishers, the company of the 2d on the left, we on the right of the pike. Captain [Daniel L.] Quaw, of Company K, whose health was poor, being the junior officer, the skirmish line was under command of the gallant [Wilson] Callwell [Colwell], of the 2d, and his commands were simply, "Forward."[45] The skirmishers pushed on up the side of the mountain and soon came in sight of the enemy's skirmishers and opened fire on them. The ground was a cultivated field with a heavy wood on the right and Company K's line extended from the woods down to the road. The field was pretty full of large stones, and now and again a huge boulder stood up and afforded both us and the enemy excellent cover. Lieutenants [John] Ticknor and [Lyman] Upham[46] directed the movement of our company, which was always "Forward," and about all they had to do was follow the men who needed no urging. Part of the men would fire and then rush forward while the others covered them and had at the rebels and then the rear line would pass through to the front and lay down while the other line kept up the fire, and in that way it was a steady advance. Where a large boulder afforded a good shelter three or four, or sometimes more, would gather there and hold it until the enemy were driven out of range. The utmost enthusiasm prevailed and our fellows were as cool and collected as if at target practice, and, in fact, on more than one occasion when gathered behind a boulder, one would ask the other to watch his shot and see where he hit.[47] After we had advanced a considerable distance I looked behind and saw the brigade following up at a short distance. One regiment was in line of battle on each side of the turnpike and another in close column by division followed them up within supporting distance.

[George E.] Chamberlain, who, like myself, was a stray waif in Company K,[48] and like myself had to suffer for all the misdeeds and mistakes, no matter by whom committed, and who had been my companion in many an hour's knapsack drill or extra tour of guard, given sometimes for our own offenses and sometimes for the offenses of others, and of whom it was said that if Dawes would stub his toe he'd put Mickey and Chamberlain on knapsack drill, and consequently we were inseparable companions and fast friends. Chamberlain, "Eph" [Ephriam] Cornish, Corporal [Franklin] Wilcox and myself kept close together and formed a group of "comrades in battle." Chamberlain, who was brave as a lion, kept continually rushing forward leading the squad, and of course we had to follow up and support him. It was now sundown and being in the shadow of the mountain it was getting dark very fast, and our fellows pushed the rebel skirmishers up to their line of battle, and our squad took shelter behind a big boulder and two of us fired from each side of it. The 7th [Wisconsin], which was the line of battle behind us, opened fire and the skirmishers who had gradually moved to the right towards the woods had uncovered their front and were fighting the rebel skirmishers at close quarters, when a heavy line of battle rose up and advanced towards the right flank of the 7th, and then came the crash of their volley by regiment. I had been troubled with mumps for several days and my jaws had now reached a respectable rotundity and Lieutenant Upham had let me have a big silk handkerchief to tie about my face, but on entering the fight I took it off as it obstructed my range of vision, and when that crash came, either a bullet split in pieces against a stone or a fragment of the boulder hit me on the sore jaw, causing exquisite pain, and I was undetermined whether to run away or swear, when Cornish groaned, "Mickey, Chamberlain is killed and I'm wounded," and then came another crashing volley and I felt a stinging, burning sensation in my right foot followed by the most excruciating pain, and as I sprang up I saw Corporal Wilcox topple over, wounded.[49] Using my musket for a jumping prop, I began to make good time for the rear. It was now quite dark and I had not gone but a few rods when I saw a line of battle coming up rapidly which proved to be our regiment that had been deployed to support the 7th, as the line that had fired on us was moving up to outflank them. I passed through Company C, and an officer that I took to be Sergeant [Edward] Whaley[50] asked me if I was wounded and told me I had better get back to the rear. Using my musket for a crutch I went down the side of the mountain a great deal faster than I had come up, and the fight which was in plain view on my right was a grand sight. In the darkness the sides of the mountain seemed in a blaze of flame, and the lines of the combatants did not appear more than three or four rods apart, but ours was steadily advancing. The pain in my foot and the angry "Zip, zip, Whing" of the bullets prevented me from dwelling long on the sight, and I made the best of time down to the turnpike, which was lit up by the flashes of a couple of Battery B's guns which were firing as guns never fired before. The two pieces made an almost continual roar and they were being pushed forward by hand at every discharge. The gap in the mountain seemed all aflame and the noise and uproar and cheers and yells were terrific.

I made my way back along the pike through the rest of the battery and soon met a body of cavalry halted in the road, and in reply to my question, "What regiment?" they answered McClellan's body guard. I went back along the pike a short distance, and finally saw a small fire in a clump of brush, and going over found several wounded and [Emory] Mitchell, of Company K, who had a very bad hernia and was not able to keep up, was waiting on them and getting coffee ready.[51] He filled my canteen with water from a brook close by, and taking the sleeve of his extra shirt and Lieutenant Upham's silk handkerchief, we rolled it up and wet it and tied it to my foot.

The sound of the battle was growing fainter, and Mitchell said our fellows were "giving 'em Wisconsin hell," and that "we had some generals now." He made me a cup of coffee and fixed his gum blanket down and let me have his knapsack for a pillow and I lay down and slept some, but Mitchell said I kept him awake all night twitching my injured foot. The next morning we went back toward the battlefield and found the hospital established in a barnyard, which was filled with wounded laying on blocks of hay and straw, and after a while Dr. [Abraham D.] Andrews[52] came around and dressed my wound and tried to extract the ball, but could not as it was wedged between the bones, and he said an operation would be necessary and that it had better be done at a hospital. We got some tea and crackers and some of the severely wounded had wine or brandy served them. An attendant offered me some of the latter, but I told him I'd take another wound sooner, and he drank it himself. We heard that the brigade had covered itself with glory and had driven the enemy steadily to the top of the pass, and had used up every round of ammunition and also that of the killed and wounded, and finally held the field with the bayonet until relieved, but our regiment, which had been missed or overlooked, held their ground all night.[53]

[As a result of his wound, Sullivan was spared the horrors of the Civil War's bloodiest day: the battle of Antietam, fought three days after South Mountain. While the limping Irishman received medical attention in Frederick City, Maryland, his comrades opened the fight along the Hagerstown Turnpike just north of Sharpsburg. The 6th Wisconsin initially swept forward in the early going, taking heavy losses, but pressing back Confederates along the Hagerstown Pike. The Black Hats stormed through a cornfield in pursuit, only to be hammered to a halt and forced back under a rebel counterattack. The regiment lost 152 killed, wounded, or missing that gruesome day.[54] Sullivan's Company K recorded three killed and eight wounded.[55]

Sullivan's piece on his experiences in the weeks following South Mountain was filled alternately with harrowing description, satiric observation, and derisive judgement.]

There were hundreds of wounded in both armies in that barnyard, and some of them were enduring fearful misery.

One who lay next to me was hit by a cannon ball, which had carried away his arm and part of his side, exposing the heart and vital organs and at every respiration their action was visible. One, a rebel, was shot through the forehead, diagonally from the temple on one side to the hair on the other, and his eyes were closed, and I heard a doctor remark, "That fellow must have no brain or he would be killed;" but I saw the fellow afterwards in the church at Middletown and he was recovering. Some time in the forenoon the ambulance train came up and we were loaded in and taken to Middletown and afterwards to Frederick City, where there was a regular hospital, with those white winged angels of mercy, the Sisters of Charity,[56] for nurses, but we did not stay long there, as room had to be made for the worst wounded at Antietam, and I was sent to Washington and placed in the house of representatives, which was temporarily converted into a hospital, where I was put under the influence of ether and an operation performed on my foot and I remained there under treatment until December 22d.[57] Two or three days before that I was ordered to report before a board, and after some scientific stares through their eye-glasses and some scientific talk about "cuspal," and "flexious" and a good deal more unintelligible jargon, I was told to return to my ward, and a few days afterwards an orderly called me to report to the office, and my discharge and final statements were handed me, and when I said that I didn't want a discharge, I was told that I did not belong to the hospital any longer and must leave. I had received no pay for six months and had no money, but one of the 56th Pennsylvania let me have enough to pay my car fare down town, and when I went to the paymaster's office it was closed and a card on the door bore the ominous words, "Closed for want of funds." Here was a fine fix to be in; turned loose in a strange city, crippled, unknown, no money, and a thousand miles from home. There were eight or ten of us in the squad and we did not know what to do, but finally we learned of a patriot, who, for patriotic considerations and a discount of 10 per cent, would cash our papers, provided we accepted state currency, and considering that his patriotism and state currency were better than none, we closed with his offer. His currency ran out before my turn came, and I got greenbacks and went on my way rejoicing. My stay at home was short, as there was no company there; only discharged invalids that had killed half the rebel army, and men who were growling about the draft, the army, and the scarcity of money; and women that were growling worse because they had to pay forty and fifty cents for a spool of thread. There was no change to be had, and every business man and merchant had cards printed good for so many cents, and after enduring it for six weeks I went to Madison, and, in answer to my query, "Could I enlist?" the clerk said, "anything owning a name could enlist," and knowing that there would be a first-class chance to get killed in the 6th within that time, I enlisted for nine months or sooner "killed."

There was a young gawk in Camp Randall that fancied himself able to butt a locomotive off the track, and having enlisted in a western regiment[58] he was very offensive in his talk about the Army of the Potomac, and when I concluded he had given me sufficient "causus belli," I admonished him by an Iron Brigade rap between the eyes and at it we went, and that time the Army of the Potomac came out victorious. Captain [George H.] Otis,[59] of the 2d, Captain [John] Callis, of the 7th,[60] and a surgeon who (I think) also belonged to the 7th, and one or two other officers were on their way back to their regiment, and myself and several enlisted men were under charge of Captain Otis. When we entered the [railroad] car Captain Otis, who had his own reasons for wishing for privacy, asked the doctor in a voice loud enough to be heard through the car, "What conclusion had been arrived at about that man; was it smallpox?" and the doctor replied that "It was not decided yet." The passengers, one after another, would glance at my face and then gather up their gripsacks and other impediments and hastily leave the car. There was no black eye, cuts or bruises visible on my face, but it was covered all over with innumerable little scabs, where the fellow had clawed me with his nails and I presented a fair appearance of a smallpox patient, and we had the car and our private amusement all to ourselves. They played the same trick at Chicago and again at Dunkirk and Elmira [Indiana] where we changed cars, and when a passenger would attempt to enter the car some one would say, "There's smallpox in this car," and he would retreat in a hurry. We reached Washington and took the steamer John Brooks for Belle Plain, where I reported to Colonel Bragg, and once more I was a member of the Iron Brigade.

NOTES

1. John Gibbon, born in Philadelphia in 1827, spent his formative years in Charlotte, North Carolina. He graduated from the U.S. Military Academy in 1847, saw service in the Mexican War, and became captain of Battery B, 4th U.S. Artillery in Kansas and the Utah Territory. At war's outbreak he remained loyal to the Union even though three brothers went South. On May 2, 1862, he was promoted to brigadier general and given command of the Western Brigade. He and Adj. Frank Haskell of the 6th Wisconsin were arguably responsible for molding the four regiments into the most formidable fighting brigade in the Union army. Gibbon rose to division command, and was instrumental in repulsing Longstreet's final assault at Gettysburg on July 3, 1863, suffering a severe wound during the action. At war's end he was a corps commander. Gibbon remained in the army and was involved in the Indian Wars. In 1885 he wrote his *Personal Recollections of the Civil War,* but these were not published until 1928. He retired from active service in 1891, and died in Baltimore in 1896 and was buried in Arlington Cemetery. *Dictionary of American Biography,* Vol. VII, pp. 236–37.

2. U.S. Pension Office, James P. Sullivan file, affidavit of April 18, 1891.

3. Bell I. Wiley, *The Life of Billy Yank* (Indianapolis, 1952), pp. 41–44; Randall C. Jimerson, *The Private Civil War* (Baton Rouge, La., 1988), pp. 41–49, 76–81. As the war progressed, it became clear that the nation could not be reunited without the eradication of slavery. In addition, Federal soldiers were becoming exposed first-hand to the evils of human bondage.

4. Quaw, of Friendship in Bad Ax (Vernon) County, enlisted as a private May 10, 1861. He rose from noncommissioned ranks to become 2nd and then 1st lieutenant of Company K. He gained the captaincy June 24, 1862, but resigned in October. He was a man of apparent abolitionist sensibilities. *Roster of Wisconsin Volunteers,* Vol. I, p. 533.

5. Union General Benjamin F. Butler first applied the term "contrabands" to escaped slaves. The incident occurred at Fort Monroe, Virginia, when he refused to return fugitive slaves to their owners. Mathews, *Dictionary of Americanisms,* p. 384.

6. As McClellan withdrew the Army of the Potomac after the futile Peninsula Campaign outside Richmond, Gen. John Pope's Army of Virginia skirmished with elements of Jackson's Corps at several Rappahannock River fords. The action Sullivan mentioned occurred August 20, 1862. E. B.

Long and Barbara Long, *The Civil War Day by Day* (Garden City, N.Y., 1971), p. 253.

7. Probably a reference to a famous race horse of the day.

8. William Jackson accompanied Rufus Dawes to Marietta, Ohio, after the officer ended his three years' service in August of 1864. Dawes assisted Jackson in gaining employment as a railroad baggage master, a position he retained for 12 years, all the while acquiring a home and other property. Jackson's brother, Moses, later migrated to Marietta with his mother and sister. William Jackson died of consumption April 7, 1886. Dawes, *Service*, pp. 314–16.

9. The most complete description of the battle is in Alan D. Gaff, *Brave Men's Tears: The Iron Brigade at the Battle of Brawner Farm* (Dayton, Ohio, 1985). See also Alan T. Nolan, *The Iron Brigade* (New York, 1961).

10. Island No. 10 and New Madrid in Tennessee were surrendered to Pope April 8, 1862. Long and Long, *Day by Day*, p. 196.

11. Pope always denied using the phrase. "A good deal of cheap wit has been expended upon a fanciful story that I published an order or wrote a letter or made a remark that my 'headquarters would be in the saddle.' It is an expression harmless and innocent enough, but it is even stated that it furnished General Lee with the basis for the only joke of his life. I think it due to army tradition, and to be the comfort of those who have so often repeated the ancient joke in the days long before the civil war, that these later wits should not be allowed with impunity to poach on this well-tilled manor. This venerable joke I first heard when a cadet at West Point . . . and I presume it could be easily traced back to the Crusades and beyond. Certainly I never used this expression or wrote or dictated it, nor does any such expression occur in any order of mine; and as it has perhaps served its time and effected its purpose, it ought to be retired," Pope wrote. John Pope, "The Second Battle of Bull Run," *Battles and Leaders of the Civil War* (New York, 1884–87) Vol. II, pp. 493–94.

12. Nathaniel Banks was a corps commander in Pope's Army of Virginia. After defeating McClellan's Army of the Potomac on the Peninsula, Lee sent Stonewall Jackson north to keep an eye on Pope's Army of Virginia. Learning of the Confederate movement, Pope sent Banks' 2nd Corps to cover. With 9,000 men, Banks hurled himself into Jackson's two divisions and won initial success. But with reinforcements, Jackson strengthened his line, rallying a successful counterattack. The Confederate commander, although he claimed the field, was nearly defeated by a substantially inferior force. Patricia L. Faust, ed., *Historical Times Illustrated Encyclopedia of the Civil War* (New York, 1986), p. 823; Long and Long, *Day by Day*, pp. 249–50.

13. Sullivan was in error. See foregoing footnote.

14. It was Confederate cavalryman J. E. B. Stuart who captured some of Pope's wagons August 22, 1862. Long and Long, *Day by Day*, p. 254.

15. The battle was fought August 25, and was considered the opening of the Second Bull Run campaign. *Ibid.*, p. 255.

16. McDowell was Sullivan's division commander.

17. Battery B, 4th U.S. Artillery, was attached to the brigade from the very first days. It was originally commanded by John Gibbon.

18. Large quantities of hardtack and pork were being destroyed lest they fall into Confederate hands. The soldiers of the brigade were not permitted to stop and fill their empty haversacks. Gibbon, however, retrieved many boxes of hardtack and ordered his artillery to transport them for his men. Dawes, *Service*, pp. 58–59.

19. Ewell was fitted with a wooden leg and returned to the field in May 1863, and fought with his corps from Gettysburg to Spotsylvania. A fall from his horse incapacitated him from further field service. *Dictionary of American Biography*, Vol VI, pp. 229–30.

20. The brigade sustained a loss of 754 men killed or wounded—33 percent of those engaged. The 6th Wisconsin lost 72 of 504 men engaged. Dawes, *Service*, pp. 64–65; Nolan, *Iron Brigade*, p. 95.

21. Charles King later attended West Point, graduating in 1866. He served in the regular army for 13 years, then became a professor of military tactics at the University of Wisconsin at Madison in 1880. He also served as an inspector and instructor for the Wisconsin National Guard. King saw duty in the Philippines during the Spanish-American war. A prolific writer, he churned out numerous fiction and nonfiction books. He retired from public life in 1931 and died in 1933 at age 88. *Dictionary of Wisconsin Biography*, pp. 206–207.

22. Flynn was Sullivan's maternal uncle. His family migrated to Wisconsin prior to the war, and he enlisted at Whitestown, Bad Ax (Vernon) County, June 23, 1861. He was wounded in September 1862, and again at Laurel Hill during the Spotsylvania campaign in May 1864. He mustered from service with the expiration of his three-year enlistment on July 15, 1864. *Roster of Wisconsin Volunteers*, Vol. I, p. 534.

23. The 2nd Wisconsin Infantry was recruited from companies in the southern third of the state in April 1861, as a three-month regiment. But in May the Federal government proclaimed that all new regiments must serve for three years; all but one of the ten companies accepted the change, and the regiment was mustered into federal service. It arrived in Washington in late June 1861—the first three-year regiment in the capital—and was joined to Gen. Irvin McDowell's Department of Northern Virginia. The Badgers were brigaded with three New York regiments under the command of Col. William T. Sherman. In mid-July 1861 the first offensive against the Confederate army was opened at Manassas, Virginia, and the brigade, led by the 2nd Wisconsin in its state-issue grey uniforms, attacked up Henry House Hill. They were repulsed, the 2nd losing 23 killed and 65 wounded or prisoners. In August 1861, the 2nd was transferred to the brigade of Rufus King of Milwaukee, and was joined to the 19th Indiana and 5th and 6th Wisconsin. On October 1, the 7th Wisconsin arrived from the Badger state and was attached to King's Brigade. Gov. Alexander Randall had hoped for an all-Wisconsin brigade, but army headquarters dashed those ideas when the 5th Wisconsin was transferred instead of the 19th Indiana. Nolan, *Iron Brigade*, pp. 4–12. For a description of the 2nd Wisconsin at First Bull Run, see Gaff, *If This Is War*.

24. Hardtack was a basic component of rations issued to soldiers of 1861–65. It was an unleavened, cracker-like staple made of flour, water, and salt, and was prepared by the men in numerous and wondrous ways.

25. Skirmishers were small groups of men in loose formation sent out to protect a unit from surprise and to probe ahead of an advancing line. They

drew the enemy's fire, determined his position, and warned the main command. Faust, *Encyclopedia*, p. 81.

26. Levi S. Gardner enlisted from Fountain City in Buffalo County on June 22, 1861. Trumbull, of Lemonweir in Juneau County, was one of the company's early enlistees. He was not so fortunate in 1863 when he was killed in the fighting at FitzHugh's Crossing April 29. *Roster of Wisconsin Volunteers*, Vol. I, pp. 534, 536.

27. The infantryman's cartridge box held 40 paper-rolled cartridges. Twenty were stored in the top of a tin divider and a like number in a compartment below. The other 20 were transferred to the top when the first were exhausted.

28. Haskell remained with John Gibbon when the general was given a division command in 1863, and was instrumental in repulsing Pickett's Charge on the third day of Gettysburg. He later was promoted to colonel of the 36th Wisconsin and was killed leading his regiment at Cold Harbor in 1864. He is remembered for his written account of the battle of Gettysburg. Frank L. Byrne and Andrew T. Weaver, eds., *Haskell of Gettysburg: His Life and Civil War Papers* (Madison, 1970).

29. Canister and grape shot were scatter-shot artillery projectiles intended as anti-personnel charges. Effective ranges were 300 to 600 yards. They were frequently used at shorter distances.

30. Simmons, of Marion, Wisconsin, enlisted May 10, 1861. He was wounded at South Mountain in 1862 and again at Petersburg in 1865. He veteranized in late 1864, but was absent wounded when the regiment mustered from service in July 1865. *Roster of Wisconsin Volunteers*, Vol. I, p. 535.

31. Zouave units took their colorful uniform designs from French troops in the Crimean War. They included white leggings, red baggy trousers, a short jacket, sash, vest, and a fez or turban. Zouave units were in both Union and Confederate armies. Faust, *Encyclopedia*, p. 850.

32. Kearny, a New Yorker with extensive military experience, distinguished himself in the Peninsula campaign outside Richmond. Two days after Bull Run, he accidentally rode into a Confederate line during the battle of Chantilly and was killed. He designated the Western Brigade as the rear guard of the retreating Federal army at Second Bull Run, and the 6th Wisconsin lay across the Warrenton Turnpike near the Stone Bridge at Cub Run. Saturday, August 31, 1862, the brigade was ordered to fall back to Washington. *Dictionary of American Biography*, Vol. X, pp. 271–72; Dawes, *Service*, p. 75; Nolan, *Iron Brigade*, pp. 109–110.

33. The regiment's loss at Second Bull Run totaled 47 killed, wounded, or missing. Dawes, *Service*, p. 74.

34. In November 1862 Porter was relieved of his command to face court martial charges leveled by Pope for disobedience, disloyalty, and misconduct in the face of the enemy. The trial found Porter guilty and he was cashiered January 21, 1863. After years of trying to clear his record, Porter was reappointed as colonel of infantry in 1886. *Dictionary of American Biography*, Vol. XV, p. 91.

35. Gouverneur K. Warren was court martialed as a result of charges leveled against him by Gen. Phil Sheridan at the battle of Five Forks, April 1, 1865. He was exonerated in 1870 and died August 8, 1882. *Ibid.*, Vol. XIX, pp. 473–74.

36. The battle of Chantilly is considered the end of the Second Bull Run campaign. Fought September 1, 1862, it took the lives of two Union divisional commanders, Isaac I. Stevens and Philip Kearny. Long and Long, *Day by Day*, p. 260.

37. Smith, of Lemonweir, enlisted on the same day as Sullivan and was his tentmate. Smith became a 1st sergeant and mustered out at the expiration of his three-year term, July 15, 1864. *Roster of Wisconsin Volunteers*, Vol. I, p. 536.

38. The near adulation of McClellan on the part of the majority of his soldiers was not shared by Sullivan; the middle-aged veteran may have been unwilling to admit that he shared their view at the time. When a rumor swept the army just before Gettysburg on July 1, 1863, that McClellan had been appointed army commander, men in the ranks cheered, lightened their step, and went into Gettysburg with added intensity. See George H. Otis, *The Second Wisconsin Infantry*, ed. by Alan D. Gaff (Dayton, Ohio, 1984), p. 83.

39. Upton's Hill lay between the Potomac River and the Loudon & Hampshire Railroad near Arlington Heights, Virginia.

40. The Long or Chain Bridge spanned the Potomac River between Washington and Arlington Heights.

41. Ambrose Burnside, famous for the rakish whiskers that bore his name, was Indiana-born. He graduated from the U.S. Military Academy in 1847, served in the war with Mexico, and resigned in 1853. He invented the breech-loading carbine that also bore his name. At war's outbreak he raised a regiment of volunteers, and became a friend of the new president, Abraham Lincoln. Burnside later became a commander of the IX Corps. He was given command of the Army of the Potomac, but failed miserably at Fredericksburg in December 1862 and in the futile "Mud March" of the following month. He thereafter led the IX Corps in Tennessee before being ordered back east, where his corps operated as an independent unit until the disaster of the Crater before Petersburg, Virginia, in June of 1864. He then left the Army. Burnside died in 1881. *Dictionary of American Biography*, Vol. III, pp. 309–13.

42. Triadelphia is five miles east of Wheeling in what is now West Virginia.

43. A "blind," in the lingo of the day, was a compulsory stake in poker. Sullivan used the term to refer to the fine levied by Bragg. Mathews, *Dictionary of Americanisms*, p. 132.

44. Lee, in another of his audacious moves, split his army, dispatching Jackson to capture Harper's Ferry. When Gen. George McClellan, who had been restored to command on September 2, discovered Lee's plan on the 13th, he failed to push the Army of the Potomac with sufficient vigor to defeat Lee's piecemeal force. Faust, *Encyclopedia*, pp. 19–20.

45. Colwell was a popular officer of the 2nd Wisconsin. He was killed leading the regiment's skirmish line that day. Pennsylvania-born, he migrated to La Crosse on the Mississippi River before the war and became a banker. At the firing on Fort Sumter, Colwell was the newly elected mayor of La Crosse. He became captain of the La Crosse Light Guard, company B of the 2nd Wisconsin. Gaff, *If This Is War*, p. 37; Dawes, *Service*, p. 81.

46. Upham, of New Lisbon in Juneau County, enlisted June 25, 1861. He

was promoted to 2nd lieutenant a year later, then made regimental quartermaster in October 1862. He resigned June 2, 1864. *Roster of Wisconsin Volunteers,* Vol. I, pp. 495, 533.

47. Few Civil War regiments conducted more than familiarization with rifle-muskets. There are but a few references in 6th Wisconsin sources about live firing. It was rare that a regiment was trained in judging distances or accurately setting sights. Sullivan did possess some knowledge about the firing mechanism of his .58-caliber Springfield, as he modified it to lighten the trigger pull. Paddy Griffith, *Battle Tactics of the Civil War* (New Haven, Conn., 1989), pp. 87–88.

48. Chamberlain enlisted at Mauston June 30, 1861. According to Dawes, the lad left a circus to enlist; his comrades agreed that he had had a hard life and had joined the army to seek relief. Rufus R. Dawes, *Mauston Star,* January 8, 1885.

49. Wilcox, of Lemonweir, was among the first enlistees in Dawes' company. His South Mountain wounds were so severe that he was discharged in March of 1863 following hospitalization and recuperation. *Roster of Wisconsin Volunteers,* Vol. I, p. 536.

50. Edward A. Whaley, Prairie du Chien, enlisted as a private in 1861. He was wounded at South Mountain and in two later battles. He rose to officer ranks, ultimately leading the 6th Wisconsin in its last campaign and losing a leg at Five Forks on April 1, 1865. After the war he was named postmaster at Prairie du Chien on the Mississippi River, and died there. *Ibid.,* p. 505.

51. Mitchell, a Yellow River sawmill hand before the war, enlisted in 1861. He served three years, mustering out July 15, 1864. *Ibid.,* p. 535.

52. Andrews was assistant regimental surgeon from October 1861 until November 1863. *Ibid.,* p. 494.

53. It was at South Mountain that the name "Iron Brigade" was first applied to the Western unit. Numerous stories and legends grew over the years relative to who was responsible for the name. It is customarily recorded that Gen. George B. McClellan uttered the name as he watched the brigade fight his way up National Road. Herdegen and Beaudot, *Railroad Cut,* p. 39–41.

54. The Iron Brigade recorded 37 killed, 251 wounded, and 30 missing, a total of 318 officers and men—25% of the brigade, more than any other Federal brigade in the battle. Nolan, *Iron Brigade,* p. 129.

55. *Ibid.,* p. 142; William J. K. Beaudot, *Sixth Wisconsin Database* (Milwaukee, 1989).

56. An order of Catholic nuns which established hospitals.

57. The second toe and a portion of his right foot were amputated.

58. Of the 52 regiments raised by Wisconsin, all but a handful served in the Western armies during the war. Frank L. Klement, *Wisconsin and the Civil War* (Madison, 1963).

59. Otis rose from corporal to captain in the 2nd Wisconsin, and served his three years. In the 1880s he serialized a history of his regiment for *The Milwaukee Sunday Telegraph.*

60. A native of North Carolina, Callis moved to Lancaster, Wisconsin Territory, with his family at age 12. He was severely wounded serving with the 7th Wisconsin July 1, 1863, at Gettysburg. After the war he moved to Alabama, where he was a member of Congress, but he returned to Wisconsin, where he died September 24, 1898, at Lancaster.

Chapter III

WORTH A MAN'S LIFE

[When Sullivan ambled back into the ranks of his comrades in the second winter camp of the war he doubtless aroused the wonder and excitement of his tent mates, many scratching their heads that the young Irishman had refused to remain amid the comforts and safety of home and kin. In the six months he had been away, significant changes had occurred in the regiment and the brigade.

The Western regiment, as a result of its dogged fight up the boulder-bordered National Road at South Mountain, had earned a new name—no longer were they the Big Hat or Black Hat Brigade, but the "Iron Brigade." Camp talk had it that Gen. George McClellan himself bestowed the sobriquet upon the Badgers and Hoosiers in the twilight of that September saturday. Later, there would be other claims as to the origin of the christening.

On his return Sullivan found that a new regiment had been added to the brigade's decimated ranks. Yet the Western soldiers exhibited studied indifference toward the new 24th Michigan, despite common geographic roots; they still had much to prove before they were accepted as equals. They were easy to spot, these Wolverines: the spanking new blue coats and standard flat-top army kepi caps marked them as fresh fish, perhaps unworthy of the hardened battle veterans they had joined. But time and blood would earn black hats and camaraderie for the Michiganders.

The November before Sullivan arrived, John Gibbon, the respected commander who, through some six months and four major battles, hammered and honed the four regiments into an awesome fighting force, had been accorded a division command. It was a bittersweet decision for the regular army officer—he lamented leaving his Westerners. Gibbon took the 6th Wisconsin's Lt. Frank Haskell, his aide, with him. Thus, two of the most important names in the evolution of the brigade were removed. But after the war, Gibbon, who remained in the military, would become intimately associated with his former charges. When the Iron Brigade Association of veterans was formed in 1880, the man some called "Boss Soldier" was elected organization president, a post he retained until his death in 1896.[1] Ultimately, in Gibbon's stead was named Indiana's Solomon Meredith, a politician who evolved into a respected brigade commander.

But these were matters about which J. P. Sullivan, in the early bloom of his forties, did not write or ruminate. The Irishman, in an article about Gettysburg written in 1882, had included a telling and humorous incident about getting a musket when he returned from Wisconsin. The quartermaster had initially issued him one of the leftover Belgian muskets, a bulky, balky affair that did as much damage to the shooter as the target. Mickey had been incensed, and he probably jawed at the ordnance sergeant for the affront. With likely little hesitation he stomped over to Col. Edward Bragg's winter quarters, asking, with the usual tinge of brashness, why the regiment could not afford to give him a new rifle-musket, one of those nice Model 1861 Springfields that most of the men shouldered. The Fond du Lac politician had been amused (he was accustomed to the young Irishman's casual regard for proper courtesy to officers); accompanying his diminutive private back to the ordnance tent, he saw to it that the young man was armed with the newer firearm.

Mickey probably mused over those incidents as he brought shape to his memories. As a middle-aged western Wisconsin farmer, he spent some of the long months of deep cold and snow bent beneath a dim lamp. More than 20 years had passed since those times, yet his disdain for incompetents seemed to fester. Thinking about this period, the name Ambrose Burnside came quickly to mind, that balding and bewhiskered army commander who had replaced the beloved George McClellan. Burnside had almost madly ordered an attempt to storm the heights near the Rappahannock River town of Fredericksburg head-on, and the result was disastrous: 12,600 Union casualties. The Iron Brigade paid for a follied assault with 65 casualties, half from the new 24th Michigan. Little more than a month later, Burnside, who in postwar years would become a ready target for much Sullivan invective, again pointed his army at Fredericksburg in another ill-conceived quest; this time the army was defeated not by Robert E. Lee but by the weather, a punishing winter storm that created a quagmire bogging men, animals, and materiel.

Returning to winter camp north of the Rappahannock, the army and the brigade and the 6th Wisconsin hunkered down to wait out the winter. In spring, the Army of the Potomac was again bestirred, this time by plan: push the army toward Chancellorsville and press the enemy where he was weak. Surely this was a prospect for victory, surmised new army general Joe Hooker. He pointed his army across the Rappahannock River, a waterway the men were finding quite familiar, on the left flank of Lee's force. Just below Fredericksburg, meanwhile, another part of Hooker's army was attempting other crossings.

Sullivan wrote about his regiment's part. While the action was a sidelight to the main thrust of the army that spring, the engagement at FitzHugh's Crossing May 1, 1863, claimed lives and limbs. But it also added to the lore of the 6th Wisconsin; Sullivan took pains to include little vignettes, humorous and sad, which added to the character of the telling.

Sullivan, when he wrote of this in 1883, again took up the cudgel against the government bureaucracy, which was tightening regulations for the granting of disability pensions. For various reasons, the Irish veteran was having difficulty securing what he considered a reasonable monthly allotment. In addition, he roundly castigated his own state for its apparent failure to compile an adequate history of his brigade. First delivered as a speech to the Iron Brigade Association, his FitzHugh's Crossing piece was published in *The Milwaukee Sunday Telegraph*, September 30, 1883.]

CHARGE OF THE IRON BRIGADE
AT FITZHUGH'S CROSSING
By J. P. Sullivan

General Sherman, in his great Atlanta campaign, correcting the impression that he had forbidden the mails to arrive or depart from camp, took occasion to say: "What the commanding general does discourage is the existence of that class of men who will not take a musket and fight, but who follow the army to pick up news for sale, speculating on a species of information which is dangerous to the army, and to our cause, and who are more used to bolster up idle and worthless officers than to notice the hard-working and meritorious, whose modesty is generally equal to their courage, and who scorn to seek the flattery of the press." Anyone who is familiar with events during the late war will recognize the force and application of the above, and must admit that the thanks of every good soldier and regiment are due the clear-headed old general who understood so well the value of the puffs and notices in the papers during the war, and was not afraid to denounce such army correspondents as spent their time in writing flattering notices of the officers who furnished them cigars, commissary whisky, and an army horse to ride. So it was with some regiments during the war. A person could not pick up a paper without finding a letter from "Army Blue," or company X, "Our special war correspondent," containing a description of the "gallant advance our regiment," the 999th Tiger or Zouaves or Bucktails made, after the enemy had fallen back, or the indominible courage of company Q displayed while drawing their ten days' rations.

The above cynicism is forced from me after reading what pretends to be a "History of the Great Rebellion," written by the late editor of the army and navy *Journal*,[2] and magazines innumerable, and exemplifies the truth of General Sherman's words so forcibly, "that the hard-working and meritorious were too modest to seek the flattery of the press." Amongst all the good troops that the union furnished for the war, there were none better than the Iron Brigade, and none that performed more daring and brilliant exploits and who merely thought it a matter of duty, yet in that history(?) of the "Great Rebellion" I am unable to find that such a brigade ever existed. Now I have no desire to say a word against any organization or detract from the reputation of anybody, but I do think our brigade is entitled to credit for some of its hard service, and daring actions, and I will now proceed to relate one of the latter.

It is hardly necessary to say a word to old soldiers about the difficulties of driving out a brave and determined enemy from a well-prepared line of breastwork, where they have been established for more than four months, and with artillery, field and siege, to sustain them, but they will understand that the difficulty is greatly increased when the charging column has to cross a river more than forty rods wide, on the clumsy pontoon boats[3] of the engineers. Such an undertaking fell to our lot at Fitz Hugh's Crossing.

About the last of April, 1863, the Iron Brigade, consisting

of the 2d, 6th and 7th Wisconsin, 19th Indiana and 24th
Michigan, under the command of Gen. Sol Meredith,[4] left
Belle Plain, where they had been in quietness since the "stick-
in-the mud campaign,"[5] and took up the line of march towards
Fredericksburg, only halting on the way to surround a New
York regiment and force them to take back their arms. They
had mutinied, claiming that their time had expired.[6] About
midnight, on the 29th, we reached the Rappahannock, a few
miles below Fredericksburg, and lay along a ditched fence
until daylight, waiting for the engineers to lay a pontoon
bridge across the river, but owing to some hitch in their
arrangements they did not get more than four or five boats in
position before daylight, and the enemy in the rifle pits and
breastworks in the other side of the river opened on them
such a hot fire that they were driven away from the river
entirely. Our brigade was then ordered down to the bank to
protect the pontoons, but it was no use, as the bank of the
river on this side slopes gradually down to the water, and was
entirely bare, if I remember right, a clover field, while the
opposite bank rose very steep from the water's edge and was
densely covered with a thriving growth of young timber down
the side of the hill to the water. The copse was full of rifle
pits, arranged for sharp-shooters and on the hill, where the
ground extended back for half a mile clear and level, there
was an elaborate system of breastworks. The rebels were
entirely concealed and all we could see was puffs of smoke,
and our fire and a heavy cannonade had no effect on them.
The pontooniers were unable to lay the bridge and our brigade
was withdrawn a little from the fire of the enemy.

While laying there under fire an incident occurred which
may be taken as an illustration of the character of our brigade
while under fire. "Billy Hancock," of company K,[7] had put on
his best uniform to avoid carrying it, and a new big hat and
an enormous big black feather, to use "Lime" [Lyman]
Upham's words, was "slinging on considerable agony." A
musket ball hit him, cutting a gash in his scalp and knocking
the top out of his hat, splitting it down the side, or, in army
parlance, "completely demoralizing it."

Picking it up[,] he [Hancock] looked at the wreck and

blurted out: "Gaul darn their ugly picture, they've split my new hat." The look of distress on his face, and his tone, set the whole command in a roar of laughter.

Things remained in that condition until about eight A.M., when our regiment was ordered to unsling knapsacks and haversacks, and a certain number of files to sling muskets. I thought [Col. Edward S.] Bragg was going to have us swim the river, but a council of generals had been held and General [James] Wadsworth[8] informed them that he had a brigade in his division that could and would cross that river, and it was decided that our brigade should charge as a forlorn hope, and may be drive the rebels away from the bank long enough to allow the pontooniers to lay the bridges. Col. Bragg made a short address, telling us to show our western breeding and our skill as oarsmen, and that we were to rush down to the river and each company take two boats and launch them and paddle and pole over as fast as possible. The regiment formed in four ranks, left in front, and Col. Bragg placed himself at the head and pulling his hat down firmer, he said, "come on, boys," and that was all the orders we got. The regiment started as hard as the men could run towards the river, and I noticed that our company [K], which was third in the line, overtook Bragg, who being small and short-legged, and having an immense pair of military boots and spurs on, was not able to keep ahead, but he reached the river with us and went over in our boat, being the second of company K. The 2d [Wisconsin] regiment[9] had also got the same orders and made the same preparations we did, and both regiments went over together, closely followed by the rest of the brigade. The Johnnies opened on us a deadly fire and our fellows fell pretty fast, but we ran right over them, straight for the river, and pushing the boats into the water we jumped in and two or three men shoved them off, and I never knew whether we rowed or sailed or poled over. Hoel Trumbull was one of our company who assisted in pushing our boat off, and he waded into the water and made a spring to get in, and some of us were assisting him when a bullet hit him in the head and he let go his hold and sank, and I was watching to see if he would come up until we were more than half way across;[10] and then, being on the upper side of the boat, I commenced firing on the rebels. Battery B [of the 4th U.S. Artillery], on our side, opened on the Johnnies furiously, and their big guns on the heights, and their infantry opened on the river and the water fairly boiled, and it is a mystery to me now how our boat escaped being sunk, but we reached the other side and our lads did not wait to go out over the front of the boat, but jumped over the sides into the mud and water and rushed up the sides of the hill, Corporal [Lewis A.] Kent[11] being the first man to reach the top. There was a little ravine where we landed, and some of our men followed up the side of it and took the Johnnies in the rifle pits in flank and rear and we gobbled a good many of them and then we rushed upon the breastworks. The rebels did their best to stop us, but it was no use; our lads were determined to capture the works and the Johnnies could not stand the press, but fell back slowly, closely followed by our men, until we got orders to halt and fall back and hold the rebel breastworks while the rest of the army crossed. "Old Daddy Wadsworth," forgetting his grey hairs and infirmities, came over with the 19th Indiana, swimming his horse behind the boat; and the brave old man went from one company to another personally thanking them, in name of the country, for their gallant conduct, and he issued an order from division headquarters complimenting officers and men, stating that he should call the attention of the president and the general of the army[12] to our brilliant charge.

The rebels took position in a sunken road and kept up a desultory fire and their batteries on the hills threw shot and shell at us with no effect, except to force the doctors who were treating the wounded, to take shelter under the brow of the hill. We charged the front of their breastworks and got batteries into position and felt able (as [Tommy] Flynn said) to "hould our own against Jiff Davis and the divil," whom most of our fellows seemed to think were intimately connected.

Hooker's rather premature order from Chancellorsville, stating that he had Lee where he would have to fight him on his own ground or seek safety of inglorious flight, was read to each regiment, and our spirits ran high with hope of soon demolishing the confederacy, but it was not long before a damper was put on them by orders to abandon the position we had so gallantly taken, and march to Hooker's aid at Chancellorsville. The pontoon bridges were covered with straw and the artillery first crossed and the infantry last. The Johnnies observed the movement and opened every available gun on the bridges, but we crossed without serious loss and took up the march for Chancellorsville, passing through Gen. Gibbon's division of the 2d corps, which had been left to support [Gen. John] Sedgwick. Gen. Gibbon, who had been our brigade commander, and who had led it in the skirmishes at Rappahannock station and White Sulphur Springs, and on the bloody fields of Gainesville, Bull Run, South Mountain and Antietam, made a short address thanking us for sustaining our high reputation, and after giving him what old "Sol" Meredith called three "backwards cheers and three more and a tiger" for the union, we trudged along on our weary march to the sound of the cannonade in front. All the afternoon and night we marched, now dragging slowly along when the head of the column met an obstruction and then rushing ahead to close up after it was passed. We crossed the river at United States Ford and soon met the usual stragglers from the front; the man whose regiment was all killed but himself, and the battery caisson that was all that was left of the battery. We pressed right on and reached the field about six A.M., and the first thing attracted our attention was a squad of Meagher's Irish Brigade[13] who, with a good deal of Irish hulabaloo, were hauling off by the drag ropes, a couple of guns belonging to their battery, from which the horses had been killed the night before, and which they had taken from under the very noses of the rebels. We struggled through the almost impenetrable undergrowth of the Wilderness and took position on the ground from which the 11th corps had so disgracefully fallen back, and Sol. Meredith, our brigade general, delivered his famous Hoosier speech,[14] "boys, unsling knapsacks and make coffee; this is our dunghill and we'll fight for our rations," alluding to the fact that each man carried ten days' rations in his knapsack, besides what he had in his haversack, and we did; we held that ground against all pressure until the enemy exhausted themselves in the attempt to destroy the Army of the Potomac which owing to the drunken mismanagement of its commander [Joseph Hooker], had been split up into two detachments, and were each beaten in detail, and then our corps was rear guard and covered the retreat until every man, horse, mule, and contraband had safely crossed, and then we formed a line on this side and protected the engineers while they took up the bridges. It is a strange coincidence that on both occasions when the Army of the Potomac had to fall back in the presence of the enemy, (at Bull Run and Chancellorsville,) the Iron Brigade was selected as rear guard, and on both occasions the steady front presented to the enemy held them at a respectful distance and yet in any of the so called histories that have come under my notice, I have not seen any mention of such a brigade. It may be owing to the fact that our men were not of the hymn singing, testament-carrying kind who spent their time in camp in writing home letters of the "Just Before the Battle Mother" variety, but they were always ready for march or battle, and when that was over they were more interested in a stag dance or penny ante than what the newspapers were saying about them. A short time since I visited the rooms of the State Historical Society at Madison and enquired if there was any record on hand of the Iron Brigade, or any of the regiments composing it, and was informed that there was nothing but a general history, and it struck me as singular that I could find records of troops of other states, but none of any of our own regiments. The only evidence I discovered showing that there ever existed such a body of men as the Iron Brigade, was a case containing a photograph of the Rebel Battle Flag[15] captured by our regiment at Gettysburg, and a short extract from the official report of General Doubleday, in regard to the part taken by the regiment in that battle.[16] I think that a state that annually appropriates thousands of dollars wrung from poor and often needy farmers to support Professors of agriculture, state fairs, and to educate lawyers, might spare a few dollars to prepare a record of the patriotism of those who gave health, wealth, life and limb, for the honor of our state.

It is very gratifying for comrades in the army to meet one

another and talk of the times when they tramped through mud knee deep, or sweetly slept on three fence rails, or when they fiercely charged and drove the enemy, or how they bravely fell back when overpowered and defeated, but most of them are prevented by poverty from taking any part in soldier's reunions, and if the State would spare a few of the dollars spent in printing volumes that not one in a hundred of the people ever see, or some equally useless and unnecessary purpose, and devote them to encouraging reunions and meetings of the late soldiers, it would have more effect in promoting patriotism and love of country than all the buncombe speeches ever delivered.[17]

The soldier with his crippled limbs and rheumatic body, who is frequently looked upon by those enjoying the benefit of his service, as a fraud, trying to obtain a pension would be more than human if he cherished any great affection for a state that neglects and suffers him to be insulted, and it may be taken for granted that he will not encourage his children to die for the country. It is also pleasant, after spending four years of one's life, and having received a half dozen wounds in the war, to be called a copperhead by one of the eleventh-hour patriots which the draft or "the hundred dollars a keow" [queue] placed in the army, simply because one cherished feelings of respect for one of the bravest and most popular corps commanders in the army.

But I did not write this to find fault with the country or to discuss politics, nor to show what somebody should or should not do, but merely to keep alive the memory of that brigade which the Military History of Wisconsin calls "The gallant corps that was the pride of our State."

Forest, Vernon County, Wis.

[At the devastating conclusion of the Chancellorsville campaign, the Army of the Potomac remained in their entrenchments for some days. It was not until the drizzling morning of May 6, 1863, that the sodden Black Hats recrossed the Rappahannock and sullenly marched back toward Fredericksburg. In all the years that remained for Sullivan and his comrades, they would fail to understand how victory was snatched from the army. The five-time wounded veteran would return to this refrain in many of his postwar writings, and he would castigate Hooker with the others he deemed wasteful of the army's good resources—its soldiers.

After catching their wind and patching themselves somewhat, four brigade regiments were selected for a mission down Virginia's "Northern Neck." To their chagrin the Westerners, minus the 7th Wisconsin, learned they were to relieve the 8th Illinois Cavalry, a regiment which had gotten itself in a tight spot while on a foraging raid. The expedition stepped off May 21, 1863.

When Sullivan recalled the episode 20 years later, it was the light-hearted aspects that came to mind. The piece, printed in *The Milwaukee Sunday Telegraph,* March 2, 1884, contained some amusing character sketches as well as some playful tweaking of the shoulder straps of the 6th Wisconsin.]

WHY THE STAFF LOST A CHICKEN SUPPER
By Mickey, of Co. K.

Among the well remembered faces of ye old-time 6th regiment, the rosy-cheeked, boyish one of our first sergeant major, and afterwards adjutant [Edward P.] B[roo]ks is indelibly impressed on the "tablets of memory" of the veterans that the fortunes of war has left surviving. How we of the high grade in the rear rank were pleased when he won (by hard and faithful service) his first straps [as a 1st lieutenant, September 13, 1862] and appeared on guard mount in all the glory of a brilliant new uniform which was, as Schriver[? possibly Ernest Schivenbachen] said "anyhow two sizes too big mit him," and how we used to note with unbounded admiration his soldierly stride, his tremendous Grecian bend and his wonderful salute *"En high Tierce,"* as he announced "Sir, the parade is formed," or presented the new guard to the officer of the day at guard mount. How we watched with inexpressible anxiety (and some with unspeakable envy,) the growth of his tow-colored and effeminate mustache, and how greatly we rejoiced when with the help of "Nigger Jack's"[18] hair dye it became visible to the naked eye when he faced the regiment at the proper distance as given in "Hardee's Tactics."[19] Although a most gallant son of Mars, he was no less a worship-

per at the shrine of Venus, and I know not how many dark-
eyed daughters of the south were smitten by his handsome,
pleasant face, and what [Tommy] Flynn would call his "civil,
purty spoken tongue." After his promotion to what Capt.
Naegle [Henry Naegely of Company G], called the "sthafe,"
B[rooks] had ample opportunity to woo the fair goddess and it
is one of his adventures in the camp of cupid that I intend to
relate in order to verify the old saying that "true love never
did run smooth."

In May, 1863, the 8th Illinois cavalry was sent on a scout
down that strip of Virginia lying between the Potomac and
the Rappahannock rivers, called by the natives the "Northern
Neck," and the 2d [Wisconsin] regiment went along to cover
their rear and assist them to collect hams, chickens, corn
dodgers, mutton, fresh pork and anything else eatable. Rumor
was in camp that the "equestrian confederacy" assisted by
some of the mud waders of the same defunct nationality, had
crossed the Rappahannock at Port Royal and Tappahannock
and had extended their lines across the neck to its narrowest
part, and were preparing to offer in true southern style the
hospitalities of Libby and Belle Isle[20] to our comrades and
friends. Our brigade was ordered to march to the rescue by
forced marches, and as we went in light marching order, and
believing our friends to be in danger, we made good time. Our
route lay through King George and Westmoreland counties,
past the spot where Washington was born, to Westmoreland
court house, a beautiful village which some of the natives
called Montrose, and others the usual "Co't Hus," and a short
distance beyond we met the cavalry and the others returning
and it was at the camp near the "Co't Hus" that B[rooks] had
the adventure referred to.

Lincoln's famous proclamation[21] had been issued the New
Years before and the kid glove policy had been abandoned to
a considerable extent, and wherever our flag went it brought
liberty and emancipation to the colored people, and, though
the slaveocracy did their best to prevent the dissemination of
the news, by some underground process the slaves had become
pretty generally informed that "Massa Linkum" would receive
all who came. The district in which we were had hitherto
almost escaped the "iron hoofs" of war, and was in a compar-

atively flourishing condition, and being well stocked with slaves, the negroes flocked to us in droves. Such a medley of sights and sounds as our brigade presented on that march was probably seldom witnessed during the war. Ox carts with one ox and a cow for the motive power, family carriages, mules, donkeys, darkies of all ages, sizes and complexions, "toting" on their heads feather beds, bed clothes, stoves, wash tubs, iron kettles, household goods of all kinds, clothing, crockery and anything else their fancy and avarice prompted; and cavalry "mud waders," darkies, donk[ies] and all were indiscriminately strung along the line of march for miles. Soldiers carrying hams on their bayonets (that the dripping might fall on the rank behind,) chickens, turkeys, ducks, geese, alive and dead, hind quarters of sheep and hogs, eggs, butter, milk, corn dodgers, and raw corn meal (that Lieut. [William N.] Remington[22] and an officer of the 19th Ind. who I think was Pension Commissioner [William W.] Dudley, ground at a mill,) and when we reached Fredericksburg the column was (including the newly enfranchised) about ten miles long. The news of our coming had spread all over the entire "Northern neck," and at each plantation and cross roads we would meet crowds of contrabands anxious to go to the land of "Canayun"[23] wid "Massa Linkum's men," while shouts of "Glory," "Bres de Lawd," "Hallelujah Jubilo" and "We's gwine wid you all," filled the air with such a joyful chorus as was never heard in all of the Northern Neck before.

The "staff" of our regiment had a peculiar weakness for piazzas,[24] and when the shadows of evening began to lengthen their eagle eyes (when not dimmed with tears at the recollection of that pitcher of cider which their host of last night did not produce,) would eagerly scan the route of march for piazzas. When one apparently suitable was discovered, B[rooks] would gallantly ride forward to reconnoiter and on his return report as to the number and appearance of the young ladies, the prospects for coffee and corn bread (provided he furnished the coffee,) and sometimes, if he thought about it, would mention the suitability of the camp ground and the chances for wood and water. On the occasion referred to, the report was favorable and soon we went into bivouac. The staff

started for the piazza and were met at the front steps by a
daughter of the South of middle age and vinegary visage who
welcomed them warmly; informed them that she was a widow;
professed the strongest union sentiments; opened her parlor
and piano; and ordered a bounteous supper to be prepared,
while, to fill the cup of their happiness, three young ladies of
most exquisitely lovely forms and beautiful, smiling faces
made their appearance, and were presented to the staff by
their doting mamma. Evadne, the eldest of the trio, who was
musically inclined, seated herself at the piano and began
soothing the days of war with the "Star Spangled banner" and
kindred melodies. Louise, the next in rank, who had made a
specialty of history, regaled them with a correct recital of the
life and times of Washington, while the flaxen haired young-
est daughter [Evangeline], attracted by B[rook]'s resemblance
to herself in capillary adornments, approached and engaged
him in a most bewitching conversation. The gallant hero, who
had stood undaunted in a dozen battle fields, was hopelessly
overpowered by the "magic of beauty" and surrendered at
discretion, and made no effort to conceal his admiration,
which was apparently reciprocated. It was evidently a case of
love at first sight. I dare not say what visions of plantations,
and cotton bales, tobacco and sugar cane with Evangeline
gracefully swinging in a hammock, "when this cruel war was
over," flitted through his mind as he listened to the music of
her soft voice.

But outside, the officers who trailed the puissant "toad
sticker" on foot and we of the musket and knapsack made our
fires, boiled our coffee, fried our "bung slide" and commented
on the singularity of the fact that at this plantation there
were no contrabands to greet us with grins and glittering
ivories and shining eyes glistening like new constellations in
the southern sky. Except a few house servants who manifested
no signs of welcome, there were no negroes about the place.
At length [Edwin C.] Jones of Co. E,[25] who was prowling
around in search of poultry, spied, away up in the garret, dark
faces and wooly polls protruding through a window. The news
spread, a ladder was raised and down came a troop of Africans,
some thirty-five or forty in number, whom their mistress

vainly believed were safely hidden from the prying eyes of the
hated Yankees. But soon she heard of the discovery and, oh,
my countrymen, what a change was there. Her black eyes
flashed fire, her vinegary face grew more acid (gone were her
welcoming smiles,) and with a voice as sweet as an army fife
concert, she eloquently and forcible ordered the staff in true
southern phrase to git "Out of this house, you Northern
mudsills, you infernal Yankee Nigger thieves; you robbers;
you desecrators of our southern soil; you cowardly hirelings."
and word was immediately sent to the kitchen for Dinah to
stop the "chicken doins." Evadne's turn[ed] up nose elevated
itself still higher. Bang went the lid on her piano and in a
tone yet shriller than her mother's, she, too, ordered the staff
to git, and the historian, in a very energetic style of elocution,
informed them of every defeat the union army had sustained
and confidently predicted for them a dog's death at the hands
of her chivalric southern army. But, "oh, frailty, thy name is
woman;" it was whispered among us outsiders that Evangeline seized "B[rooks]" by the hair with the fair hands he had
been admiring, and there is no saying what the result would
have been had not some one interposed and released poor
"B[rooks]."

Sullenly the staff left the room; slowly they retired to the
far end of the piazza; sadly they ordered their servants to
prepare supper of coffee, bacon and hardtack. But no power
could drive them from that piazza; that was their last ditch,
and there they resolved to stay or die. Also, for visions of
Evangeline in the hammock and Northern Neck Plantations,
gone like the baseless fabric of a dream! To us who had been
the innocent cause of that tempest and who heard with
affright the shrill voices of the ladies and beheld with awe the
staff retreat, the newly emancipated brought hoe-cake and
eatables innumerable and unlike the staff we had reason to
rejoice in our "chicken doins."

For days "B[rook]s'" usually genial countenance wore a look
of settled gloom that not even a rumored extra issue of
commissary [whiskey] could wholly remove.[26]

NOTES

1. Herdegen and Beaudot, *Railroad Cut,* pp. 269–70.

2. Charles Carleton Coffin, who also wrote under the pseudonym "Carleton."

3. Pontoon boats were heavy, 31-foot, flat-bottomed affairs usually employed in bridging rivers. Canvas pontoons, 21 feet long, were lighter craft designed for transportation. It is likely the brigade used the former in making its crossing. Faust, *Encyclopedia,* p. 591–92.

4. Meredith, the colonel of the 19th Indiana, succeeded John Gibbon to command of the brigade.

5. Burnside, in an attempt to again cross the Rappahannock and succeed where he had failed in December, ordered his army from the winter camps on January 22, 1863, for what became the "Mud March." Men, animals, and materiel quickly bogged down when a winter storm turned roads into a quagmire. On the following day, the Federals agonizingly extricated themselves and returned to their old camps opposite Fredericksburg. At the conclusion of the failed campaign, Burnside, full of recriminations, moved to dismiss his subordinates. On January 25, Lincoln replaced Burnside with Joseph Hooker as commander of the Army of the Potomac. Long and Long, *Day by Day,* pp. 314–15.

6. Of the incident on April 28, 1863, Rufus Dawes wrote: "The mutiny was a small affair of a few two years men of the 24th New York, who claimed that their time had expired. A few pointed remarks by [Division Commander] General [James] Wadsworth, rendered pungent by the presence of our regiment with loaded muskets, brought them to their senses and they quietly fell in." Dawes, *Service,* p. 135.

7. William D. and Wallace B. Hancock were brothers. The former enlisted in June 1861, and the latter in March 1863. Both were wounded at Gettysburg. William was taken prisoner at Petersburg in 1864 and was killed by a rebel guard at a Salisbury, North Carolina, prison; Wallace was killed near Petersburg in June 1864. *Roster of Wisconsin Volunteers,* Vol. I, p. 534.

8. Wadsworth, popular among the men in ranks, was a white-haired division commander in the spring of 1863. Born in Connecticut, he was 53 when the war commenced. A friend said of him, "He was the truest and most thoroughly loyal American I ever knew." Despite his lack of military experience, Wadsworth quickly displayed organizational and command skills as well as concern for his soldiers. In December 1862, after Fredericksburg, he was accorded command of the I Corps' 1st Division, which included the Iron Brigade. His mettle was tested at Gettysburg, and he later commanded the 4th Division of the V Corps. In the battle of the Wilderness, Wadsworth was shot in the head; he died two days later in a Confederate field hospital. *Dictionary of American Biography,* Vol. XIX, pp. 308–309.

9. Sullivan is in error. Rufus R. Dawes identified the 24th Michigan as the other regiment. Dawes, *Service,* p. 136.

10. Trumble was listed as killed in action. *Roster of Wisconsin Volunteers,* Vol. I, p. 536.

11. Kent was a Virginian by upbringing, and a college student in Wisconsin at war's outset. He enlisted as a private soldier, ultimately winning command of Company A. As a captain, he became the final field commander of the 6th Wisconsin. In war's aftermath he was a newspaperman; he spent his final years in Oakland, California, dying there July 21, 1921. Wm. J. K. Beaudot, "A Virginian in the Iron Brigade," *Blue & Gray Magazine,* April 1990, pp. 26–30.

12. In his official report of the action, Wadsworth singled out Colonels Bragg and Henry Morrow of the 24th Michigan, and "the gallant men under their command, for the heroic manner in which they crossed the Rappahannock and seized the heights on the opposite shore. . . ." *War of the Rebellion, Official Records of the Union and Confederate Armies* (Washington, 1889–1900), Vol. 25, Part 1, p. 262.

13. Irish-born Thomas Francis Meagher, a fiery proponent of independence for his native land, was banished in 1849 by the British government. He escaped from Tasmania, and made his way to America in the early 1850s. In 1861 he organized a Zouave company which became part of the 69th New York State Militia, commanded by Michael Corcoran. The unit fought at First Bull Run in Sherman's Brigade. The following winter, Meagher organized the Irish Brigade in New York City, and he was appointed brigadier general by the president. The unit participated in all the campaigns of the Army of the Potomac and was remembered for its hopeless charge upon the entrenched enemy position at Fredericksburg in December 1862. Meagher thereafter was refused permission to recruit and determined to leave the army, but his resignation was not accepted, and in 1864 and 1865 he was assigned duty in the rear of Sherman's army. He finally left the service in May 1865 and traveled west to Montana. He served in the territorial government. At Fort Benton on July 1, 1867, Meagher drowned under mysterious circumstances; his body was never recovered. *Dictionary of American Biography,* Vol. XIII, pp. 481–82; Warner, *Generals in Blue,* pp. 317–18.

14. Only one year later, Sullivan, the 6th Wisconsin, and the brigade would once again grope through the sinister tangle of The Wilderness.

15. The flag was that of the 2nd Mississippi Infantry.

16. *OR,* Series 1, Vol. 27, Part 1, pp. 243–57.

17. Sullivan had been invited by Edward S. Bragg to address the Iron Brigade Association reunion meeting at La Crosse, Wisconsin, in September 1883. The loquacious veteran was the first enlisted man accorded the honor, and he spoke about the action at FitzHugh's Crossing. *La Crosse Republican and Leader,* September 22, 1883; *La Crosse Chronicle,* September 13, 1883; *Milwaukee Sunday Telegraph,* September 30, 1883.

18. A black barber from Fond du Lac who accompanied Company E to war.

19. Reference to William J. Hardee's *Rifle and Light Infantry Tractics,* a translation from a French drill manual which was published in the United States in 1855 and 1861. Griffith, *Battle Tactics,* pp. 100–101, 224.

20. Sites of Confederate prison camps.

21. The final draft of the Emancipation Proclamation was issued January 1, 1863.

22. Remington, of Mauston, enlisted as a common soldier in May of 1861;

he quickly distinguished himself, rising through the ranks to become an officer in October 1862. Twice wounded, he was promoted to captain of Company K and resigned because of ill health on October 11, 1864. After spending some years in Wisconsin, he and his family removed to Nebraska where he died prematurely at age 46 on September 12, 1886. His body was returned to Wisconsin for burial. Herdegen and Beaudot, *Railroad Cut,* pp. 261–62.

23. Probably a reference to "Canaan," the "promised land" of the Bible.

24. Sullivan is referring to the porch or veranda common to large Virginia homes.

25. Jones, a Shawano County farm boy, enlisted in Bragg's Company E on June 18, 1861, identifying his home as "Cosmopolite." He was, according to Watrous, the "most awkward soldier in drill or parade, but perfectly fearless in a fight." He faithfully served his term, re-enlisted, was wounded during the Spotsylvania campaign, and mustered out in July of 1865. *Roster of Wisconsin Volunteers,* Vol. I, p. 514; Jerome A. Watrous Papers, State Historical Society of Wisconsin.

26. Brooks, popular to Mickey's pen, was a somewhat controversial figure who was, in war's aftermath, criticized by one comrade for a sad incident in 1864. A newspaperman in Janesville before the war, Brooks enlisted and was assigned to Company D where he became quartermaster sergeant. His leap to officer ranks and regimental adjutant came quickly, the latter dated April 1, 1863. It was in this capacity that he led a 30-man detail into North Carolina below Petersburg in June 1864. "His military career was obscured somewhat," wrote Jerome Watrous in 1893. "He surrendered his force . . . the second day out and most of those thirty men died in prison, or have been wrecks ever since." Only Brooks and a handful returned. From July 1864, Brooks served as 1st lieutenant of Company F, mustering out in January 1865. He returned to the newspaper business, becoming editor of the *Washington Republican* before moving back to the Midwest and settling at Peoria, Illinois. He died in 1893, and was buried at Arlington National Cemetery. "His life was not what he expected it would be, and was in some respects a disappointment to his friends. He had many good qualities. Let us forget his mistakes," Watrous eulogized. *Milwaukee Telegraph,* May 13, 1893, August 11, 1896; *Roster of Wisconsin Volunteers,* Vol. I, pp. 494, 509, 517.

Chapter IV

EVERYTHING STOOD STILL

[Sullivan's most popular piece was the first that he wrote and had published—his account of the battle of Gettysburg. The fight that first day of July 1863 all but demolished the famed Iron Brigade, which was engaged west of town along Willoughby Run and in McPherson's Woods. Sullivan's regiment fought not with its celebrated brigade that bloody morning, but "singly and alone" on another part of the field. Initially held in reserve, the 6th Wisconsin was ordered north to the Chambersburg Pike, where Union regiments had given way under a strong Confederate attack. The regiment made a sudden charge into the flank of the advancing Confederate brigade and there was a sharp, brief fight in an unfinished railroad cut before the Johnnies fled, leaving behind 232 prisoners and the battle flag of the 2nd Mississippi Infantry. The cost was frightful. Of the 340 men who marched to Gettysburg with the 6th Wisconsin, more than 160 were killed, wounded, or missing. The successful charge set the stage for the ultimate Union victory, but 6th Wisconsin men, at the time and thereafter, always felt their great achievement was overlooked in the accounts of the epic battle.

It was late 1881 when J. P. Sullivan resolved to set the record straight. He was still working his "worthless" 40 acres of rolling Vernon County land, and it was a hard-scrabble existence. The 40-year-old veteran had a wife and growing family—George, born during the war years, was now 17, and much help out in the fields; Anna, called "Fannie," was 8; John, 7, and the baby, James, 4. There is no indication as to what prompted Sullivan to begin writing about his war experiences. Perhaps he was touched by the beginnings of the veterans' movement that would soon swell and surge over the nation's political shore. A Grand Army of the Republic encampment had been held in Milwaukee in 1880, and tens of thousands of veterans had quickened the city with meetings, marches, and martial displays. Many of Sullivan's former comrades gathered in a local hall to talk about forming an Iron Brigade Association. There is no record that the Irishman joined them at that time, but the following year, during a large reunion at Milwaukee of the Army of the Cumberland, the Iron Brigade Association formally adopted an organizational structure and elected officers.

More and more, Gettysburg came to symbolize the turning point of the war, and certainly Sullivan's memories of that battle were sharpest. He also worried that his old regiment was not getting recognition for its service there—a charge he felt was as bold and brave as any in military history. "Ours was not a mad dash, but a steady, cool, straight-forward advance against a greatly superior force . . .," he wrote of that Wednesday morning west of Gettysburg, grumbling in print that no poet laureate had written about it, as Alfred Tennyson had glorified the lesser charge (at least in Sullivan's thinking) of the Light Brigade at Balaclava in the Crimean War. The charge of his 6th Wisconsin, he wrote with bitterness, "is forgotten by all, except a few veterans and cripples, and the wives and mothers who lost all they held dear."

His was a soldier-in-the-rank view of Gettysburg, and Sullivan again displayed an almost casual indifference to the death of comrades in battle—he stripped a cartridge box from a fallen friend without a pause or reflection, did not lament the loss of the company sergeant shot to death before his eyes, and rolled a dead cavalry officer off a hospital bed to secure a place to sleep. It was an important story because it detailed a significant action in the very opening infantry battle at Gettysburg and recalled what it was like to be a wounded Union soldier behind Confederate lines in the town during the final two days of fighting. He also watched, from the cupola of the railroad depot, the doomed, final grand assault of the Army of Northern Virginia—what by 1880 some were calling "the high tide of the Confederacy"—and how, in that instant, "everything stood still."

In a rambling postscript to his recollections, Sullivan offered an acerbic assessment of those who criticized the pensions paid to veterans, and he savaged newspaper editors who flayed former Gen. Winfield Scott Hancock, the Democratic presidential candidate in the campaign of 1880. He delivered something of a diatribe against detractors he called "long range patriots," against the "meddling interferences of the politican and the bull-headed Senator," and against those who failed in their duty to country, whom he derided as the "Coffee Cooling Brigade" of malingerers and shirkers.

When Sullivan completed his lengthy article, the editor at the *Mauston Star* agreed to print it, and it appeared in two consecutive weekly issues March 22 and 29, 1883. The newspaper editor in nearby Viroqua saw the dispatch and published it in the *Vernon County Broadcaster–Censor* August 1 and 8 of the same year. Across the state, in Milwaukee, another of Sullivan's old 6th Wisconsin comrades, Jerome A. Watrous, was scouting for good stories to print in his weekly, *The Milwaukee Sunday Telegraph*. Watrous had come down from Fond du Lac in 1879 and bought into the society paper. Now he was working to gain subscribers for the paper, particularly among veterans who enjoyed his regular features about the war. The pieces were, for the most part, written by men who had seen the "elephant" of battle. Old comrades, who had not seen each other for two decades, were also making contact through the newspaper, discovering what had become of those youthful soldiers.

Sullivan's story of Gettysburg began on the morning of July 1, 1863. He did not, however, describe the grueling, dry, weeks-long June march north by the Army of the Potomac from the Rappahanock River near Fredericksburg, Virginia. As the long columns of dust-coated soldiers, wagons, animals, and implements of war passed the old Bull Run battlefield near mid-month, Lt. Col. Rufus Dawes had written to his sweetheart in Ohio that the men were "tired, sore, sleepy, hungry, dusty and dirty as pigs. I had no wink of sleep for two nights. Our army is in a great hurry for something." Lee and his Confederate Army of Northern Virginia were once again prowling toward Union territory as they had done almost a year before. Sullivan and his regiment crossed the Potomac River into Maryland June 26, and the final day of the month encamped at Marsh Creek just inside Pennsylvania. This account of the 6th Wisconsin at Gettysburg was completed by Sullivan February 13, 1883.]

THE CHARGE OF THE IRON BRIGADE
AT GETTYSBURG
By Mickey, of Company "K."

The first day of July [1863] dawned cloudy and rainy. We were awakened by the reveille before daylight, and preparing a hearty[1] breakfast of coffee and hardtack, we packed up traps and marched out of the field where we had encamped, and took up the line of march along what was called the Baltimore "Pike," towards Harrisburg, Pa. The day was cool and pleasant and our fellows seemed in good spirits, and now and again a

song would break out along the line. We had a German
Company F, the turners,[2] of Milwaukee, and amongst them
were some very good singers, and that day they struck up a
soul stirring song in German, such as only Germans can sing.
I remember we all took step to the time and when they had
concluded, we gave them three rousing cheers. Then Co. K
boys sang, and with about as much melody as a government
mule. They commenced:

> On the distant prairie where the heifer wild,
> Stole into the cabbage in the midnight mild,
> [Watrous added the next two lines:]
> Every one that knew her said she was a thief
> And should be killed and quartered and issued out for beef.

There was more of the same nature, but I have forgotten it.
I only know there was a grand chorus in which we all took
part, from Capt. [John] Ticknor down to the drummers.

> On the distant prairie, hoop de dooden doo.
> (Repeat ad libitum.)

It was kept up from one end of the line to the other, [Tommy]
Flynn, of Co. K, winding up with "Paddy's Wedding," which
made music enough for one day. It may seem odd for men to
be marching toward their death, singing, shouting and joking
as if it were a street parade or holiday show.

About 7 o'clock that morning the cavalry and horse artillery
came up on the gallop and we opened up right and left and let
them pass through as we marched along. Flynn gave them a
parting benediction, as follows: "May the divil fly away with
the roofs of your jackets; yez are going ahead now to get us
into a scrape and thin walk off and let us fight it out like ye
always do." Cannonading could be faintly heard to the right,
and word passed through the ranks that [Gen. John] Buford[3]
had found the Johnnies over at York or Hanover. [James D.]
Wood, of the 2d Wis. [Sullivan erroneously identified him as
"Woods" of the 19th Indiana], our brigade adjutant general,
rode along the brigade shouting, "Boys, 'Little Mac' is in
command of the Army of the Potomac." And our fellows
cheered like mad,[4] glad to be rid of such vainglorious fools as

hind quarters in the saddle [John Pope], and old-stick-in-the-mud [Burnside], to say nothing about drunken Joe [Hooker], who had Lee where he would have to fight him on his own ground or seek safety in inglorious flight. Our fellows thought Hooker did the inglorious part to perfection on that occasion.[5] Before we were done cheering, Gettysburg came in sight and our lads straightened up to pass through in good style, and the brigade band struck up the "Red, White and Blue," when all at once hell broke loose (as Flynn put it,) in front. The cavalry had found the Johnnies and they were driving them back on us. The band swung out to one side and began "Yankee Doodle" in double quick time and "Forward, double quick," sang out the colonel [Rufus R. Dawes], and the decisive battle of the war had begun.

The regiment turned off to the left towards the seminary, and over the ridge on the double quick and then we saw the rebs driving the cavalry over a ridge in front, and at the same time a heavy line of battle rose over a ridge on our right and advanced towards us on our right flank. Down the slope they came and then it seemed as if the ground had opened and swallowed them up—but we soon found that they were still on top of it—as they opened a tremendous fire on us, from an old railroad cut. Just then, what appeared to me like a very boyish looking staff officer[6] galloped up to our commanding officer and I heard him say Gen. [John] Reynolds is killed and Gen. [Abner] Doubleday is in command[7] and directs your regiment, and that was all I heard as we were marching all the time. "By company into line, on right company," sang out Col. Dawes. "Load at will, load," ordered Captain [John] Ticknor, and our boys began to fall fast before we got into line.[8] We swung into line and the order was, "Forward." We advanced over a meadow that had been cut a short time before and was now green and smooth, crossed a fence, through a stubble field, up to a road [Chambersburg Pike] with a fence on each side of it. In the road our fellows straightened up their lines and waited for all hands to get over the fence and opened fire on the Johnnies, and then I found my gun would not go off. When I rejoined the regiment at Belle Plain in 1863[9] there were a good many old guns on hand and a few new ones [Model 1861 Springfield rifle-muskets]; the regimental ordnance Sergeant gave me one of the old ones,[10] and I indignantly went to Col. Bragg and wanted to know if the regiment could not afford to give me a good musket, and he went with me to the ordnance Sergeant and said, in his usual jesting manner: "Serg't, this is the man that fought the whole rebel army at Bull Run, let him choose a gun for himself." I selected one with a curly stock and I mounted it with some silver ornaments and fixed the screw in a stock against the dog [sear] so it worked almost as easy as a squrirel gun, and I felt very proud of it. Once on general inspection, Gen. [James S.] Wadsworth [division commander] asked me why I put that screw in my gun stock, and I told him, so that I could hit a canteen at one-hundred yards, and he asked me no more questions. We climbed over the fence and I tried my gun again, and finding it had two loads in it I went to our Adjutant [Edward Brooks] who was just in rear of our company and said: "Brooks, my gun won't go off."[11] "Here, take this," he said, and handed me one he had picked up, and telling him not to lose mine, I went back into place in the line and fired it off, but when I loaded up and tried again it would not go, and then I knew my [percussion] caps were bad. I went to Ticknor and told him my caps were bad. He said, "take Crawford's," pointing to a corporal of our company who had just dropped dead [John A. Crawford of Baraboo] and we rolled him over and I took the cartridge box and buckled it on myself.

As I turned around I saw Capt. Ticknor start for the rear in a spread out, staggering sort of way [and after] a few feet he fell. As I reached the line, First Sergeant Erastus Smith,[12] my tent mate started for the rear saying "Jerkey" (our nick name for Capt. Ticknor) is shot and I think he's killed, and I am going to see about him."[13] We were then within a few feet of the railroad cut and were ordered to fix bayonets and charge, which we did. Some of the Johnnies threw down their guns and surrendered. Some would fire and then throw down their guns and cry, I surrender, and some of them broke for the rear. I jumped into the railroad cut and a rebel officer handed me his sword and passed through the cut with the intention of stopping the Johnnies, who were limbering to the rear. Just

as I climbed up the side of the cut a big rebel broke and run
for the rear, and I called on him to halt, to which he paid no
attention, and I flung the rebel sword at him with all my
might, but I never knew whether it hit or not,[14] for just as I
turned to throw the sword, a bullet hit me on the left shoulder
and knocked me down as quick as if I had been hit with a
sledge hammer. The first thought I had was that some rebel
had hit me with the butt of his gun, for I felt numb and
stunned, but I was not long in finding out what was the
matter. I think that when I turned to throw the sword it saved
my life, as otherwise I would have been shot square through
the body. Sergt. [Albert] Tarbox[15] came up the side of the cut
and seeing me says, they've got you down, Mickey, have they,
and then fell forward dead. Some of the damned rebs who had
surrendered having shot him as he straightened up. They did
a good deal of that kind of work that day. In my experience of
battles before or since, I never saw so many men killed in
such a short time, as it was not more than fifteen or twenty
minutes from the time we saw the rebels until we had them,
officers, colors and all. Frank Wallar, of Co. I, got their flag,
and I learned afterwards that twenty-seven of our men were
killed or wounded trying to get it. I believe Wallar was
wounded, but he kept the flag and afterwards received a medal
from Congress for it.[16] After a while I began to feel better,
and like a true Irishman I spoke to myself to see if I was dead
or only speechless, and finding it was only the latter, I picked
up my gun and tried to shoulder it, but I found that my left
arm was powerless and so I went around to the other side of
the cut where our fellows had a heavy line of prisoners, and a
very thin skirmish line of themselves, and took my place
outside the rebs, intending to help guard them, but I felt sick
and faint and the blood was running down inside my clothes
and dropping from my pants leg and my shoe was full and
running over. I had a canteen of fresh milk that an old
Pennsylvania Dutchman had given me that morning, and one
of the rebs took it off for me and held it while I took a big
swig, which helped me a good bit.

"Old Waddy" [Watrous changed it to "Old Daddy Wadsworth"] had brought up the cavalry to help guard the prison-

ers, and seeing my condition he said, "My man, you are too badly hurt to be here." He called a cavalry Sergeant and directed him to assist me on his horse and take me back to the hospital, which had been established in the city, and not to leave me until he saw me in care of a doctor. The streets were filled with ladies and citizens who had wine and refreshments of all kinds on tables and trays, and in their hands, and urged them on every wounded man, and assisted them in every way. By the way, an old citizen named [John] Burns joined our fellows in the morning and fought like a tiger. I never heard what became of him.[17] The Sergeant brought me to the court house, which had been converted into a hospital, and there I found "Old Syntax" Dr. [John C.] Hall and Dr. [Oscar F.] Bartlett[18] and a good many more quinines [doctors], citizens and military, busy cutting up and patching up the biggest part of the Sixth Regiment, and in due time I was put together with sticking plaster and bandages and was served some good strong coffee that the citizens brought in, and feeling faint I lay down on the floor and tried to rest myself, and after awhile I felt well enough to look around and see how many of Company K had got punched. I found that nearly every man in the company was in the same fix I was, and some a great deal worse. Gene [Eugene P.] Rose had lost a leg, Abe [Abram G.] Fletcher had his thigh cut off (for all the world like a sugar cured ham.) Bill [William H.] Van Wie was grunting about a crack he had got. [Peter A.] Everson had a hole in his thigh big enough to put one's fist in, Wallace [B.] Hancock was shot in the arm and Billy [Wallace's brother, William D.] in the breast. Sile [Silas W.] Temple and Charley Crawford were in a corner together. Chauncy [Chauncey] Wilcox had his arm off and Lou [Lorenzo] Pratt was hit in the leg.[19] Hugh Talty [of Lisbon] had got his canteen filled with whisky by one of the citizens and didn't feel his wound and was bragging how "the Ould Sixth, be gob, could niver be whipt, be gob." There were more of them at the railroad depot, but I didn't know who they were, anyhow I thought there were enough here out of the little squad of a company that went into the fight that morning.[20]

All of a sudden some one rushed in and said that the 11th

corps had broke and run and the rebs were driving our fellows through the town. Sure enough, solid shot and shell began to crash through the court house and burst in the yard. The doctors ordered all who could march to leave and put up a hospital flag on the court house, and after a bit no more shot struck near it. By-and-by a rebel officer came in and demanded our surrender. The doctors told him there was nobody there only medical men and severely wounded, and the band men who were nurses. After some palaver and a drink or two of hospital brandy, the reb told our doctors to have the nurses tie a white string around their arm and the wounded to keep inside, and they would not be disturbed. I was mad as the devil to think that all our hard fighting that morning had went for nothing, and here was over two hundred of our brigade all smashed to pieces, to say nothing of all that were at the other hospitals. The poor wounded fellows cursed the "Flying Moon" Corps freely and [Oliver O.] Howard for a bible thumping hypocrite [Watrous expunged the Howard reference],[21] and Hugh Talty wanted to go out whip the "d—-d cowards be gob," but some one told him that the rebels would gobble him and take him to Libby [Prison] and that took the fight out of Hugh. After a while things quieted down and the firing ceased. Along towards night I began to skirmish around for some better place to sleep than the floor of the court house, where, having no blankets or knapsack for a pillow, I was not very comfortable. [William D.] Hancock said our fellows had a good place in the railroad depot, and we went there. I slept with a dead officer who had been mortally wounded in the cavalry fight, and some citizen had brought out a feather bed and some bed clothes, and had fixed him on it; not being able to roll him off I lay down with him and some time in the night I went to sleep.

The rebels plundered the stores and houses in the city and we could see them going with pails of sugar, molasses and groceries of all kinds; clothing and bales of goods, silks, calico and cloth. They were good to our wounded boys and shared their stolen whisky, tobacco and baker's bread freely, but the rebel officers were surly, and one of them wanted a rebel soldier to take a good pair of balmoral shoes I had on, but I told him there would be an Irish row first; and the fellow said they would not fit him, that they were too small: they had not yet fairly begun to strip our wounded and prisoners. Hays's brigade of Louisiana Tigers was stationed in Gettysburg, and they felt very jubilant over yesterday's battle, exultingly told us that "you uns" were whipped and they were going to take Washington, Baltimore and Philadelphia and end the "wah." Our fellows, although they felt down in the mouth enough, defiantly told them that they would have to whip the Army of the Potomac first, and if half the rebel army was barely able to whip part of the First Corps they would find a different job when [Generals Winfield Scott] Hancock, [Daniel] Sickles, [George] Meade, [John] Sedgwick and [Henry] Slocum would come up with the 2d, 3d, 5th, 6th and 12th corps, and if Howard spent his time in running, there were plenty of fighting men in the Army of the Potomac [again Watrous expunged the caustic remark about Howard] and McClellan was in command and would serve Lee worse than he did at Antietam. That kind of took the brag out of them and we did not hear any more about "you uns" being whipped. I saw Gen. [Jubal] Early and Staff riding through the city. He appeared to me to be a short, pussy, gray haired, bull-headed Reb with no great amount of intelligence in his look [Watrous erased the phrase about intelligence], but the rebs say he was a fighting devil, and we were willing to agree with them.

The day [Thursday, July 2, 1863] passed quietly enough. Skirmishing was going on and now and again a *bum-anade* would break out. The rebel army all came up and the fields back of the town were full of their wagons and cattle that I suppose they had taken from the poor farmers. Their artillery was moving out to the right of the town towards the seminary, and some of our fellows who had climbed up to the observatory on top of the railroad depot said that their army was massing on our centre and right flank. Two or three times during the day some one came around for our names to parole us, and the boys would tell them the worst, jawbreaking name they could think of, we all belonged to the 199th Wisconsin, and that McClellan would parole us to-morrow. Anyhow we never heard anything about it afterwards as they did not have time next day to do anything but look out for themselves. The citizens had left the city and there were scant arrangements for the wounded, but during the forenoon Dr. Bartlett and old Syntax [Hall] got a mess-room fixed up for us in a saloon and basement kitchen, and we got some coffee, tea and crackers, and the Johnnies brought in their wounded and we were all mixed together.

The rebs gathered up what prisoners they could and started them off for Richmond. Billy Hancock and myself rolled the dead officer off the bed and took possession by divine right, but my wound gave me a good deal of bother, and I did not enjoy our conquest very much. What added to our uneasiness was the fact that the rebs might clean out the army of the Potomac and take Washington, then "Old Abe" and the country was gone for certain. The reb wounded said that Lee had reinforcements from [P. G. T.] Beauregard and [Gen. Braxton] Bragg's armies, and that Charleston and Savannah had left the Home Guard in the works at Richmond, and were going to end the war in this battle, and things looked mighty blue. Ewell's corps moved out to the left of the town. About eight or nine o'clock they charged our fellows and drove them out of their breastworks [around Culp's Hill], but the next morning they were driven out again. Thursday[22] dawned fine and clear, everything seemed as still as if there was not a soldier within a thousand miles. About eight o'clock a *bum-anade* began, and our fellows done well out of the breastworks [on Culp's Hill] we had taken the night before. Our lookout in the observatory said that all their artillery was gathering on the right of the town and their infantry was being massed in solid blocks. We knew they meant to make trouble pretty soon. After dinner about two o'clock, the Fife Major who was in the observatory came down and said that the Johnnies were moving. Just then "bang, bang" went a couple of guns, and then such a roar of artillery as I have ever heard before or since. Bull Run was not a patching; the ground shook, and the depot building fairly trembled. Our fellows answered just as loud, and it seemed as if the last day had come. I got one of the band boys to help me, and hanging onto the railing of the stairs I climbed to the cupola and looking over towards the

right of the town [south] I saw what appeared like a whole
rebel army in a chunk start for our lines with their infernal
squealing yell [Pickett's Charge].[23] It seemed as if everything
stood still inside of me for a second or two, and then I began
to pray. Now I never was and am not yet, noted for the
frequency and fervency of my prayers, but that time I prayed
from the bottom of my heart that they would catch h--l, and
they did. It seemed as if the fire from our lines doubled and
doubled again, and I could see long streaks of light through
the rebel columns, but they went forward. I was afraid they
would capture our guns, but all of a sudden they seemed to
melt away as our infantry opened on them, and then we could
hear the Northern cheer. We knew that the rebs were scooped,
and the old Army of the Potomac was victorious. There were
ten or fifteen of us in the observatory, and they were wild
with joy, some cried, others shook hands, and all joined in
[the] best cheer we could get up. I forgot all about my wound,
and was very forcibly reminded of it when I went to shout as I
had to sit down to keep from falling. The other wounded down
below joined in the cheer, and a rebel officer came in and
wanted to know what was the matter, and when told that Lee
was cleaned, he growled out if we d---d Yankees were able to
cheer we were able to go to Richmond. But our fellows felt
good anyway, and the reb went out and we saw no more of
him.

Afterwards we could see that it was all up with the Johnnies; the wagons began to hustle off, and the cattle were
driven after them. The streets were filled with wounded and
stragglers from the front, and everything indicated that Lee
had been badly beaten. Our fellows were as much pleased as
if the paymaster had just come into camp, and night settled
down quietly. My wound had now got so far along that the
numbness had left and was very painful, and I was unable to
sleep during the night, and I could hear the roll of artillery
wagons all night on the retreat, and after daylight woke
[William] Hancock and we went out into the street intending
to try and reach the regiment. It was raining a drizzling sort
of rain and I had no coat on and Hancock went back for one of
the bed quilts for me, but before he returned a skirmish line

came down the street, followed by a support and the battle
flag of the 11th Corps, and then I knew that our fellows had
Gettysburg. I told the officer about the artillery moving all
night, and he sent an Orderly off to Headquarters with the
information, and his command passed on through the town
after the rebs. After breakfast Dr. Bartlett advised all who
could walk to go to Littlestown, seven or eight miles distant,
as they would stand a better show for there than was possible
here, as the town was overflowing with wounded rebels and
then a limping squadron with broomsticks for crutches, and
any means of assistance they could lay their hands on started
out on the pike towards Cemetery Hill where we found the
regiment [6th Wisconsin] about the size of a decent company
supporting a battery in the center of the horse shoe in which
our line was formed [on Culp's Hill]. Company K had seven or
eight men, First Sergeant [Erastus] Smith in charge, and
Corporal Billy [William S.] Campbell the only other officer of
any kind left.[24] Smith and myself compared notes and found
that the company had lost five killed and eighteen wounded
out of the thirty-three who went into battle on the morning of
the first. I believe Lieut. Col. Dawes was the only field officer
left in the brigade, and more than two-thirds of the company
officers of our regiment were killed or wounded, and the other
regiments of the brigade were cut up just as bad. Old Sol
Meredith, Brigadier General, was wounded, and five regiments would not make one. The Second lost its Colonel
[George H. Stevens] and Col. [Lucius] Fairchild had lost an
arm, and the major [John Mansfield] was wounded. Lieut. Col.
[John B.] Callis of the 7th, had lost a leg, and the 19th Indiana
was in as bad a fix as any.[25] I don't know whether Col. [Henry
A.] Morrow, of the 24th Michigan, was wounded or not.[26] I was
told that General Wadsworth shed tears over his good men,
his Iron Brigade, and I believe he did, for if there was a patriot
in the army it was him. I understand, at least it was currently
believed in the Army of the Potomac that he served from the
time he raised the regiment in 1861 until he was killed in the
Wilderness in 1864, without any pay or remuneration of any
kind from the Government, except feed for his own horse. I
believe that was the first, last and only fight which the brigade

was in that Col. [Edward S.] Bragg was not present. Where he was I don't know but I think he was sick in hospital.[27] Capt. [John] Ticknor, of Co. "K" and Sergeant Albert Tarbox, Corporals John Crawford and Abraham Fletcher, and Privates James M. Scoville were killed.[28] Lieut. Wm. N. Remington, Sergt. Wm. H. Van Wie and Privates Silas Temple, Chas. Crawford, Peter A. Everson, Wm. D. Hancock, Wallace B. Hancock, James P. Sullivan, Lorenzo Pratt, Eugene P. Rose, William Revels, Hugh Talty, Chauncey Wilcox, and some others who were not among those at the Court House, were wounded. After remaining a short time with Smith, I took up the line of march for first corps hospital two miles off, where I stayed that night and the next morning I again started for Littlestown, as the surgeons told us the wounded were being sent to Harrisburg and Philadelphia from that point. I made about two miles that day, and slept in a barn with twenty-five or thirty more wounded. The old Pennsylvania farmer furnished us with quilts, supper and breakfast. In the morning he took a spring wagon and carried myself and three others to Littlestown, where we were loaded on freight cars and taken to Baltimore where the citizens supplied us with every luxury, and the next day I was sent to Philadelphia and taken to the Germantown Hospital, Ward B, with twenty-nine others of the Sixth and Seventh, and it was a long time before I was able to get back to the regiment.[29]

[Sullivan took the opportunity of closing his Gettysburg piece with a lengthy diatribe against the newspapers, government bureaucrats, and "long range patriots" who sat out the war only to criticize the pension-drawing soldiers in the postwar years. He also waved the political flag, trumpeting the election of veteran candidates. Apologists for the former Confederacy, during the 1880s, were also engaged in a war of words extolling the prowess of Southern armies and generals during the late war. Sullivan more than bristled, and fought these writers as well as Eastern authors.]

Above, taken from notes written on the plates, in a copy of "Casey's Tactics,"[30] from memory, is a correct and faithful account of the famous charge of the old Iron Brigade, so far as it came under my observation and although it may seem more

like an account of my personal actions, it must not be thought
of as a soldier in battle, who does his duty, has limited means
of observing what transpires outside his own immediate vicinity, and though it may be very easy to write imaginary
accounts of troops during a battle, they lack the force of being
true. There must be many persons living who remember of
the above facts, and may be willing to corroborate my statements.

Gettysburg was the high point of the war. Had Lee been
victorious, and defeated the Army of the Potomac there was
nothing to stand between him and Washington, Philadelphia
and New York, and there is no foreseeing what might have
been the result. The old Army of the Potomac was found fault
with a good deal, by some of the "On to Richmond" editors
and the "long range patriots," but it could always be counted
upon when half decently handled. The final collapse of the
Rebellion proved that Lee was the mainstay of the confederacy, and the Army of the Potomac, notwithstanding the inefficiency of some of its commanders, and the meddling
interference of the politican and the bull-headed Senator, was
able to beat Lee if it had anything like a chance. Antietam
and Gettysburg showed that if through ignorance and mismanagement Lee had beaten it at [Second] Bull Run and
Chancellorsville, the same army, with diminished numbers,
could almost immediately after, give Lee a terrible beating.

I believe there is no instance on record where the loss was
so heavy (being over 70 percent,) for the number of men
engaged, as the Iron Brigade lost at Gettysburg. There may
be cases where troops have charged fortifications or entrenched troops and suffered as heavily, but it must be remembered that our fighting was all done in an open field, and
with the exception of the railroad cut, on which our regiment
charged, the rebs had no protection whatever. The famous
charge of the Light Brigade at Balaclava, of which so much
has been said, and for writing a silly poem describing what
he saw, Tennyson achieved his fame, does not compare to it.
Ours was not a dash, but a steady, cool, straight-forward
advance against a greatly superior force, and notwithstanding
the severity of our loss, we took more prisoners, including a

Brigadier General, than we had men when we entered the fight. No poet laureate has written about it, and no sentimental young lady dressed in Stars and Stripes has recited it to an enthusiastic audience, as I have witnessed Tennyson's poem, but it is forgotten by all, except the few veterans and cripples, and the wives and mothers who lost all they held dear. If one of the surviving cripples is drawing a meager trifle of a pension, there are plenty of "long range patriots," willing to support the Government at a safe distance from danger, where they could make money out of the blood of the soldier, that are ready to exclaim: "Oh, he's all right; he draws a pension!" coupled with the sneering remark: "He's no more entitled to it than I am." This may seem strange, but there must be many living who have felt their blood boil when they heard it. An example may be cited in the case of Gen. Hancock,[31] who selected the ground and formed our lines, and who was severely wounded in the final attempt of the rebels to break through our lines. No abuse was too much, or too severe, and the vile scurrility of partisan newspapers was disgusting to all who knew the history of the man during the war, and all because he was foolish enough to allow his name to be used as a candidate for office. I also have proof in my own person, for having, about six years ago, homesteaded a worthless forty acres of land, now after living in Wisconsin Territory and State forty-three years, (all my life), some one in the Land Department at Washington wants proof that my father became a naturalized citizen, before I can obtain a patent. They did not want such proof in 1863, when my brother, seven years my senior, was enrolled for the draft. He did not claim exemption on the ground of being an alien, but after taking his chances and not being drawn, he enlisted in the old Eagle Regiment [8th Wisconsin Infantry], and served with it until the close of the war.[32]

I hope it will not be long before the soldiers will understand in which direction their interests lie, and act accordingly. I always have and always will support a soldier for any office, regardless of the party which nominated him, or what ticket he was on, and if all soldiers would do the same[,] the brother-in-law and cousin-in-the army kind of patriots who are so anxious to serve the country would have to limber to the rear and take their place among what our fellows used to call the "Coffee Cooling Brigade."

Forest, Vernon Co., Wis., February 13, 1883

[About a year after writing his Gettysburg reminiscences, Sullivan was disposed to twice write about the great battle in defense of his 6th Wisconsin. As a reader of *The National Tribune*, a national soldier newspaper published weekly in Washington, D.C., the Irishman's ire was raised by a piece which appeared in the June 5, 1884, issue by Col. William Hofmann of the 56th Pennsylvania,[33] and again on March 26, 1885, by a Gettysburg account written by a pseudonymous author named "Carleton"—Charles Carleton Coffin, a war correspondent and editor. The latter piece was a chapter in a series entitled "Saving the Nation, The Story of the War Retold for Our Boys and Girls." Coffin erroneously failed to include the 6th Wisconsin among the " 'Iron men' of the West," and later stated that General Doubleday halted the Badger regiment and "100 men of the 149th Pa." near the Seminary in reserve. After the unit was ordered to advance, and the charge made on the railroad cut, Coffin wrote, "Adjutant (Edward) Brooks, with a company shuts the eastern end (of the cut to prevent the Confederate escape)." Mickey vented his fury in a rebuttal which was published in *The Tribune* May 14, 1885.]

Gettysburg: A Member of the 6th Wis. Takes Issue with 'Carleton.'

To the Editor: I have noticed in your paper various articles concerning the opening fight at Gettysburg, but not being controversially inclined, I have refrained from correcting them; but "Carleton's" article in your issue of March 26 is the last straw that breaks the back of my patience. So far as my knowledge extends, "Carleton's" statements are a tissue of errors from beginning to end. He first omits the 6th Wis. from the "Iron Brigade," then assigns the 156th Pa. and the 146th Pa. to Wadsworth's Division, and commends the 6th Wis. and 100 men of the 149th Pa. (What Brigade?) at the Seminary, describes the tremendous fire of the other two regiments of

Cutler's Brigade across the excavation to escape which the Confederates rush into the trap of the cut; how Adjutant Brooks closes the eastern end with a company, and the pitiless storm that causes the enemy to lift their hands in token of surrender. If Adjutant Brooks, Col. Dawes, or any man of the 6th Wis. who was present in that charge, will admit that there is a word of truth in "Carleton's" description of it, I am willing to allow "Carleton" to "down an ass." The drifting cannon smoke which thickened the atmosphere must be in the fumes of "Carleton's" imagination, which became over-heated while conjuring up the statements he puts forth as history. Gen. Sheridan says Whitelaw Reid[34] wrote a description of the battle of Shiloh from his view of the field obtained in Cincinnati, and I judge by the tone of "Carleton's" article that it was written while surely entrenched behind newspaper gossip.

The setting forth such mental dribble as history is an outrage upon the men who stood between the Union and destruction on that memorable 1st day of July. While the 6th Wis. always felt towards other regiments' claims as Prince Henry did towards Falstaff in regard to the killing of Hotspur, yet we do think that persons who attest to write history should state facts. "Carleton" has probably outlived his usefulness as a historian, and had better give way to one who can learn the facts first and write their history afterwards.

Now I desire to write a few facts (whether it is history or not) about the actions of the 6th Wis. on the morning of July 1, 1863. About 10 a.m. we heard skirmishing on our left front, and immediately started towards the Seminary, and just after we had started[,] a line of battle of the enemy rose over a ridge on our right front—or, more correctly speaking, in a right oblique direction—and immediately opened fire on our column. Our regiment formed a line of battle "by company into line on the right company" and advanced towards the enemy, who were advancing and firing on our regiment at the same time, until they reached the railroad cut, which they occupied. We did not fire a shot until the road with a fence on each side of it was reached. In this road we halted a moment until all hands came up, when the command was again

"Forward!" and from there to the railroad cut, a distance of 150 or perhaps 200 yards, our men fired two or three rounds, loading and firing at will as we advanced. All the while the enemy kept up a deadly fire and our killed and wounded lay thick on the grass between the road and cut. Upon reaching the cut [,] bayonets and clubbed muskets were used by the 6th Wis., and the rebs were clubbed and bayoneted into surrendering. Some of them would throw down their guns and cry "I surrender," and immediately pick them up and shoot some of our unsuspecting men. A few of them escaped to the rear, but finally their commanding officer [Maj. John Blair of the 2nd Mississippi] gave his sword to Lieut.-Col. Rufus R. Dawes, who commanded the 6th Wis., and Corp. Frank A. Wallar, of Co. I, 6th Wis., captured their colors after a desperate struggle that occurred over them. The 6th Wis. received no support morally or physically, from any New York or Pennsylvania regiment, but charged alone and unaided. The 6th Wis. lost 40 killed and 82 wounded between the Seminary and the railroad cut, and if necessary I can and will furnish the name of each individual.

—*JAMES P. SULLIVAN, CO. K, 6TH WIS.*

[Sullivan also responded to a long account of the 56th Pennsylvania's role in the opening infantry fighting at Gettysburg written by the former colonel of that organization, William Hofmann. Hofmann asserted, probably correctly, that his regiment fired the first volley by a Union infantry regiment at the epic battle, and disputed claims by 2nd Wisconsin men that their unit was the first to engage the Confederates. Sullivan identified Hofmann both as colonel and general. The Pennsylvanian was a colonel at Gettysburg and subsequently was promoted to the higher grade. Sullivan's letter was printed June 21, 1885, in *The Milwaukee Sunday Telegraph*.]

THE SIXTH WIS. AT GETTYSBURG

To the Editor National Tribune.

My attention has been attracted by the article in your issue of June 5, 1884, from Col. Hofmann, of the 56th Pennsylvania, in regard to the action of the 147th New York at the opening of the Battle of Gettysburg, and also the article in your issue of April 2, 1884, from Capt. J.V. Pierce, 147th N.Y. Both of those writers agree substantially upon one point—that General Cutler's brigade formed line of battle on the ridge just beyond the Seminary Ridge, or what Gen'l Hofmann calls the second ridge, and north of the old railroad cut; or in General Hofmann's words: "How the line was formed." When Cutler's brigade of infantry, in the following order, 76th N.Y., 56th Pa., 147th N.Y. and 95th N.Y. and 14th Brooklyn arrived upon the ground about 10 A.M. July 1st [1863], after crossing the Seminary Ridge, just south of the Seminary buildings and descending in column into the low ground in front of it; the three leading regiments were moved north across the turnpike and north of the railroad grading when the line of battle was formed, facing west, with the left of the left regiment— the 147th N.Y.—resting near the railroad cut of the second ridge." Now, unless I am suffering from an overexcited imagination, that is the identical spot where the 6th Wisconsin captured the 2nd Mississippi, and the route described by Col. Hofmann is the route followed by the 6th Wisconsin when going into battle on the morning of July 1st, 1863. Gen. Hofmann asserts that the 6th Wisconsin was placed in reserve at the Seminary and when the enemy outflanked and drove Cutler's brigade, that the 6th Wisconsin and 14th Brooklyn under Lieut-Col. Fowler, of the 14th Brooklyn, advanced and captured the enemy in the cut who, owing to the depth of the cut, were deprived of their fire. General Hofmann is in error in every particular (in regard to the 6th Wisconsin.) The 6th Wisconsin was not in reserve at the Seminary before it captured the enemy in the cut; the 14th Brooklyn was nowhere in sight, nor did it take part in the charge at all. We were not under Lieut.Col. Fowler,[35] but Col. Dawes of the 6th Wis. commanded and directed all the movements of that charge. That, so far from the enemy's being deprived of their fire, the 6th Wis. lost 40 killed and 80 wounded in advancing from the Seminary to the railroad cut.

The facts in the case in regard to the movements of the 6th Wis. are as follows: About 10 A.M., July 1st, 1863, when about three-fourths of a mile from Gettysburg on the Emmittsburg Pike, the 6th regiment heard desultory firing in front and immediately started on the double quick, turning off towards the left to the Seminary (passing to the left of the Seminary a short distance.) On reaching the top of the Seminary ridge our cavalry became visible on the top of the ridge beyond, skirmishing with the enemy, whom we could not see as they were beyond the ridge. Simultaneous with our arrival at the Seminary a line of battle rose over a ridge on our right flank and front or in military parlance in a right oblique direction to our line of march. Lieut. Col. Dawes immediately ordered "by company into line on right company," and we advanced toward the enemy, making a slight wheel toward the right. The enemy also advanced, making a quarter wheel to the right as they did so, and occupied the unused R.R. cut which was deep enough to be about breast high and from which they poured on us a withering fire.

The 6th advanced steadily without halt or waver until it reached a road with a stake and rider fence on each side of it. In the road, the line halted a moment and opened fire, using the fence as a breastwork, but the command was again "Forward," and we climbed over the fence and advanced over a smooth piece of ground to the railroad cut, and after a hand to hand fight the enemy surrendered. After the surrender and before the prisoners were marched off the division rearguard, which contained some of the 14th Brooklyn, came up and assisted in guarding them, (the prisoners greatly outnumbering what was left of the 6th Wisconsin,) and that was the only way in which the 14th Brooklyn took part in that charge. General Wadsworth also brought up some cavalry and he sent the writer to the city on a cavalry sergeant's horse and my personal knowledge of events at that location ended with that circumstance.

I wish also to state that the 147th N.Y. were not in sight, and had nothing to do with that charge, and why they are entitled the credit for the capture of the enemy in the railroad cut is beyond my comprehension. General Hofmann will please explain why, if his left regiment had its left resting on the railroad cut, the enemy should find it necessary to open fire on our regiment on the Seminary Ridge before we had got into line of battle, if his brigade had already engaged with them? Had Cutler's brigade been driven entirely off the field in the short time it took us to double quick from the Emmittsburg Pike to Seminary Ridge? Or did the events described by General Hofmann occur after I had left the field.

The writer remembers Col. Hofmann distinctly as the brave and gallant young commander of the 56th Pennsylvania, nearly all through the war, and can only reconcile his statements with my knowledge of events at the opening of the battle of Gettysburg by supposing the events he describes to have occurred after my departure from the field, and if that is so, what becomes of his claim to have opened the battle? I will also say that the Battery Meredith's [Iron] brigade followed on that morning was a horse battery of 6 pounder rifled guns which accompanied a cavalry brigade that passed through our column while on the march.

I would suggest that the editor call on Hon. Rufus R. Dawes of Marinette [Marietta], Ohio, who commanded the 6th Wisconsin on that day, and who was not the victim of an "over-excited imagination," or too much commissary [whiskey], on that or any other occasion, for a statement of the events as they occurred that morning. Yours in F., C. and L. [fraternity, comradeship and loyalty],

James P. Sullivan
Sergeant, Col. K, 6th Wis. Vet. Vols.

NOTES

1. Editor Jerome A. Watrous of *The Sunday Telegraph* changed it to read "scanty" breakfast.

2. "Turners" was an Americanized term referring to the German gymnastic societies of the day, *Turnverein*, which proliferated in cities such as Milwaukee with large immigrant population. Company F, however, was known as the Citizens Corps, Milwaukee. It was recruited almost exclusively among the German wards of the city by ponderous Wilhelm Lindwurm. But he had resigned as captain late in 1861, as did the company's 1st lieutenant, Frederick Schumacher. Next in rank, Werner von Bachelle, was killed at Antietam. At Gettysburg, Company F was led by another immigrant, 1st Lt. Oscar Graetz. Rud[olph] Koss, *Milwaukee* (Milwaukee,

1871), p. 221; *Milwaukee Sentinel*, May 10, 1861; *The Blackhat*, No. 33; *Roster of Wisconsin Volunteers*, Vol. I, p. 516.

3. Buford, a Kentuckian by birth, graduated from West Point in 1848, and saw service in Texas, New Mexico, and Kansas, and against the Sioux. In July 1862, Gen. John Pope plucked Buford from an unimportant post in Washington and made him brigadier general of the reserve brigade of cavalry. He performed well during the Second Bull Run campaign and was grievously wounded on August 30, 1862, but was soon back in service. Buford thereafter became chief of cavalry for the Army of the Potomac. In command of the cavalry division during the Gettysburg campaign, he drove back the advance of A. P. Hill's Confederate corps on June 30, 1863, and held the Rebel surge at bay the following day until the arrival of elements of the I Corps, which included the Iron Brigade. The cavalry division was heavily engaged during the remainder of 1863. In November, Buford was given leave because of failing health, and he died in Washington on December 16, 1863. *Dictionary of American Biography*, Vol. III, pp. 243–44.

4. It is curious that the army reacted so joyously to the news that McClellan was back in command. His generalship was found sadly wanting in the Peninsula campaign and at Antietam; more judicious use of the army on both occasions may have proved successful. But McClellan was a conservative general, a brilliant organizer and equipper who cared for his men and ensured they were properly fed and clothed.

5. Editor Watrous expunged all critical references to the army commanders by Sullivan. Watrous was reticent about printing caustic and overly critical material in his publication, perhaps because he felt that veterans should present a united rank to the nation.

6. Lt. Benjamin T. Marten of Gen. Abner Doubleday's staff.

7. Abner Doubleday, often credited with the origination of baseball, was a New Yorker. He graduated from West Point in 1842 and saw action in the Mexican and Seminole Wars. In Charleston, South Carolina, at war's outbreak, he aimed the first replying shot at Confederate batteries from Union Ft. Sumter. In early 1862 he was appointed brigadier general and commanded a brigade in Irvin McDowell's corps. At South Mountain he succeeded to division command. When I Corps commander John Reynolds was killed early on the morning of July 1, 1863, Doubleday assumed command and directed the delaying action against the Confederates. He saw further action during the war and mustered from service in January 1866. He died in 1893 and was buried at Arlington National Cemetery. *Ibid.*, Vol. V, pp. 391–92.

8. Company K was on the right center of the two-rank battle line as it charged toward the railroad cut.

9. He had re-enlisted after being discharged for his South Mountain foot wound.

10. The 6th Wisconsin was initially issued Belgian rifles. When the regiment was later issued Springfields, the ordnance sergeant apparently still maintained many of the foreign-made guns. "They are the Belgian Rifle and are good for secesh at a thousand yards distance," one Badger said of the old rifles. *Appleton Crescent*, October 19, 1861.

11. In the din and confusion of battle, many soldiers unknowingly double or triple loaded their rifle-muskets, unaware that the guns had not fired.

12. Smith, of Lemonweir, Juneau County, was one of the initial enlistees in Dawes' company. He was promoted to 1st sergeant and served his three years, mustering out July 15, 1864. *Roster of Wisconsin Volunteers,* Vol. I, p. 536.

13. Ticknor, of Wernersville, died of his wound. *Ibid.,* p. 533.

14. The target of Sullivan's thrown sword was probably A. H. Belo, who was in command of the 55th North Carolina. In a talk by Belo before the Sterling Price Camp of Dallas, Texas, January 20, 1900, Belo recalled: "One officer, seeing me, threw his sword at me and said: 'Kill that officer, and we will capture that command.' One of my men, however, picked him off and we were able to get out of the railroad cut after a severe struggle." Belo, seeing the sword Sullivan was carrying, apparently assumed he was a Federal officer. A. H. Belo, "The Battle of Gettysburg," *Confederate Veteran,* 1900, pp. 165–68.

15. Tarbox, one of the "Yellow River crowd" from Necedah in Juneau County, enlisted June 26, 1861. He moved up through noncommissioned officer ranks to sergeant. He was wounded at Antietam. Tarbox is buried in the National Cemetery at Gettysburg. *Roster of Wisconsin Volunteers,* Vol. I, p. 536; Samuel P. Bates, *The Battle of Gettysburg* (Philadelphia, 1875), p. 330.

16. Wallar, a farmer from DeSoto in Bad Ax (Vernon) County, with his brother Sam, enlisted in the Anderson Guard, Company I, in July 1861. He ended the war as 1st lieutenant of his company, and afterward farmed in Wisconsin and Dakota Territory. He died in April 1911 at age 71. His body was returned to Wisconsin and buried at Retreat on the Mississippi River. He was awarded the Medal of Honor for his capture of the 2nd Mississippi flag. *The Gettysburg Magazine,* No. 4, January, 1991, *Roster of Wisconsin Volunteers,* Vol. I, p. 529; *The Blackhat,* No. 27.

17. Burns, of course, became a Gettysburg folk hero. A veteran of the war of 1812, he was a cobbler in Gettysburg when the battle occurred. He grabbed his flintlock musket and presented himself for duty. The 72-year-old veteran fought with the 50th Pennsylvania and later with regiments of the Iron Brigade. He was wounded three times. Burns was briefly held prisoner by the Confederates. After the battle, he was presented to President Abraham Lincoln during the dedication of the National Cemetery on November 18, 1863. Burns died in 1872. Faust, *Encyclopedia,* p. 96.

18. Hall, of Juda, Wisconsin, was regimental surgeon from October 1862 to war's end. Bartlett, of East Troy, was assistant surgeon from June 1861 until October 1862, when he transferred to the 3rd Wisconsin. The assistant surgeon at Gettysburg was probably Abraham D. Andrews of River Falls. *Roster of Wisconsin Volunteers,* Vol. I, p. 494.

19. Rose, of the village of Lemonweir, would be discharged for disability January 14, 1864; Fletcher, also of Lemonweir, died July 5 of his wounds; Van Wie's wound was not serious, and he ultimately rose to 1st lieutenant of Company K, serving until the final muster in July 1865; Everson of Mauston was discharged because of his wounds May 11, 1864; Wallace Hancock of Mauston survived, but was killed in action at Petersburg on June 18, 1864; his brother William, of rural Clifton, also survived, only to be taken prisoner the following summer at Petersburg, and was killed by a Confederate guard at Salisbury, North Carolina, November 27, 1864; Tem-

ple, of Newport, survived his wound and mustered out July 15, 1864, at the expiration of his term; Crawford, of Kildare, who had sustained an earlier wound at South Mountain, re-enlisted, rose to become sergeant, and answered the final muster July 14, 1865; Wilcox, of Lemonweir, survived and mustered out July 15, 1864, at the end of his term; Pratt, of Lemonweir, served until war's end, mustering out July 14, 1865. *Ibid.*, pp. 533–36.

20. The Iron Brigade led the casualty list for the entire Union army during the three-day battle. The 6th Wisconsin lost 48% of its number in about 15 to 20 minutes in the very opening of the infantry fight July 1, 1863. Company K, on the right center of the line, sustained 23 casualties— five killed outright, including Capt. John Ticknor; two others receiving mortal wounds; 14 wounded who never returned to ranks, and one missing. Only seven or eight of 34 remained in ranks. Beaudot, *Sixth Wisconsin Database*; Dawes, *Service*, p. 184; Nolan, *Iron Brigade*, p. 256.

21. Oliver O. Howard's XI Corps was identified by a corps badge in the shape of a quarter moon. Because of the heavy Germanic content of its component regiments and brigades and the impression that it performed badly at Chancellorsville and Gettysburg, the unit bore a despised reputation. Maine-born Howard graduated from West Point in 1854 and seven years later, at war's outbreak, became colonel of the 3rd Maine Infantry. He rose to general by September 1861, and participated in First Bull Run and the Peninsula Campaign, losing an arm at Fair Oaks. He returned to duty in time to see action at Second Bull Run, South Mountain, Antietam, Fredericksburg, and Chancellorsville. His conduct at the latter battle, when Jackson fell upon the flank of his corps and scattered it, was suspect. At Gettysburg, his XI Corps attempted to establish defensive lines north and west of the town on July 1, but his units were pushed in piecemeal and broken by the advancing Confederates. The Union brigades broke and retreated through the town. After Gettysburg, he was sent West and participated in the Atlanta Campaign and in the March to the Sea. He maintained a strong Biblical bent and was appointed to the Freedman's Bureau by Lincoln, but his service was clouded by incompetence. He died in 1909 at age 79. *Dictionary of American Biography*, Vol. IX, pp. 279–81.

22. Sullivan was mistaken. July 3, 1863, was a Friday.

23. The advance on the Union center commenced about 3 P.M., preceded by a 90-minute artillery bombardment of Cemetery Ridge. Then, about 13,000 Confederate infantry marched almost a mile over open ground to assault the Federal center. The assault drew its name from Gen. George Pickett's Virginia Division, but numerous other Confederate States' regiments participated.

24. Killed was Capt. John Ticknor and wounded was 1st Lt. William N. Remington. *Roster of Wisconsin Volunteers*, Vol. I, p. 533.

25. William Dudley, a 19th Indiana officer who lost a leg at Gettysburg, made a careful study of the official reports and corresponded with surviving Iron Brigade officers. His casualty figures are accepted:

	Total	Killed	Captured or Wounded	Missing	Total	Remaining
Brig. and Staff	8	0	3		3	5
19th Indiana	288	27	133	50	210	78
24th Michigan	496	79	237	83	399	97
2nd Wisconsin	302	27	153	53	233	69
6th Wisconsin	344	30	117	20	167	177
7th Wisconsin	343	27	109	43	178	165
Brigade Guard	102		22		22	80
Totals	1883	189	774	49	1212	671

Dawes, *Service*, p. 184; Nolan, *Iron Brigade*, pp. 256, 365–66, *fn* 68; William W. Dudley, *The Iron Brigade at Gettysburg, 1878, Official Report of the Part Borne by the 1st Brigade, 1st Division, 1st Army Corps* (Cincinnati, 1879). See also William F. Fox, *Regimental Losses in the American Civil War* (Albany, N.Y., 1889), p. 117.

26. Morrow suffered a scalp wound. Nolan, *Iron Brigade*, p. 256.

27. Bragg was convalescing from an injury. On May 31, 1863, Dawes wrote to his sweetheart in Ohio that Bragg had been kicked in the foot a few days before by Major Hauser's "ugly little horse." Five days later, he again wrote that Bragg was still "quite ill," "wholly unfit for duty in the field," and did not take part in the campaign. Dawes, *Service*, pp. 146–47.

28. Scoville was apparently not buried at the National Cemetery at Gettysburg. In addition to Fletcher and Tarbox of Company K, others of the 6th Wisconsin buried in the Gettysburg National Cemetery were: Pvt. Uriah Palmer of Company A; Cpl. James A. Kelley, Cpl. William E. Evans and Pvt. Henry Anderson of Company B; 2nd Lt. Orrin Chapman and Pvt. Levi Stedman of Company C; Sgt. William Gallup of Company D; Pvts. Edward Leaman and Frank King of Company E; Pvt. Charles Haare of Company F; Pvt. Lewis H. Eggleston and Ernest Schivenbachen of Company H, and 1st Sg. Andrew Miller of Company I. Bates, *Gettysburg*, pp. 329–30.

29. It was while recuperating from his Gettysburg wound that the young soldier met his future wife, Angeline Shaeffer. She was perhaps a nurse or volunteer at the Cuyler Hospital.

30. A reference to another of the military manuals of the day, Silas Casey's three-volume *Infantry Tactics for the Instruction, Exercise and Manuevers of the Soldier.*

31. Winfield Scott Hancock, regarded by many as one of the ablest Union generals, had his finest hour at Gettysburg. On July 1, 1863, he established the Federal position on Cemetery Ridge; on the afternoon of July 2 he thwarted Longstreet's assault, and on July 3 he repulsed Lee's final assault on the center of the Federal line. Hancock was severely wounded, however, and never fully regained his elan. He served in active field command until November 1864. In 1866 he was honored by Congress for his service. In 1880 he was nominated for the presidency, but lost to James A. Garfield by a small popular margin and 59 electoral votes. He died six years later. *Dictionary of American Biography*, Vol. VIII, pp. 221–22.

32. The 8th Wisconsin received national attention for its pet—an eagle named "Old Abe." John Sullivan enlisted in that regiment from the Town of

Greenwood, Vernon County, in August 1864. He was assigned to Company I and served with the unit until mustered out in September 1865. *Roster of Wisconsin Volunteers*, Vol. I, p. 599.

33. John William Hofmann was the colonel of the 56th Pennsylvania. Born in Philadelphia in 1824, he was breveted brigadier general in the summer of 1864 for constant and efficient service. After the war he was a hosiery merchant and died in 1902. Roger D. Hunt and Jack R. Brown, *Brevet Brigadier Generals in Blue* (Gaithersburg, Md., 1990), p. 288.

34. Reid was at first political correspondent and later city editor at the *Cincinnati Gazette*. In the latter capacity the 24-year-old newspaperman, headquartered in Washington, D.C., covered political as well as military affairs. He accompanied Gen. William Rosecrans during the West Virginia campaign, and was in the field at Shiloh and Gettysburg. *Ibid.*, Vol. XV, pp. 482–86.

35. There was confusion over credit for the successful attack because Col. Edward B. Fowler of the 14th Brooklyn (officially the 84th New York) in his official report, filed July 9, 1863, claimed he had ordered the charge on the unfinished railroad cut. *OR*, Series 1, Vol. 27, Part 1, pp. 286–87. Rufus Dawes, in his war memoir, noted: "Colonel E.B. Fowler fourteen Brooklyn, in his official report, has given the impression that he ordered the sixth Wisconsin regiment to make this charge. He gave us no orders whatever. I did not know he was on the field until the charge was over." Dawes, *Service*, p. 167. For a full discussion of the controversy, see Herdegen and Beaudot, *Railroad Cut*, Appendix II, pp. 287–99.

Chapter V

THE FIGHT FOR THE WELDON ROAD

[Months passed before Sullivan, along with thousands of other wounded soldiers, could return to his regiment. The Irishman was at Philadelphia's Cuyler Hospital the remainder of the 1863. While his shot-up shoulder mended, the feisty veteran likely was as much a nettle to the medical staff as he was to the officers of his regiment; after all, he had seen the elephant and had been blooded and would have little truck with behind-the-line martinets.

But during this period Sullivan did meet someone who touched him—Angeline Shaeffer, a young Philadelphia woman working as a nurse at Cuyler Hospital. She was attracted to the diminutive and brash young soldier as much for his blarney as for his tough-edged Western demeanor. As Sullivan's recuperation progressed, a romance blossomed. That relationship reached the full bloom of marriage in February the next year.

But Sullivan did not write about those days. Moreover, he failed to write about any of his regiment's engagements in 1864 and 1865 save one—the Battle of Weldon Railroad south of Petersburg, Virginia. While he expended considerable energies reconstructing the engagement (a piece Jerome Watrous published in his Milwaukee newspaper the summer of 1885), he also wrote two humorous pieces that were more generic than particular, but no other Sullivan battle accounts of the final 21 months of the war ever appeared in print.

Those latter months, contrasted with the descriptions of storied charges and stand-up fights from Gainesville to Gettysburg, lacked grandeur and glory. To the memory of a middle-aged veteran as well as in actual fact, 1864 and 1865 were characterized more by grinding attrition and gritty survival; such was not the stuff of storytelling.

General George Gordon Meade ordered the Army of the Potomac in a somewhat timorous pursuit of Lee's Confederates in the days that followed Gettysburg. Then, after the Rebel army made a largely uncontested return to Virginia, Meade made no more than tentative movements, feints, and probes along the Rappahannock River lines.

In August a new stand of colors was sent to the 6th Wisconsin, and the hallowed national flag carried through Gettysburg was reverentially returned to the state. Lt. Col. Rufus R. Dawes wrote:

> ... the tattered folds and splintered staff bear witness more eloquently than words to the conduct of the men who rallied around it from Gainesville to Gettysburg. We send it to the people of Wisconsin knowing what they expect of us, and we promise that the past shall be an earnest of the future, under the beautiful standard they have sent us.[1]

Here was a watershed event—the emblem of the old regiment retired and a new one raised. Soon, the legion of early enlistees, the "Boys of '61" who had survived to this point, would be further diminished; death, severe wounds, and disease would claim hundreds; more would refuse to serve beyond their three-year enlistment. This, coupled with the growing number of bounty-paid enlistees and the arrival of draftees, would make the 6th Wisconsin nearly a stranger to itself.

There was another flag, one donated by subscribers in Wisconsin, Indiana, and Michigan, that captured the attention of the Western soldiers in the post-Gettysburg days. A blue silken banner emblazoned with the five regimental names was presented to the brigade with appropriate ceremony in September. There was also the song that the 6th Wisconsin's Loyd Harris had commissioned from a Milwaukee music publisher, "The Iron Brigade Quickstep." It had been completed, and hundreds of copies of the sheet music—subscribed to at 50 cents a piece—were distributed. While the music-minded Harris had good intentions, the resulting creation by a famous Milwaukee music publisher was less than desired; even Colonel Dawes remembered its lack of artfulness when he wrote his war memoirs 25 years later.

The flag and the tune were ironic, as the unalloyed character of the vaunted Iron Brigade had begun to be transformed in mid-July. Because of the enormous loss sustained by the Western men in those battles of 1862 and 1863, a nine-month Pennsylvania regiment, the 167th, was added to the brigade. The association, however short-lived, got off to a bad start when the Keystone State unit refused to march because their enlistment, the soldiers claimed, had expired. Such foolishness was unacceptable, and the 6th along with the 2nd and 7th Wisconsin were ordered to prod the Pennsylvanians with loaded muskets. The Pennsylvanians were removed in August. But in their stead were the four companies of the 1st New York Sharpshooters as well as the 7th Indiana, transferred into the brigade on the heels of the departing Pennsylvanians. They were to march with the black hats for a year. In the months to come, more Eastern regiments would be grafted onto the brigade.

Such galling events were compounded by the arrival of conscripts, new men who had been drafted and others who had enlisted to secure a healthy monetary bonus. Admittedly such men were needed to bring regiments to some semblance of field strength; but, as typified by the comments of Rufus R. Dawes, the veterans saw the arrivals as a "sorry looking set."[2]

More symbolism occurred those closing months of 1863. While marching near the old Gainesville battlefield, Division Commander Lysander Cutler discovered that the men of Wisconsin and Indiana who had fallen nearly 16 months before had been left unburied. He ordered details from all regiments to the grisly and unsettling task of providing decent internment for their dead comrades.

Also in November, Edward P. Brooks, the handsome young adjutant whose earlier caperings Sullivan had chronicled, was captured. It was another exemplar of comely Southern womanhood who led the Madison lad into his captors' hands. His eye for petticoats would cost him several months in Libby Prison. Meanwhile, the ineffectual effort by Meade to punch across the Rapidan River near Mine Run, Virginia, and plunge south to Richmond closed 1863.

Unknown to Sullivan or any soldier in the ranks of the Army of the Potomac, the new year was filled with ominous portent: beginning in spring and for more than six weeks, the great blue mass would march into a caldron seething with maiming and death. It would sustain thousands of casualties, and emerge, like the 6th Wisconsin, quite different than when the campaign started.

As the last days of 1863 still played out, the paramount concern was the veteran question. Throughout the Army of the Potomac, early regiments, such as the 6th Wisconsin, were nearing the completion of three years' service. The Calico Boys, encamped near Culpeper and the Rappahannock River in early winter fastness, knotted to discuss the issue of re-enlisting. There were many, early on, who were determined to remain, to see this thing through. Two-thirds of their number were needed to ensure that the 6th Wisconsin would remain a viable regiment; if less remained, the unit would cease to exist. By late December, 217 of the "Boys of '61" had made their choice, induced by a 30-day furlough and a $400 bonus; with 10 other men, the requisite number had been attained.

Pvt. James P. Sullivan, recuperated once again, returned to the

winter camp in much the same manner as he had a year before—
battered and scarred but feisty and spoiling to have at the Rebels.
On January 22, his second enlistment having expired, he took the
oath for the third time in the war. He would damn well march until
this thing ended.

Early spring was another period of disruption for Sullivan and
the Western soldiers. U. S. Grant, promoted to lieutenant general,
was named the top military commander, and he came East to direct
the entire war effort. On March 29, under a chilling Virginia drizzle,
he reviewed Meade's Army of the Potomac. As he passed, Eastern
regiments rended the air with thundering cheers and huzzahs;
Grant gave no acknowledgement. Dawes turned to the 6th Wisconsin
and gave his men instructions. The Ohioan saluted the general in
proper fashion, and the Badger soldiers, as prescribed in military
manuals, remained motionless and maintained stony silence. Grant
paused at the lack of display, doffed his hat and bowed from his
horse. After the review was concluded, the soldiers again knotted
together, nodding that the new commander "wants soldiers, not
yaupers."[3]

That month, too, much more changed. The bloodied and under-
strength I Corps was disbanded. Its components were distributed to
the V Corps. No longer would the Westerners be the first brigade in
the Army of the Potomac; they were moved to the 4th Division of
the corps commanded by Gouverneur K. Warren, one of the heroes
of Gettysburg. And there was another discomfiting change. The
initial enlistment of the 2nd Wisconsin expired, and an insufficient
number had deigned to take the oath again. Only two companies of
veterans and newer enlistees determined to stay the course: they
were designated as an Independent Battalion. Before the spring
campaigns commenced, the remains of the 2nd Wisconsin were
removed from the brigade to serve as division provost guard.

And thus, a spring offensive, designed by yet another commander,
was about to commence. The setting of the opening battle of Grant's
offensive might have been conjured in the midst of a nightmare. It
came in an area called simply "the Wilderness"—a vast brooding
thicket of scrub pine stands, threaded with underbrush, brambles,
and other creeping, clutching growths. In early May the Army of
the Potomac was intent only upon passing through as quickly as
possible to push toward the Rebel capital. But, as was so often the
case, a battle was initiated. For two days the 6th Wisconsin and the
Iron Brigade thrashed about in the thicket. And for the first time in
their experience, the Western men, after gaining initial success,

shuddered from the shock of a Rebel counterattack and reeled backwards. On the next day, no greater success was achieved by Grant's columns.

The cost to the 6th Wisconsin: 63 casualties, including three highly qualified officers—Maj. Philip Plummer, one of the young English brothers from Prairie du Chien, and Capt. Rollin Converse of Prescott were killed; and Mauston attorney John Kellogg, one of Dawes' close friends, was captured and presumed killed. The ordeal of May and June continued almost immediately at Laurel Hill and Spotsylvania Court House some miles south. The 6th Wisconsin sustained the heaviest losses in those days of attacks: 83 men— about one-quarter of the casualties in the brigade; Sullivan's Company K suffered one killed and four wounded. Still, Grant pressed his men on. The roll of battles passed almost unabated: Jericho Ford, North Anna, Bethesda Church. Always Robert E. Lee's men were behind earthworks and in strong defensive positions; assaults were almost certain to fail. As Company A's Mair Pointon recalled, it was "Grab a root"—lie down and hope a Rebel bullet or shell would not find a Wisconsin mark. In late May, Dawes wrote: "I have had no full night's sleep since May 7th. . . . Day after day, and night after night, we have marched, fought and dug entrenchments; I have not changed my clothing since May third."[4]

During the Cold Harbor campaign in early June, Dawes would record the crushing cost of the spring offensive on his regiment: some 170 killed and wounded. ". . . my sensibilities were deadened by this constant, wearing pressure," the Ohioan would recall a quarter of a century later. Finally, in mid-June, the Army of the Potomac crossed the James River and the investment of the last Confederate bastion at Petersburg commenced in earnest. War weariness mounted, unsteadying even Dawes: ". . . in another hopeless assault (on Confederate defenses) there was enacted a horrid massacre of our corps." The 6th Wisconsin counted five killed and 35 wounded. Two of Sullivan's friends were among the slain—Wallace Hancock, brother of Billy, who had enlisted in March 1863, and Sgt. Linneaus Westcott of Lindinia, who had marched with the company since May 1861. In early May the regiment had counted 380 men in its ranks. By the last day in July, 227 had been killed, wounded, or were missing. Nearly 60% of the 6th Wisconsin was gone.

These were grim matters that James P. Sullivan, in his middle years, failed to record. His dark Irish sensibility might have been expected to have led him to write of such scenes. But he chose not do so. In March 1885, before the hard Wisconsin winter had loosened its grip on the Vernon county soil, Sullivan pulled together his notes on the Battle of Weldon Railroad. Here, perhaps, Sullivan found some bit of high drama and what glory remained in that war of attrition which unfolded in late 1864 and early 1865.

In August 1864 General Grant determined to sever Lee's remaining rail links between Petersburg and destinations south. He ordered the V Corps to grab the line running to Weldon, North Carolina. The site of the attack was near a country inn known variously as Yellow or Globe Tavern. Sullivan's description of the three-day engagement was published in *The Milwaukee Sunday Telegraph* in two parts, June 28 and July 5, 1885.]

THE FIGHT FOR THE WELDON ROAD
By Mickey, of Co. K.

In overhauling some old letters and papers a short time ago, I found a yellow, dingy parchment, folded up small, in the manner I used to have during the war, to admit of being carried in the pocket of a diary, and opening it, I read:

> The commanding Officer of the 6th Wisconsin, Vet. Vols.: To all who shall see these presents, greeting: Know ye, that reposing special trust and confidence in the patriotism, valor, fidelity and abilities of   , I do hereby appoint him sergeant in Co. K, 6th regiment of Wisconsin veteran volunteers, to rank as such from the 1st day of August, 1864. * * * *
>
> Thomas Kerr,
> Major Comd'g 6th Wis.

By the Commanding Officer,
  J. A. Watrous,
    1st Lt. and Ad't 6th Wis.

It reminded me of the time when it was given to me, for what Gen'l [Edward S.] Bragg was pleased to call "good conduct;" and consulting my diary for August, 1864, I saw the following entries:

> Thursday, 18th, marched at daylight. Reached Weldon Rail Road at noon; [Gen. Romeyn] Ayers' division in possession; made coffee; Rebs attacked at 3 P.M. and got decidedly scooped;

hot. Friday, 19th, moved out to right and went out on picket line; nasty, rainy, drizzling day. Reb sharpshooters busy; killed our adjutant [Cuyler Babcock].[5] [Confederate Gen. William] Mahone's graybacks got in rear and placed us between two fires and we had to hyper to save our bacon. 7th regiment gobbled. 9th corps came up in rear of Rebs and gave them hell, with compound interest. Rainy, cold. Saturday, 20th, in breast-works; sat around all day in rain and mud; everything soaking wet; no fires; no coffee; lived on condensed milk and hardtack. Sunday, 21st, clear and bright; hung out blankets and things to dry; 7th regiment got back, having given the Johnnies the slip and taken some prisoners. Rebs charged [Gen. Charles] Griffin on our left and got Paddy's drumming; in afternoon tried us and got another. Hit with shell and knocked out for some time; feel better; good for duty yet; head feels like a band of iron pressing on; volunteered to go out and drive Reb skirmishers off; led skirmish line and cleaned out Reb rifle pits; head and neck sore and stiff; promoted to sergeant. Warm and pleasant.

Stirring up my memory I wrote the following account of how I came to get that same dingy, folded parchment. After the mine [Crater] fiasco the Iron Brigade lay quietly in their trenches for a couple of weeks. About the middle of August our corps [V] was marched out of their place in line and moved about four miles to the rear. All sorts of rumors prevailed in regard to the meaning of it and our probable destination. Some had it that we were to be sent north to enforce the draft; others that Gen. [Gouverneur K.] Warren [V Corps com-mander] was to have a separate command; and others that we were destined for an attack on Mobile; while some (among them myself) were perfectly indifferent. Col. [Rufus R.] Dawes, whose time had expired, received his discharge[6] and the regiment was placed under the command of Captain Thomas Kerr, who was awaiting his commission to major.[7] We would pack up, fall in and march in some direction every day; and finally, at daylight, on the 18th, we marched out; left in front, which had been the style since leaving Culpepper, and it was generally understood that we were destined for an attack on the Weldon Road, which was by no means an agreeable prospect. Shortly after the charge of June 18th, the

6th corps had been sent out to take that road and had been disastrously repulsed, and not long afterwards the 2d corps went out and met with the same luck; and now it was the 5th corps' turn. Our brigade by discharge of the non veterans, deaths, wounds and other casualties had been reduced to less than a thousand men, and the corps would scarcely muster ten thousand, but our confidence in Warren's abilities was unlimited, and most of the officers and men were veterans who had been tried on more than a score of battlefields, and we felt able to hold our own against any reasonable amount of Johnny Rebs. I noticed, though, that the buoyant feeling that used to characterize the brigade on the march was absent, and there were no songs and jests as there had been in the earlier years of the war. The almost continual fighting since spring, and so many defeats and disappointments had a depressing effect on the hilarity of our fellows, and we trudged along in almost absolute silence. The day was intensely hot and water not to be had by hook or by crook, and the boys suffered severely in consequence. When I was almost exhausted George Washington Allen [one of the regiment's contraband black servants], one of the F.F.V.'s[8] who had espoused the Union cause and liberty and had joined the mess of First Sergeant [Erastus] Smith, [Tommy] Flynn and myself during our first advance beyond Fredericksburg, in 1862, as general utility boy, and whose dazzling purity of complexion had caused Smith to re-christen him "pink" and who had been promoted since the regiment veteranized, and was now footman, coachman, waterdrawer, wood-stealer and "waitah, sah for Genwel Bwagg, sah," came along with a canteen of fresh water, and stepping up to me as he used to do before his advancement to his high office, he said, "Want a drink, Mickey?" and handed me the canteen. It was hardly necessary to say I drank. About 11 o'clock[,] firing was heard in front and we were ordered to close up and hurry along and soon after we came out of the woods into a big opening where stood what was called the Yellow House, or Yellow Tavern. Ayer's division[9] had the railroad and was driving the Johnnies toward Petersburg, while [Charles] Griffin's[10] fellows were busy tearing up the track and throwing up breastworks on the other side. Warren rode up to Bragg with a pleasant expression on his face and in his cheery tone, said "we have the road," and directed Bragg to halt 20 minutes for coffee and then be ready to support Ayers. About 3 o'clock the rebels came down the railroad in our front and made a furious attack on Ayers' division on the left of the railroad, but we repulsed those in our front and advanced a considerable distance, which endangered those who were fighting Ayers of being flanked, so they gave up the fight and fell back and we held the ground all night. Early the next morning our brigade was sent to the right and deployed as skirmishers to extend as far as possible and attempt connection with the left of the line in front of Petersburg. The rebel sharp-shooters were mighty busy, and one of them shot the acting adjutant, Cuyler Babcock, through the head, as he sat at the foot of a tree wrapped up in a poncho, and he was gasping and dying for some time before he was dead. An orderly brought Bragg a dispatch and after he read it we fell in and leaving Co. G, 2d U.S. sharpshooters,[11] which was attached to our brigade in the breastworks, we marched back and took a position (at right angles to our former one) in a slight breastwork that someone had thrown up some time before. Mahone, who had been raised in that neighborhood and was familiar with all the highways and byways, marched his division by an old road to our right and rear and burst into the opening 80 or 100 rods distant, ten or twelve thousand strong. The 7th Wisconsin had been sent to the right, and the 19th [Indiana] and 24th [Michigan] were on the left. The 2d [Wisconsin] had been reduced to two companies and was now a battalion under the command of Major [Dennis B. Dailey] Daily,[12] and there was nothing to meet that torrent of greybacks but our diminutive regiment, less than two hundred strong. The rebels in front where we had just left, made an attack, sweeping away the sharpshooters like chaff, who being armed with heavy telescope rifles, after their first volley, were helpless against a charge. As soon as the rebels heard the first volley from Mahone the battle broke out all along the line in front, and we were in a *cul-de-sac* of fire. Gen. Bragg said that if we would save ourselves we would have to get out of that, and we stood not on the order of our going, but went at once, and lively, too. Mahone's rebels closed up on us and we ran directly along their front under the fire of each successive rebel regiment, as we passed and they tried to head us off, but failed. After we got out of the *sac* we came to a fence with a ditch on each side of it, and the dirt from each had been thrown together and stakes driven in to which a couple of boards were nailed and when we reached it Bragg shouted "halt," and said we would try them there awhile. Our fellows opened fire and bothered Mahone's rebels some, but the Johnnies in front, who had swept away the thin skirmish line in front of them, came up on our left and rear and gave [us] a volley in our flanks. Bragg shouted for every man to break for a barn that was in sight, and we rallied around it and again opened fire on the rebels who were coming up on three sides of us, but one might as well try to dam the Mississippi with a chip, and before they surrounded us Bragg ordered us to run for the Yellow House, which we did, under a perfect storm of bullets. One shot struck an officer who was in front of me, in the back of the head and it seemed to me it knocked the whole top of his head off [Company G's Capt. John Timmons]. Bragg, who was a short distance to my left and who was doing his level best to beat Dexter's time, said "there goes Billy Campbell,[13] shot through the head," and I thought it was him. Frank Wallar, of Company I,[14] was color bearer and carried the National colors, and when we were almost to the Yellow House a fellow who was crouching in a ditch that was half filled with water ordered him and Bragg and myself to halt, saying he was provost guard and was stationed there to stop runaway stragglers. Wallar, with the pike [finial] on the end of the flag staff, and I with my bayonet, punched the fellow out of the ditch and started him forward, telling him to go where we had been and see if he would stay there as long as we had. The 9th corps, which should have taken the place our brigade vainly endeavored to fill, but was delayed, owing to the muddy condition of the roads, now came up in rear of Mahone, and Griffin's division rallied to our support and drove back the rebels in front and Mahone was caught in the trap he had set for us. The 9th corps pitched in in good earnest and gave Mahone what our fellows who enjoyed the situation called "Merry Hell," and Mahone and his Johnnie's had a good chance to show their speed and they were sent back jumping, with severe loss.

THE FIGHT FOR THE WELDON ROAD
[Part 2]
By Mickey, of Co. K

I went back on the battle field to look after Billy Campbell and secure any papers and property he might have on his person intending to send the same to his friends in Mauston. The 11th Pa. had charged over the ground and their killed lay scattered around and some of the severely wounded were calling for water. A middle aged man who was mortally wounded and fast dying called to me for water. I gave him what I had in my canteen and he told me to take his diary containing a tin type picture of his wife and two children and something over $11 in money and send it and his watch to the address inside the diary which I promised and did[;] afterwards I received a regular caustic letter from his wife for my pains, because there was not more money. After doing what I could to make him comfortable I went on to where the officer of our regiment had fallen who proved to be Lieut. [John] Timmons of Co. G.[15] An officer and a squad of New York artillery men had examined the body and taken his watch and papers but on learning that I belonged to the same regiment they handed them to me and when I went back I gave them to General Bragg. Night set in cold and rainy and Jim Roades[16] who had in some of his raids jayhawked an old fashioned copper bottomed coffee-pot that would hold two or three gallons, put it on the fire and each man furnished water and coffee and we made a regimental supper. Bragg whose culinary department had disappeared in the melee, taking a cup with us. The boys felt good and were as jubilant as though we had won a victory, for they felt that though we had been overpowered and compelled to run it was better than to lie down and surrender and partake of the noted hospitality and excellent fare of the confederacy at Libby, Belle Isle or Andersonville, and though the Rebs had tried their favorite game of a flank movement we had not lost our credit and still held the road. The 7th [Wisconsin] regiment was reported gobbled up entire and our fellows felt very sorry for the loss of our good "Huckleberry Regiment." We lay around in the mud and rain all that night and the next morning we marched across the railroad and took position in the works Griffin's men had thrown up the first day. The day was very cold and the rain came down in sheets and our fellows sat on their knapsacks and haunches with rubber blankets over their heads in vain efforts to keep dry. Every thing was soaking wet so that we could not make fires and were obliged to do without our much needed coffee; we passed a very uncomfortable day and night. The next morning dawned fair, the sun shone bright and warm and our chaps hung out their blankets and shirts to dry. During the forenoon the 7th regiment which had marched around Mahone through a gap in the rebel lines came up, bringing with them the rebel picket line which they had taken in out of the wet, and our brigade, which had supposed them lost, turned out and gave them quite an ovation. About ten o'clock we heard rebel bugles behind the woods, and the artillerymen said the call was "harness up," and Paddy Hart ordered his battery to open fire with solid shot for fifteen hundred yards. Before noon the rebels moved around and came out of the woods on our left and rear and charged Griffin's division,[17] but they went back empty handed, and we could see through a small opening in the woods another column forming in our front. Our skirmishers were withdrawn and we waited patiently expecting to get satisfaction for the chase they gave us, Friday, and we did. About two o'clock a charging column came out of the woods and advanced over the open ground in our front. Our batteries opened on them with double shotted canister and cut lanes through them, but they came on with their heads down and arms at a trail; the rain had damaged our ammunition a great deal, and many of the guns would not fire, so we could not receive them as heartily as we wished. We got orders "to fix bayonets to repel charge," but when they were within a few rods of us they threw themselves down in a small ravine and surrendered, while the supporting column which was exposed to fire of the cannon loaded to muzzle with canister, broke and ran for the rear despite the efforts of their officers to rally them. I had a good position alongside of a gate post which afforded me an excellent rest, when I fired, and I was doing my best to "welcome them to hospitable graves" when a shell burst and the next thing I knew I was lying down in the trench and Campbell and [William] Van Wie[18] were sprinkling water on me from canteens. After a bit I sat up and Van Wie pulled a sliver out of the back of my neck and my head felt as though a band of iron was tightening about it. The Rebs had been taken in and new supplies of ammunition brought up in rubber blankets. The Rebs who had fallen back were being rallied for another charge and an officer on a gray horse was particularly conspicuous in his efforts to form them and the sharpshooters with their telescope rifles and now and again one of our chaps with their muskets were trying to give him a quietus but could not succeed. Jared Williams, of company K,[19] who was a noted good shot, put the powder from two cartridges in his gun and patched his ball; taking rest on the gate post where I had been, he fired and the Reb tumbled out of his saddle, and the horse dashed off behind the woods.[20] We learned afterwards from rebel sources that it was General Higenbotham, of Florida, and his death put a damper on the charge, and all they did was send out skirmishers which advanced to the shelter of some willows that fringed a creek, and commenced killing off our battery horses, and firing at any one whose head appeared above the breastworks. Skirmishers were sent out to drive them off, but they only went three or four rods in front and took position in a triangular work that had been built to cover the gate, and they had no more effect than if they had remained in the breastworks. We stood it a short time, but then got angry, and Bragg called for volunteers to go out and drive them off, and I offered myself as the corporal, to lead them. Lieut. Campbell said if I felt well enough to go, and I did; and brought those who were in the lunette, out, and we made those Rebs skip for the woods in a hurry.[21] When I returned, Billy Campbell said I was promoted sergeant by order of Bragg, for good conduct on the battle-field, and some time afterwards I received that faded, dingy parchment.

Forest, March 31st, 1885

[The wounds Sullivan sustained were much more aggravated than he suspected then or when he wrote about it two decades later. A gunshot wound to his right thigh was bloody and difficult to staunch. Worse, however, the shell splinters had entered his back and neck. Regimental surgeon John C. Hall treated the Irishman in the field, and no hospitalization was required. But 42 years later one of the causes of the old veteran's death were those Rebel shell fragments lodged near his brain.[22]

Sometime in the aftermath of the fight for Weldon Railroad another series of disruptions were visited upon the men of Wisconsin, Indiana, and Michigan. The V Corps' 4th Division was broken up, and the Iron Brigade transferred to the 3rd under the command of Gen. Samuel Crawford. The famous tall, felt black hats, proud emblem for a band of hard-fighting Badgers, Hoosiers, and Wolverines, had only months ago crowned every man in the brigade. Now, however, the new realignment brought more Eastern units into the once all-Western brigade; they wore the standard Federal-issue blue cap. There is evidence that in the latter stages of the war, starting in the winter of 1864–65, the Model 1858 black hats were no longer issued to the 6th Wisconsin. Many soldiers, however, retained the black hats for as long as possible. It must have been dismaying to Sergeant Sullivan and his marching mates when three more Pennsylvania regiments, the 143rd, 149th, and 150th, were added. In their postwar writings, Sullivan and others fairly well overlooked the Easterners; and in the histories of those Pennsylvania and other regiments, scant note was made of the association with the Western units. Then in September, the 7th Indiana was merged with the 19th; less than a month later, the identity of the 19th was expunged from the roll when it was merged with the 20th Indiana and removed from the brigade. This was a particularly emotional disassociation, and for weeks afterward, old Hoosier black hats wandered back to their brothers in the old brigade, only to be rounded up and corralled back in the new regiment.

The fight at Weldon Railroad had secured General Grant a toehold south of Petersburg for the Army of the Potomac. For the remaining nine months of the war, Grant determined, Warren's V Corps would spearhead a series of thrusts toward the South Side Railroad, a line that cut southwest of the Confederate bastion and connected with Danville, Virginia. The link was not only a source of supply, but an escape route to be used if the defenses around Petersburg crumbled. The land in which Sergeant Sullivan and his comrades marched and fought in those months was timbered and cut with innumerable and, to the Union forces, largely uncharted streams. Snow and rain quickly turned the land into a boggy, adhesive nightmare. Connections and communications between units were lost in much the same fashion as occurred in the Wilderness. An initial lunge toward the rail line was taken at Burgess' Mill on the vital Boydtown Plank Road in late October (the battle was sometimes referred to as First Hatcher's Run, after the stream that coursed nearby). But the effort by the V and II Corps, largely uncoordinated, was beaten back by the Rebel opposition. The casualties to the 6th Wisconsin and the brigade were relatively few; but among the wounded was Sgt. James P. Sullivan, who received a gunshot to his already scarred right thigh.[23] The fight raised exasperation and ire among the men in the ranks: here again was an example of inept generalship.

But Sullivan, in his postwar life, did not write of these days. Perhaps he deigned that such confusion and ineptitude were unworthy of his creative skills. What he did reveal were two humorous episodes which characterized camp life in those latter days of war. As a bearer of sergeant chevrons, Sullivan had, uncharacteristically, been accorded responsibilities. He was a significant cog in the Company K machinery, and in one account, published in *The Milwaukee Sunday Telegraph* January 25, 1885, the salty veteran described a drill for draftees.]

A SQUAD DRILL
By Mickey, of Co. K.

In the fall of 1864 the 6th regiment was reinforced by about five hundred new men whom the tyrannical government at Washington had induced to serve the country, and Company K received some fifty or more for its quota, and amongst them a diminutive son of Erin named Stephen Thomas,[24] and a former subject of Koenig Wilhelm, called August Wallschlaeger.[25] Thomas was a man about five feet in height and probably weighed 120 pounds, while Wallschlaeger was over six feet and of proportions that would delight the heart of old

Frederick the Great; but both were alike in one thing, it was impossible for them to keep "step."

After the return from the "Weldon raid" [December 7–11, 1864] to camp near the Jerusalem Plank Road [the area south of Petersburg and the South Side Railroad], Colonel [John] Kellog[26] undertook to transform the aforesaid five hundred patriots into drilled soldiers, and company and squad drill was the order of the day, much to the disgust of the veterans. Finding that he could do nothing with them in the company drill, where they were only a disgusting element, Capt. [Andrew] Gallup[27] directed the writer to take Thomas and Wallschlaeger and drill them in marching in close order until they would learn the step, and the following is an attempt to describe one of the many drills that occurred under his supervision.

After explaining the principles of the direct step in quick time,[28] and laying particular stress on the direction to step off promptly with the left foot at the command march, I inquired if they understood what I had just explained to them.

"Yis," "yaw," was the answer.

"Squad, forward, march!"

Thomas started off with the right foot, and Wallschlaeger with the left, and the result was that Wallschlaeger's No. 13 "governments" raked Thomas from the calf of his leg down to his heel.

"Thaneman Dhioul, he'll take the heel av me," said Thomas.

Another explanation to step off with the left foot at the word, march, another "yis" and "yaw," and again the command forward, march. "Left, left." Scrape goes the No. 13. "Oh, Jasus." "Silence in the ranks;" left, left. Scrape with the No. 13. "Bad luck to ye, ye Omadhaun. "Silence in the ranks; left, left, right, left." Scrape with the governments. "Howly murdher in mint." "No talking on drill; left, left." Scrape goes the 13. "Sarjunt hould on a minit til I hit that agit (idiot)." "Thomas, you'll git into the guard house if you don't be still; left, left;" scrape. "Tare and ouns, fhy did I iver come to Americky at all," and when poor Thomas' patience was entirely gone, the command was given, "right about, march," and one turned one way, and the other another until they faced each other, and Thomas immediately wanted to "strike him," but was prevented and faced to the front, and they were again instructed to "left face" and the principles of the direct step in quick time, Thomas, all the while muttering in an undertone, "what he'd do to the Omadhaun of a Dutchman whin he got into camp." "Left, face," and now Wallschlaeger was in front; Thomas walked pigion toed in a mincing choppy step of about one hundred and fifty [paces] per minute, while Wallschlaeger raised his feet about a foot from the ground and strode with elephantine proportions and deliberation, and somehow Thomas always managed to kick him on the ankles when he missed step.

"Squad, forward, march, left, left," kick. "Dunner and blitzen," Thomas get step. "Left, left," kick. "Shwinekoup," "silence in the ranks; left, left," kick, kick. "Py Got, nochamahl du spitz-poop." "Thomas get the step; left, left, right, left;" kick, kick, kick. "For dumle aisel Ich wullen schlaggen du von de koup." "How the divil kin I keep step fhin ye don't march right." "Silence in the ranks, left, left;" kick, kick, kick, kick. "Krites, dunnerwasser hergot sacremento." "Halt, front," and Wallschlaeger made a grab for Thomas to "Smize him awie," but I interrupted and again the step is explained with particular injunctions to bring the left foot to the ground at the word left, while Wallschlaeger, in a stage aside was threatening in voluble German to exterminate Thomas when the drill was over.

"Right, face, forward, march." Again the right foot starts off, and again the 13's rake down the leg. "Blood an ouns, he won't lave a leg undher me," growled Thomas. "Vell you mak him no right," says Wallschlaeger. "The divil blow ye, ye big Urishkan," returns Thomas, and after another explanation, and assisted by a vigorous push with my foot on the left leg of Thomas, they go off together with the left foot—left, left, right, left; Thomas misses a step and gets his feet between Wallschlaeger's legs, tripping himself up, and he pitches headlong. "Orah sargint, did ye iver see the loikes o' that omadhaun?" "Vell, py Got, you makes your feet go mit my legs in." "Silence, both of you."

"Forward, march; left, left, right;" scrape comes down the government. "Bad cess to yer clumsy crubeens." "Wallschlaeger, don't step so long. Left, left; right, left;" scrape with the right government; scrape goes the left 13. "Chrean Tharig and Dhioul, will ye keep off me heels; I won't be able to take a step for a month." "Vell, you valk anyhow too fast mit your feets; don't could valks like dot fast." "Stop your talking. Halt; front, face." Another explanation of the steps in quick time; another left face and again Wallschlaeger is in front. "Forward, march;" Wallschlaeger starts off in about common time[29] and Thomas is dancing along behind, trying to get step with him; "faster, Wallschlaeger, left, left, right, left," kick. "Du Lumpe. "Left, left; right, left." Kick. "Du for Domte Irlandois aisel." "An shure no one could march afther yure stippin." "No talking in the ranks. Left. Thomas, step longer. Left, left; right, left. Kick, kick. "Gott for damn, Gott for damn, Gott for damn." "An phy don't ye walk wid littler stips, thin," and Wallschlaeger lets loose a volley of German oaths enough to almost annihilate poor Thomas, but seeing the drummer preparing to sound recall, I march them by the front where each one has his own step, so that they may recover their tempers, and when ranks were broken Thomas would say, "that last drill was fust rate;" and Wallschlaeger, "Dot is anyhow, a goot vay," and their beligerent intentions would be postponed indefinitely.

Wallschlaeger and Thomas proved to be good soldiers, and although the latter (as Hugh Talty "rest his soul" would say) "couldn't shoot and hit a barn if he was within it, but he was a divil in a charge."[30]

[It was the final winter camp of the war for Sullivan, the men of the Sixth Wisconsin, the Brigade and the Army of the Potomac. Whether or not the men in the ranks sensed the end was but a handful of months away is not known. More maiming and death surely lay ahead, the soldeirs knew that much; the Rebels had lost no determination and the war was not yet won. The camps south of Petersburg were no less cold and damp, no less cheerless in those sumplike surroundings than they had been for three previous winters. In February 1865 a stir rippled through the brigade camp: the unit was being removed from the V Corps and the seat of war, and sent to duty up north. The seven regiments were marched to the James River in preparation for departure, when entreaties by General Warren were partially heeded. The 6th and 7th Wisconsin would remain in the V Corps. It may have been that the six-month association with the 143th, 149th, and 150th Pennsylvania would not be much missed; they had, however, grown more accustomed to the 1st New York Sharpshooters with whom they had marched and fought for over a year and a half. But it was the removal of the 24th Michigan that proved the most emotional: these hard-fighting Wolverines had become an integral part of the Western brigade at Gettysburg; they had earned their black hats and grown to be brother soldiers.

Sullivan did not write about those events when he was setting his war recollections to paper 20 years later. Nor did he mention that he was charged with desertion and lost his sergeant stripes. During that last war winter, Sullivan was granted a furlough to visit his wife, pregnant with their first child, in Philadelphia. Upon his return, he looked up his uncle, Tommy Flynn, and the two left the 6th Wisconsin camp without authorization. They were first listed as "absent without leave" and finally as deserters, but both turned up somewhat red-faced a few days later; doubtless, the two Irishmen concluded missing a few roll calls while the war was in winter's ebb was not a serious indiscretion. The result, however, was that Sullivan was reduced to a back rank private with the "rag tag and bobtail" of Company K once again.

And, thus, the final campaigns of the war commenced. The ranks of the 6th and 7th Wisconsin had been bulked by numerous late enlistees and drafted men. In March a final Eastern regiment, the 91st New York, a converted artillery outfit, had been added to the brigade. Milwaukee Irishman Tom Kerr was major now, and would lead the regiment. And Col. John Kellogg, white-haired and shrunken from his months' long captivity, had returned to lead the brigade in its final campaigns. Sullivan and many of the "Boys of '61" may have been shocked by the colonel's appearance. The new men in ranks did not even know who he was.

The spring campaign was another grinding and punishing one. At Hatcher's Run in early February, a desultory and largely ineffectual attempt to capture the South Side Railroad cost the regiment 103 men—nearly half of the brigade's total loss; Company K accounted for 13 casualties, the majority of whom were draftees. Two months later, Grant again hurled the V Corps against Lee's desperate remnants at Gravelly Run. On the next day, April 1, 1865, the

whispy Rebel defenses were breeched at Five Forks. The losses in
the 6th Wisconsin were 119 in those two days. One of Company K's
draftees, Anthony Frembgen of Paris, Wisconsin, was the last man
killed in the unit. The war had now little more than a score of days
to run. And James P. Sullivan was a father—Angeline had given
birth to a son, christened George, March 23. There was likely
hurrahing and celebration in the camp when word finally reached
the new father. A new generation of Sullivans was American-born.

The middle-aged veteran wrote nothing about his reaction to
becoming a father, or of the final campaign. These latter fights
lacked the snap and sparkle of earlier years, and failed to ignite his
pen. What he did recreate, however, was another incident of camp
life in those final months of war that tickled the fancy of his readers.
It was a story of the company mule that was likely told at Iron
Brigade Association gatherings in the 1880s and was published by
Watrous's *Telegraph* January 4, 1885.

Editor Watrous, a proponent of temperance and other rectitudi-
nous movements was somewhat careful about impressions given to
civilian readers. Sullivan's candid recollections of foraging and
thievery prompted Watrous, who wrote under the penname "Camp
Fire," to provide an explanatory introduction to Sullivan's piece.]

[A] hasty glance at "Mickey's" letter really does leave the
impression that the mule was stolen; that he was stolen
several times, but the customs of the day were such that it
was not called stealing. It was variously termed "taking
things," "foraging" and "allowing things to stick to his fin-
gers." And the custom was confined to no particular regiment,
brigade, division, corps or army. Nor did any one religious
denomination have a monopoly. The road was open to "take
things" to the Methodist, Baptist, Presbyterian, Catholic or a
Congregationalist as it was to an Episcopalian, and if one
denomination seemed to be getting the start of another in
collecting things without permission, there was not that showing of jealousy and bitterness which is made at times in civil
life; the defeated denominations went to work with renewed
zeal, and if the foraging was poor, they would step around on
a dark night and "take" things which the more fortunate
denomination had slipped into camp, and thus even up matters. "Foraging," or, as some people in their ignorance term
it, "stealing," was not confined to either of the political par-

ties. Both did it. A Company D democrat would "take" the colonel's canteen of poteen [liquor] as readily as a Company E republican would scare the major's black cook away and carry to his own tent the delicious noonday meal. The reader must keep in mind the fact that not a little of the "taking" was done for mischief. And there is another thing which should be kept in mind. For instance: When "Pip," supposing it was he who "took" Co. K's mule from the Virginia farm, was about to retire with his new found property, and the farmer reminded him that he had not liquidated, the chances are that "Pip" apologized for his forgetfulness and immediately drew his check on the bank of Mukwa, or gave him a note for sixty days. If it was a note, and the farmer said he would feel better if it was endorsed, why "Pip," largehearted, generous, straight dealing man that he was, didn't hesitate a minute to put the name of J. P. Sullivan, Lieut. Bill Van Wie, Capt. [William] Remington or any other Co. K man's name on its back. So a great deal of what people at home had the habit of calling stealing was not stealing at all. Like Pip's mule deal, it was straight business. The boys, when the people [local farmers] were around, simply took chickens, sheep, hogs, horses, hams, flour, cows and other things which their profession seemed to demand, and gave notes or checks. I don't suppose all of the notes and checks have been cashed. As like as not the holders never presented the checks at the banks or put the notes into the hands of lawyers for collection. If that is so, the fault is their own, not that of the boys. And, I suppose a good many of those notes were signed by boys whose spirits were marching upon the golden paves of heaven before the paper came due. I saw a Co. D man give a "poor white trash" a note for two chickens which read: "I promise to pay the bearer four bits for two dead hens the day after he is inaugurated President of the United States."

[Sullivan's piece followed.]

COMPANY K'S MULE
By Mickey, of Co. K

Company K had a mule. How it came by it is "one of the things that no fellow can find out," you know. Certain it is, there was no transfer and delivery of property when company K became owner of the aforementioned useful animal, but one morning the quadruped appeared at the end of company K's street and was added to the personnel of the company. It was suspected by the knowing ones that company K was indebted to the "abstracting" abilities of "Pip," (of whom the boys used to say that he could scent a loose contraband horse a mile off) for that latest acquisition to its diversified personal property, but from whatever source the company acquired the title, the fact remained, "allee samee"—company K had a mule.

When the fog raised on the morning referred to, and the animal became visible, considerable discussion arose in regard to what was the proper class of animal to which the quadruped belonged. Some held that it was a mule, others that it was a donkey; more thought it might be a goat, and some remarked dubiously that it looked like a horse; but Hugh Talty contradicted that, flatly, by saying, in his clear Irish brogue, "it's not a horse at all, that's in it, but a rale jackass." Having settled the question of the species, and that company K was possessed of the animal in "fee simple," it was determined that he should have a title according to his rank and standing, and all the famous quadrupeds of history, ancient and modern, including "Pegazzuz," "Bucephalus," "Copenhagen," "Old Whitey," "Knight of Malta," etc., were mentioned, but none seemed appropriate, and some of the distinguished and extinguished generals of our army were named, but rejected, and at last one genius, remembering Beauregard's famous beauty and booty order, intimated that if he was not a beauty he certainly was a booty; and advised that the animal should be named Beauregard, after the Bull Run hero, and it was adopted, as the boys said, "pusillanimously," and in course of time the name became contracted to Bory and finally to "Old Boo," and as "Old Boo," company K's mule became a celebrity.

"Old Boo," like a good many more of the "galvanized Yankees," during and since the war, found his connection with the dominant party profitable, and a very visible change was soon effected in his appearance and feeling, which was no doubt owing to various surreptitious nocturnal and diurnal

visits company K paid to "Bobby Robert's" department, and
to the haversacks, pockets and armfuls of grain and hay which
were obtained, and in course of time "Old Boo" waxed slick
and fat and dexterous with his heels, and company K thought
"Old Boo" could sing the "Quartermaster's call" equal to any
equine or bovine in the service; and the boys were ready to
risk their six month's pay, and an installment, that Beauregard could out-kick, out-holler, out-buck, out-eat and carry
the biggest pack of any mule with two or four or any amount
of legs or ears in the Army of the Potomac.

After Phil Sheridan had made an April fool of Lee at Five
Forks, and forced the surrender at Appomattox, the army
returned to Washington and camped around the city, and "Old
Boo," like Othello, found his occupation gone, and the boys
being more interested in home and friends than about the
expiring rebellion, "Old Boo" found himself neglected and was
relegated with the rest of the regimental animals to the
wagon train and about that time rations became very scarce,
whether owing to the fact that the war being over the government wished to economize or that expecting soon to be out of
a job, the commissaries were trying to feather their nests, was
not known, but it was known that company K was mighty
hungry; and various were the expedients resorted to, to supply
the demand; for a while things could be obtained on credit,
based on assurance that the paymaster was coming next week;
and when it failed, peddler wagons were rolled on, and sharp
eyed and sharper tongued pie women were made the subject
of diverse harmless tricks which always resulted in their
disposing of their wares and a visit to the captain [Andrew
Gallup of Lisbon], who, they were informed, would pay company K's bills, and who would tell them much to their disappointment, that he did not buy pies for the company; but ere
long peddlers and pie women fought shy of the command and
some thing had to be done.

A council of war, (or rather of grub) was held, to which none
but veterans, tried and true, were admitted and after discuss-
ing and dismissing various projects, one was submitted and
adopted without a dissenting voice. The next morning "Old
Boo" was missing, and about 9 o'clock the captain was in-

formed that "Old Boo" was stolen, and was requested to send
a detail in search of the company property, and after being
armed with proper passes and orders to take one mule, the
property of company K, etc., the party started for Washington
and obtained the assistance of a "patrol," and after awhile
they met some strange soldiers who told them that they had
seen a party of soldiers bring such a looking mule to a certain
stable, kept by one of the shylocks who were ready to buy
anything on which five hundred per cent could be made; and
"Old Boo" was found in a stall, contentedly munching hay.
After a heated discussion and threats to arrest the stable
keeper, "Old Boo" was brought out and company K's detail
marched off in triumph, and at the Georgetown end of the
"Aqueduct bridge," they again met the party of strange soldiers who had informed them where the mule might be found,
and who had various and numerous parcels and packages
which were awaiting transportation to their camp, and "Old
Boo" was loaded with the said parcels and the parties went
along together amid much exultant laughter and noisy dem-
onstrations, which a stranger might find difficult to see cause
for.

"There was a sound of revelry by night," in company K's
street that evening, and oysters, sardines, canned fruit, fine
cut and plug were plenty. A feast was spread and edibles and
bibibles were plentifully disposed of by company K and its
invited guests, (some of whom wore shoulder straps), and for
several days supplies of all kinds were plenty, and the pie
women debts were liquidated with interest at fifty per cent,
"but after a feast comes a famine," and in a short time
company K's treasury was again empty, and about that time
Beauregard was again stolen ('twas reported, by some of the
Yorkers.) Again he was brought back to camp in triumph and
his return was celebrated by another feast and for a short
time company K was supplied with the luxuries of the season.
Shortly afterwards orders were received directing our regiment to report to Louisville, Ky., and Beauregard was stolen
for the fourth time, but the party found a good deal of
difficulty in disposing of him, but at length an intelligent
contraband was found who intended establishing himself in

business within the shadow of the Goddess of Liberty, on the capitol, and who "done reckoned dat mooel ud make a right peart dray hoss," and producing a roll of greenbacks from his dirty black silk neck handkerchief, he became the owner of the gallant Beauregard and for all the writer knows, "Old Boo" may still be a "right peart dray hoss."

Written for *The Sunday Telegraph*.

NOTES

1. Dawes, *Service*, p. 196.
2. *Ibid.*, p. 202.
3. *Ibid.*, pp. 241–42.
4. *Ibid.*, p. 277.
5. Babcock, of Beetown in Grant County, Wisconsin, enlisted in May 1861 and moved up noncommissioned officer ranks to become sergeant major in April 1863. He was promoted to regimental adjutant a year later and was killed at Weldon Railroad, August 19, 1864. *Roster of Wisconsin Volunteers*, Vol. I, pp. 494, 495, 505.
6. Dawes had finally been accorded promotion to full colonel July 5, 1864; he mustered out upon expiration of his enlistment August 10, 1864.
7. Kerr, of Milwaukee, was another Irish immigrant. He joined the Montgomery Guards, Company D, as a private soldier in 1861, and worked his way through the ranks to become major. He was wounded several times, and was one of the regiment's final field commanders. He survived the war, living impecuniously in Milwaukee until his death in 1893. Kerr was a regular participant in postwar Iron Brigade Association gatherings. *Milwaukee History*, Vol. II, No. 4, Winter, 1988; *The Blackhat*, Nos. 39 and 40.
8. Sullivan's reference was to the "First Families of Virginia," a cruel soldier description of the ex-slaves working as strikers.
9. A New Yorker by birth, Romeyn B. Ayres graduated from the U.S. Military Academy in 1847 and became a career officer. In the war's early actions, he commanded the 5th U.S. Artillery and later was promoted to brigade and division command, ending the conflict with brevets to brigadier and major general at age 41. He remained in the army after the war, and died in 1888. Ezra J. Warner, *Generals in Blue* (Baton Rouge, 1964), pp. 13–14; *Dictionary of American Biography*, Vol. I, pp. 443–45.
10. Griffin, an Ohioan, graduated with Ayres from West Point in 1847. At the battle of Five Forks, April 1, 1865, the 41-year-old would succeed Gouverneur K. Warren as V Corps commander when Phil Sheridan removed the latter. *Ibid.*, pp. 190–91; *Dictionary of American Biography*, Vol. VII, pp. 617–18.
11. The U.S. (or Berdan's) Sharpshooters were organized in the summer of 1861 by New Yorker Hiram Berdan, an inventor and top amateur rifle shot. Recruits were accepted on the basis of a marksmanship test. One company was raised in Wisconsin: Company G, 1st Regiment. Eventually a

total of two regiments were organized and armed with special .52-caliber Sharps' rifles, outfitted with double-set triggers. The Sharpshooters wore a distinctive very dark green uniform. Faust, *Encyclopedia*, pp. 56–57; Roger D. Hunt and Jack R. Brown, *Brevet Brigadier Generals in Blue* (Gaithersburg, Md., 1990), p. 513; Richard L. Smallwood-Roberts, ed., *The Scout, Newsletter of Company "G," 1st Regt. U.S.S.S., Wisconsin's "Badger Scouts" in Berdan's Sharpshooters*, Volume I, Issue 1.

12. Dailey, an Irish immigrant to Ohio, interrupted plans to attend law school to enlist in the 2nd Wisconsin Infantry, rose through the ranks to attain captain's bars, and was breveted major for gallantry. He led two companies that formed the Wisconsin Independent Battalion, which served as division provost guard. At the battle of Weldon Railroad, August 21, 1864, Dailey impetously rode into attacking South Carolina troops, demanding their surrender. He was shot from his horse by Confederate Gen. Johnson Hagood. Recovering from his wound, Dailey was among the 2nd Wisconsin veterans merged into the 6th Wisconsin in November 1864. Dailey rose to major and served through the spring 1865 campaign. Dailey migrated to Council Bluffs, Iowa, where he practiced law until his death March 25, 1898. William J. K. Beaudot, "The Bravest Act of the War," *Virginia Country's Civil War Quarterly*, Vol. VI, 1986; *The Blackhat*, Nos. 22 and 23.

13. William S. Campbell, of Mauston, Juneau County, enlisted in the Lemonweir Minute Men in May 1861. He rose through ranks to become 1st lieutenant in July 1863, but resigned in October 1864. Campbell was killed before his paperwork was completed. *Roster of Wisconsin Volunteers*, Vol. I, p. 533.

14. Francis A. Wallar, a 24-year-old sergeant of Company I at Weldon Railroad, had enlisted from Bad Ax County, Town of DeSoto, in July 1861 with his brother Samuel. As a corporal, his heroic deed in capturing the 2nd Mississippi flag earned him high honor and he would be awarded the Congressional Medal of Honor. He returned to farming for some 20 years in Wisconsin before migrating to Dakota Territory in 1883. He died at age 70 in 1911. Wm. J. K. Beaudot, "Francis Asbury Wallar; A Medal of Honor at Gettysburg," *Gettysburg Magazine*, No. 4, January 1991; *The Blackhat*, No. 37.

15. Timmons, of Beloit in southern Wisconsin, enlisted as a private in the Beloit Star Rifles, Company G, in June 1861. He was promoted to 1st lieutenant in December 1862 and to captain in August 1864. He was wounded at Laurel Hill and killed in action at Weldon Railroad August 19, 1864. *Roster of Wisconsin Volunteers*, Vol. I, p. 520.

16. James H. Rhoades, of Middleton in Dane County, enlisted in January 1864. A corporal, he was wounded in the Spotsylvania campaign and mustered from service with the regiment in July 1865. *Ibid.*, p. 535.

17. Charles Griffin was an Ohioan and West Point graduate who saw action during the Mexican War. Ordered to organize a field battery, he led it at First Bull Run and earned promotion. He gained a general's star during the Peninsula Campaign. He successively commanded a brigade and a division. Absent due to illness during Gettysburg, he later led his division of the V Corps through the Spring Campaign of 1864. After the war, Griffin commanded the District of Texas and he died of yellow fever in Galveston in 1867. Warner, *Generals in Blue*, pp. 190–91.

18. William H. Van Wie enlisted in the "Lemonweir Minute Men" from Lindina in Juneau County in June 1861. He was promoted to corporal and sergeant and late in the war to 1st lieutenant. After the war, he was a merchant in Mauston. *Ibid.*, p. 533.

19. Jared Williams enlisted February 1, 1862, from Ontario in western Wisconsin. He served until war's end. *Ibid.*, p. 536.

20. The standard load for a Civil War .58-caliber rifle-musket was 60 grains of FFg black powder. Doubling it to 120 grains would have flattened bullet tragectory dramatically.

21. A lunette was a two- or three-sided fort with the rear open to interior lines. Faust, *Encyclopedia*, p. 464.

22. Certificate of Death, October 1906; U.S. Pension Office, James P. Sullivan File, Affidavit of March 30, 1874.

23. *Ibid.*

24. Thomas, of Plymouth, Wisconsin, was drafted October 31, 1864.

25. The *Roster of Wisconsin Volunteers* spells his name Wallschlager. From Liberty, Wisconsin, he was drafted September 30, 1864.

26. Kellogg was captured in the Battle of the Wilderness in May 1864. After a harrowing escape from rebel prison, he returned to command the Iron Brigade in November 1864. The Brigade was then comprised of the 6th and 7th Wisconsin and the 91st New York.

27. Gallup, who enlisted as a private soldier in June 1861, rose through the ranks to become captain of Company K in December 1864. He served to the end of the war. *Roster of Wisconsin Volunteers*, Vol. I, p. 533.

28. "Quick Time" was 110 26-inch paces per minute.

29. "Common time" was 90 26-inch paces per minute.

30. Thomas and Wallschlaeger fought in the spring campaigns of 1865; the former mustered out with the regiment July 14, 1865, while the latter was absent sick at the final roll call.

AFTERWORD

James P. Sullivan, a graying, bewhiskered man of 42, had only a few times since the war days experienced a town as large as La Crosse, Wisconsin, a commerce stop on the Mississippi River. The veteran of the "old 6th Wisconsin" had seen big cities during his war years, of course—visiting the nation's capital as an impressionable young private and recuperating from his Gettysburg wound in Philadelphia. He had also marched victoriously through the devastated rebel capital of Richmond, Virginia, in the spring of 1865. But since returning home to the Badger State two decades before, the Irishman's travels had been more modest, limited to the unprepossessing hamlets and villages near his farm in western Wisconsin, with an occasional turn in Madison and Milwaukee, and a brief attempt at homesteading in the Dakota Territory. The past several years he had, with indifferent success, been attempting to wrest a living for himself and his family from a "worthless forty acres over by" Hillsboro in Vernon County.

La Crosse, where Sullivan found himself that mid-September of 1883, was one of Wisconsin's largest and most prosperous cities, with a population crowding toward 22,000. The middle-aged man may have recalled that when he returned home with a disability discharge in the middle of the war he had been troubled by a seeming preoccupation with commerce and profit by the folks at home while his comrades were still in the field in Virginia. He had re-enlisted with his "old black hat" regiment and would stay for two and a half more years of fighting. Certainly, times had changed, and he was a man of maturity and perspective now, but Sullivan never had been at ease in such tight and frenzied surroundings. City Point, Virginia, had looked something like this two decades before when Grant's soldiers, Sullivan among them, were attempting to corral Lee's men in Petersburg.

Dominated by craggy, 570-foot Grandad Bluff, La Crosse squatted on a narrow, oblong stretch of river terrace. Scores of stern- and side-wheeled river packets churned the murky Mississippi River waters along the dockside. Warehouses seemed fairly to bulge with materials and merchandise. Workers, a great variegated army, swarmed about barrels, crates, and containers. Ponderous dray horses, straining in harness at laden wagons, clumped upon the brick streets of the central business district. In the wealthier residential sections of town, ranks of sprawling brick and stone mansions, built by the barons of lumbering, milling, brewing, and related industries, stood at elegant attention in tree-shaded precincts.[1]

Was this, then, a portent of America in the new century? For many of the veterans, like Sullivan, such changes were difficult to fathom. Not only was the nation rushing madly toward an urban future, but the values and motivations so significant in sustaining them through four bloody years of civil war seemed to be eroding. The homefolk during 1861–65 had been unable to understand what their soldier sons were experiencing, and now the children of these veterans were embracing such concerns as balance sheets and influence. Little wonder that a growing number of old soldiers sought solace in reunions of their old units, where they could relive youthful days, filtering out the cold, dampness, and death of the war years and recreating a sunnier memory "of a hundred circling camps."

J. P. Sullivan was in La Crosse for just such a purpose—he was to address his old comrades gathered for the third reunion of the Iron Brigade Association. The veterans' organization had been formed in Milwaukee in 1880, not only as a means of maintaining contact with former tentmates and to honor the memory of fallen comrades, but also to politic for soldier pensions and other matters, to hear old war stories, and to relive the days of glory and adventure.

The Irishman had, by the mid-1880s, gained some measure of notoriety through his war writings; they had been published in a few newspapers in Wisconsin. His old colonel and association chairman, Edward S. Bragg, had invited Sullivan to deliver a speech to his old friends on Friday, September 14, the anniversary of the battle at South Mountain in 1862. Despite the modesty of his postwar achievements, Sullivan would be the first enlisted man to address the organization.[2]

Likely dressed in the best suit his means would allow, Sullivan had traveled by buggy from his small Vernon County farm Thursday to Viroqua. Once aboard the Chicago & North Western rail car, he perhaps poured over a sheaf of notes, readying himself for the important speech. At the old Neuman Store on Main Street in La Crosse the next morning, Sullivan and scores of other Iron Brigade veterans rallied. There and at later meetings, he met many with whom he had marched and fought two decades past. He found his old messmate, Charley Crawford, who had journeyed west from Tomah. Bill Van Wie, his old Company K comrade, had traveled over from Mauston, where he was a merchant. It did not seem possible that so many years had passed since these men, young men then, had enlisted in Capt. Rufus Dawes' company of volunteers and marched off to be soldiers.

Sullivan also ran into Earl "Bona" Rogers, his friend from Vernon County, who still bore a resemblance to Napoleon. And he found Ed Whaley, now postmaster down river in Prairie du Chien, whose cork and wooden appendage was a painful reminder of the leg he had given at Weldon Railroad in Virginia in 1864. Sullivan also paid his respects to the "Tall Sycamore," Joseph Marston, who had ridden across the state from Appleton to attend the reunion. And there was the old regiment's surgeon, Doc John Hall, whom the boys still called "Old Syntax" because of his command of vocabulary; he had patched up the soldier hurts and ailments of many of the men who gathered that day.

Gregarious Jerome Watrous, the Milwaukee newspaperman, was evident, too, busy scribbling notes about the meetings, greetings, and goings-on that he would print in his *Sunday Telegraph*. All the way upriver from St. Louis had traveled affable Loyd Harris, one of the fine singers of the 6th Wisconsin who, along with a few others, had entertained the boys in the Washington camps and on the march. Little Aleck Johnson, the fresh-faced drummer boy, had trekked up from Patch Grove in Grant County to attend; the youthful vigor was still apparent, but his face was no longer smooth and hairless.

Of the 150 brigade veterans who signed the roll at Neuman Store, 57 identified the 6th Wisconsin as their regiment. For Sullivan and others, it was warming to embrace old friends, to fight back the tears of joyful reunion. The years since the war had marked most of the men with deep lines and gray hair; most, like Mickey, evinced the thickness of middle age; many trod with lame and weary steps. But at least for a few days, years would turn back and they would again be the "Boys of '61"—those patriotic children of the Republic who flocked to the old flag after the firing on Ft. Sumter.

The stolid three-story, red-brick Germania Hall on 5th and Ferry Streets served as headquarters for the Association's two-day fête. The interior was festooned with flags, bunting, and banners; wreaths enshrined names and visages of brigade heroes. For Sullivan and others of "Old Company K," the prominently emblazoned name of Johnny Ticknor was particularly poignant. He was the likeable young sawmill worker who had risen through the ranks of his company to become captain. But his promise of leadership was cut short that hot morning of July 1, 1863, at Gettysburg, when he went down under a torrent of rebel lead during the furious charge on an unfinished railroad cut full of rebels.

At the opening session, "Bona" Rogers called attention to the names adorning the walls, the men being honored. But he also noted that "all others though their names did not appear were equally remembered and honored, who had fought the good fight on earth and had been called to join the great army . . . into the regions of the hereafter." Rogers also delivered a eulogy for John Kellogg, a Company K man who escaped rebel imprisonment and returned to the field to lead the remnant of the Iron Brigade in the final campaigns of the war. He had died February 10th. Sullivan recalled Kellogg from his days in Mauston as district attorney; and he may have remembered when he returned to Virginia, his hair snow white and his body shrunken.[3]

Also remembered at that opening session was the 6th Wisconsin's trumpet-voiced major, John Hauser. A German immigrant with experience in European wars, Hauser was remembered for his clarion commands, the sometimes comic amalgam of English and German that seemed to bellow above the battle din. Hauser, too, had recently died in Milwaukee, and Watrous asked comrades to pay heed to his memory.

At Friday's gathering, Bragg introduced Mickey Sullivan with appropriate fanfare. Watrous' notebook contained a thumbnail sketch of the Irishman. He is a "man of note," the newspaperman wrote. ". . . but he is not the smooth-faced boy of '61, side whiskers and whitening hair tell of twenty-two years flown."

From notes Sullivan read his recollections of the harrowing action on the Rappahannock River during the Chancellorsville campaign in 1863. While the fight at FitzHugh's Crossing was a sidelight and did not alter the course of the Union defeat in the battle, it was carried out with elan and at tragic human cost. Sullivan's oration cast Bragg, the "Little Colonel," in a humorous but favorable light. The diminutive Bragg had led the force which frantically paddled across the river under steady fire from rebel sharpshooters and pickets. They had gained the far shore, swept away the enemy, and established a precious foothold. To the chagrin of those who survived, what they had won in blood was abandoned only hours later under orders from the army commander.[4]

FitzHugh's Crossing was perhaps an emblematic action for Sullivan to choose. Like so many other fights in which the Iron Brigade was involved, the action was overlooked or minimized by Eastern writers and putative historians who were chronicling the war. "[I]n any of the so-called histories that have come under my notice," Sullivan said, "I have not seen any mention of such a brigade." And for this reason, Mickey gave himself a charge—to set the record of the war straight, to arrest the obfuscation and reams of rhetoric that shrouded the accomplishments of the Western brigade. "[I] did not write . . . to find fault with the country or to discuss politics, nor to show what somebody should or should not do," he concluded that Friday at Germania Hall in La Crosse, "but merely to keep alive the memory of that brigade which the Military History of Wisconsin calls "The gallant corps that was the pride of our state.""[5]

But he did have another purpose: to fire a salvo at those who attempted to deny just pension rights to a crippled and rheumatic former soldier such as he. He was critical of a state that "neglects and suffers him to be insulted [by] eleventh-hour patriots and bounty men."

If Sullivan had dreams of great attainment and enrichment, they were never to be realized. He lacked the resources, connections, and plain old Irish luck. For a man of common means, fighting for survival amid the buffeting economic conditions of postwar Wisconsin lacked the drama of dodging rebel bullets. But it had to be done. With his wife, Angeline, and months' old son, George, the scarred veteran returned home in the late summer of 1865 to an uncertain future. The skills he could bring to bear were less than impressive. He had spent his youth in his father's fields and had been a hired hand when the war broke out. He had honed some innate writing talents in war diaries, but it would be years until these brought him recognition.

Wisconsin's farm economy was in a postwar lull. Then the Panic of 1873 ushered in more hardship, and the worst depression in U.S. history created severe constriction of money and credit. Meanwhile, during the 1870s, three more children were born to Angeline and Mickey; Anna in 1872, John in 1875, and James in 1878.

New land in Wisconsin was selling for $1.25 an acre, and in 1870 Sullivan somehow scraped together funds for a small homestead in Vernon County.[6] Part of Wisconsin's western upland, Vernon County boomed with newcomers after the war, boasting a population of over 23,000. Black and white oaks and elms clumped on grassy heights which were interspersed by cultivated meadows and hilly pasture-

land. The county was cut with frequent rivulets and river trenches—
branches of the Wisconsin and Mississippi River systems. Entirely
rural in character, Vernon County had but a scattering of small
towns. Forest Township, where Mickey purchased 40 acres, was
described as "very rough," but fine farmland was available on bluffs.
Less than a thousand souls dotted the township in 1880, and that
was barely exceeded a decade later.[7]

The new decade accelerated changes that were beginning to
penetrate Wisconsin and affect the lives of men like Mickey Sullivan. A Republican Party faction thwarted a third term for President
U. S. Grant and the nomination went to another war veteran, James
Garfield. In June 1880, the Grand Army of the Republic made its
presence felt when 140,000 former soldiers gathered in Milwaukee
for a sprawling reunion. Many old Black Hats were there, and they
assembled in a small hotel to form an association to preserve the
record of their achievements. The national veterans movement bur-
geoned in the next few years, and began pressuring sympathetic
politicians, many of whom were veterans themselves, for more
liberal and expanded benefits.

Meanwhile, Sullivan continued fitfully in his attempt to wrest
subsistence from the often stubborn western Wisconsin soil. And
during the implacable winters which seized the upper Midwest,
Sullivan began sorting through his war memories, trying to put
things in perspective, attempting to measure what he had experienced against the torrent of words in the soldier press and in the
books of the day.

It may have been coincidence that one of Wisconsin's snowiest
winters, the 1881–82 season, and the publication of Jefferson Davis's apologia for his administration, *The Rise and Fall of the Confederate Government*, were somehow wedded in Sullivan's mind. He was
moved to sort through notes, diaries, and letters and compose his
recollections of the 6th Wisconsin's charge on the railroad cut at
Gettysburg. He sent the manuscript to the editor of the nearby
Mauston Star, where it was published in the aftermath of the annual
reunion of old Company K in 1883.

Sullivan quickly warmed to this writing business, encouraged,
first, by Congressman Bragg, who invited the Irishman to the La
Crosse reunion, and, second, by Jerome Watrous, who published the
Gettysburg piece in his Milwaukee weekly. Over the next half dozen
years Sullivan churned out evocative and sometimes caustic pieces
on battles and incidents of war.[8]

Sullivan's anger over contemporary assessment of the war, and of its politicans and generals, was apparent within his lines as well as between. Watrous sometimes edited the Irishman's harsher judgments and softened his caustic criticisms, but what remained was telling.

Sullivan also used his budding confidence with the printed word to serve as a vent to frustrations with postwar life as well as past military life. For example, for the March 1, 1884, issue of *The Telegraph*, Sullivan restated a theme he had trumpeted some six months previously in La Crosse:

> **HE RETURNS THANKS HILLSBORO, FEB. 22.**—I wish to thank *The Sunday Telegraph* for that able editorial "There must be a Remedy," and would have done so sooner but was prevented by illness.
>
> If more influential Journals like yours would speak out in plain terms on the same subjects, there would be a different state of things from the present. Presidents of examining boards would not tell a veteran who had received three or four severe wounds in the service and was seriously disabled otherwise, that he saw "no reason why he was not able to do a full day's work in a harvest field." I hope you will continue the fire with your heaviest guns until all the red tape, spies and the disgraceful methods of fancying every soldier to be a perjured, lying rascal until he can prove it different, are blown where we sent the Rebellion. Very respectfully your friend and comrad,
>
> MICKEY

In the ensuing years, more poured from Sullivan's pen—accounts of Gainesville, Second Bull Run, and the expedition to Virginia's Northern Neck, where some of his regiment's officers received deserved comeuppance. He gained readers and notoriety, and Watrous' newspaper grew in circulation. Prompted by his old friend Charley Crawford, Sullivan promised more, the while revealing some details about his circumstances:

> Will *The Sunday Telegraph* please give my respects to Charley Crawford and tell him that I have taken the field for the spring campaign, and am heavily engaged all along the line, "horse, foot and dragoon's," selecting strong positions for my small grain; preparing to deploy my awkward Irish potatoes into line; plant my corn batteries; consulting my assistant adjutant general in regard to her kitchen garden and flower beds; and using my ablest strategy to keep on the right side of

that autocrat of American farmers, the "hired man." When I again retire to winter quarters, and my principal duty will consist of disposing of my ration of "hominy and hog," if *THE SUNDAY TELEGRAPH* will kindly spare me space, I will try to enlighten its readers upon the most scientific method of making "Spit Devils" from thirty pound rifle shells, and describe the famous "Kats" mentioned in his letter, which included such acknowledged talent as [John] "Kilmartin [of Company D]," "Jones," [Charles] "West," [James W.] "Knapp," "Tomp [Andrew R. Thompson]," [Erastus?] "Packard [of Company G]," "Charley Crawford," "Pip," "[John?] Kennedy," "Mickey," etc., and also give the adventures of Co. K's mules; in the meantime my best wishes to all the old braves of the Iron Brigade.[9]

Sullivan, in time, made good on those promises, producing additional episodic and humorous sketches. He spared no one his satiric pen, not even himself. He created a piece about his experiences as a sergeant, drilling two clod-footed draftees in 1864. He also drafted his recollections of an unsung battle at Weldon Railroad in August of the same year.

It was likely, albeit he did not sign the muster roll, that Mickey made the journey to Lancaster, Wisconsin, in late August 1884 to attend the fifth annual Iron Brigade Association conclave. It was a special gathering as it was the only one to which the respected Rufus R. Dawes journeyed. The breveted general and former Ohio congressman traveled north from his home in Marietta to meet old comrades and deliver a speech about great deeds and valor.

Dawes would, years later, recall the diminutive, light-hearted Irishman who marched in the back rank of his company and caused not a small amount of consternation among the young officers. When Dawes published his war memoirs six years later, he wrote: "For genuine sallies of humor at unexpected times, I never have seen his equal. He was a heroic soldier, and he was shot and severely wounded three times in battle." Mickey and little Hugh Talty, Dawes wrote, "softened the suffering of many by their unconquerable good humor and genuine wit. Such men are of priceless value in any army."[10]

Sullivan by then had become a member of the Grand Army of the Republic, and he reported to editor Jerome Watrous about one event at Ontario, a gathering typical of the hundreds of small-town G.A.R. meetings across the country in the 1880s. J. P. Sullivan, the old war veteran, was almost as spirited as Sullivan, the young soldier, as indicated in his March 22, 1885, report to *The Milwaukee Sunday Telegraph*:

CAMP-FIRE AT ONTARIO

By MICKEY OF CO. K

James H. Williams Post, No. 1548, had a very enjoyable camp-fire, and although the mercury stood at twenty below, and a keen, cutting wind was blowing during the day, the attendance was such as to demonstrate that the old "boys" still hold a warm place in the hearts of the people.

From an early hour until after sundown, Ontario presented the appearance familiar during the time when Wisconsin's sons were gathering and "swiftly forming in the ranks of war," to vindicate, on nearly every battle field of the war, the honor of this state which some chivalric southern braga-docia had seen fit to asperse when returning a "joint resolution of the legislature," pledging the state to support the laws and constitution of the Union.

At 1 P.M., the martial band struck up an air familiar to soldier ears and the "squeaking of the wry-necked pipe," and "ruba-dub-dub," "boom, boom, boom," the resonant drum re-minded the "boys" of the days when they left the "girls" behind them," "with promises to return with honor or not at all." Then the Ontario silver cornet band took up the gauntlet thrown down by the "sheepskin fiddlers," and finished a choice selection of National and Grand Army aires, after which they led the way to the dining room and "breathed out" appropriate melodies while the guests were filling the seats. The hall was beautifully and tastefully decorated with guidons designating the corps badges, interspersed with evergreens and small flags. A regulation size storm flag 10×20, stretched across the end of the hall, above which were swords crossed over the charter of the Post, the name and number of the Post in beautiful letters, portraits of Washington, Lincoln, Garfield, different generals of the war and pictures of war scenes. Stacks of arms, swords, cartridge boxes, etc., were in appropriate places and the chandelier in the center of the room was framed in a grand pyramid of flags of different sizes, the tables were loaded with ye succulent "army bean" baked to a delicious crispness and surmounted by pieces of old fashioned S.B. [sow belly] mounted "en barbette," while piles of genuine hard tack stood guard at proper intervals, but not having been left over from the war of 1812, it had not yet attained that toothsome solidity which characterized the "grape shot" our common uncle doled out to us with such persistent economy during the war. For nearly an hour every one was busy disposing of the edibles, occupying intervals between reliefs with laughable anecdotes, "When our regiment was in front of Petersburg," "During the march to the Sea," "At Kalorama Heights," "Smoky Hollow," "Camp Misery," "Camp General starvation," etc., etc. When every one had taken in a double deck load, the singing and fun began, Comrade Dunlap[11] of Wm. A. Barstow Post, Kendall [in neighboring Monroe County], capping the climax with "Mary had a little lamb," (with variations,) to the tune of "Rally round the Flag," all hands joining in the chorus, whether they had music in the souls or not, "Hurrah, Boys, for Mary, Hurrah for the Lamb," etc., and amid much various mirth, the company dispersed to meet again at the evening session.

At 6 P.M., Commander Marsden[12] rapped the assembly to order. The cornet band played Yankee Doodle, and the first toast was: "The Boys in Blue," to which comrade William Sandon, of Post 14, department of Dakota, responded with a touching recitation which was warmly received. The band played "Hail Columbia," and "Marching through Georgia" was sung by the entire audience, the sweet voices of the ladies blending with the hoarser ones of the gray haired vets in "Hurrah, Hurrah, we bring the jubilee." "The Grand Army" was responded to by Comrade Dunlap, of Wm. A. Barstow Post, Kendall, and Comrade J.P. Sullivan, of Henry Didiot Post, Hillsborough, the former reciting in a very impressive manner Mrs. Kate B. Sherwood's ode to the Grand Army, and the latter an appropriate eulogy on the subjects of the Grand Army and our honored dead. The cornet band rendered, in very effective style, the "Red, White and Blue." More Grand

Army odes were sung, after which occurred the event of the evening. In response to the "Presidents of the United States," the 6-year-old son of Comrade W.E. Davies, of James H. Williams Post, took the floor and recited a lengthy poem in a manner that elicited applause such as could only be heard on the battle field when re-enforcements relieve some hard-pressed part of the line, or when the news of some great victory was received in camp. To say that he took the house by storm is putting it mild, indeed. When the applause sub-sided the commander announced that remarks by the com-rades would be in order, and after some amusing remarks by Comrade Hutchinson, Comrade Dunlap took the floor and in an able and lengthy address, set forth the prize object, pro-gress and benefits of the Grand Army, and was vociferously applauded. The band played "Rally round the Flag," and all rose and sung the closing ode of the G.A.R., when the com-mander, in a few happy remarks, thanked the friends of the Post for their kindness and declared the meeting closed, to prepare for the dance which followed, and which was kept up vigorously until 5:30 A.M., next morning, when the musicians put away their instruments, remarking "that they did not want to kill 'em quite dead this time."

The Post had also hired the roller rink for the afternoon and evening and those who did not wish to shake the light fantastic, had an opportunity to display or witness the poetry of motion on wheels, and occasionally a gymnastic evolution.

Next morning, after much hand-shaking and warm good byes, and "take care of yourself old boy," the comrades sepa-rated, feeling that they had added one more pleasant recollec-tion to their memories.[13]

While Mickey Sullivan would produce two more lengthy battle accounts in 1885, life changes were crowding the Irishman's imme-diate horizon. Middle-age, infirmity, and tragedy would convince him that his farming days needed to end. Despite being but 45, Sullivan began experiencing more pronounced effects of war wounds and service. He had always been troubled by minor discomforts, but by the late 1880s these became more insistent. He had to engage a hired man to assist in working the 40-acre farm. Then, sometime after 1885, young Anna, called Fannie, and James Sullivan died, carried away by one of the periodic epidemics that swept the Middle West.[14]

In the mid-1890s Sullivan came to the decision that he could no longer sustain the effort to coax a living from the Vernon County soil. Why not study for the bar, he may have asked, and become a pension agent or the like. So the Sullivans moved a few miles north and west, to Ontario, a community of some 350 near the Kickapoo River and in the shadow of the Wildcat Mountain. On September 1, 1897, James P. Sullivan was officially admitted to the State Bar of Wisconsin. One of his four examiners was Gilbert Woodward, who had served in the old 2nd Wisconsin of the "Iron Brigade of the West." Five months later he spent $65 for a vacant lot on Ontario's square and a short time later the county's weekly newspaper proclaimed that "Mr. Sullivan's law office stands on his own soil."[15]

Mickey soon became a man of some consequence in the village; writer, war veteran, and attorney were important attributes, and he became village clerk. He also took up an old toot horn in the community's cornet band, carried the national flag at the head of Independence Day parades, and painted his law office a patriotic red, white, and blue.

But Sullivan's family life was troubled in the 1890s. His first son, George, was involved in a shooting and ultimately convicted of manslaughter and given a sentence in the Waupun State Prison. Shortly thereafter Sullivan divorced Angeline, his wife of 30 years. His life in those years could be followed in the brief mentions he received in the weekly newspapers of Vernon County:

1898—J.P. Sullivan has asked to be [Spanish-American War] recruiting officer.

1899—State versus Bill Allen for resisting an officer will be heard in Baldwin's Court. J.P. Sullivan, attorney for State. B.C. Smith, attorney for defendant.

1899—Bessie Gorham versus Bill Allen, attachment suit in Sullivan's Court. (Judgement of $7 rendered and $6.23 costs, against defendant).

Jan. 18, 1899—J.P. Sullivan and Mrs. Bessie Gorham of our village [Ontario] were married last Sun. in Hillsboro. At this writing they are keeping house in his residence of Red, White, and Blue over in "JimTown."

1899—Case of Sullivan against Chicago and Northwestern railroad for the loss of his dog, "Pom," began in Judge Francisca's court the 10th inst. It will be prosecuted to a finish. (Plaintiff got a judgement of $5 and costs. The trial took two days).

Feb. 4, 1899—J.P. Sullivan, who was dangerously ill, is now recovering.

1899—J.P. Sullivan attended a law suit in Justice Fulmer's Court a week ago.

1900—The village of Ontario has experienced a "blind pig" prosecution on last Thurs. John Shaker, charged with selling liquor without a license, was arraigned and tried before Justice J.P. Sullivan.

His marriage to Bessie Gorham created some adjustments. The white-headed old veteran, who subtracted at least three years from his age for the U.S. Census taker of 1900, now was the step-father of three little ones, all under ten years of age. He was solvent, owning a house free of mortgage, and he continued his law practice. The second marriage produced a son, christened James Fitz.[16]

But there were few years left to Sullivan and he may have known it. He was a father of young children, but he was stooped and weakened by persistent illness. He had, for several years, taken the 30-mile trek from Ontario to Mauston in neighboring Juneau County for the annual January Company K Reunion. In 1900, unable to make the trip and bear up under the numbing Wisconsin January, he declined the invitation to attend. Instead, he communicated his feelings by pecking out a poem on a typewriter. He wrote about hardships, marches, and dangers, of "stirring times in the dim misty past."

> I would like to see Mauston and talk of the times,
> When we drilled on the school house square.
> With Ticknor and Dawes with Kellogg and Crane,
> When right face and left wheel and right about march
> Seemed like tricks of the magical art,
> When to make the salute like old "Cap" Holden did
> Was the highest aim of my heart.

He would ask old comrades, in his unpolished poesy, to remember him not as in days gone when he planned "to play some confounded

fool trick / Or suffering for his green ways." He concluded with
another nod to "fast passing years" leading to "Mortality's goal."[17]

So the scarred old veteran of the 6th Wisconsin ended his years
tapping out doggerel in his office on Main Street. Receding were the
sarcasm and criticism of his earlier writings; Mickey was becoming
unabashedly patriotic. And the former ambivalence he carried
about freed slaves found no place in his latter jottings. He wrote of
the "patriot's fervid thrill" and the "wisdom of our leaders;" and of
men "free from [the] slaver's snare." In a piece he titled "The Old
Veteran's Request," he concluded:

> But five and thirty years past, I am old and feeble too.
> I ask my country to recall what, I then tried to do.
> When on war's chance its life was staked I gave it full and free,
> I ask it now its strong and great, to be kind and just to me.[18]

In one of his final poetic flights, weary Mickey Sullivan composed
a paean to his old brigade, a 16-stanza effort that cataloged the
unit's action from Gainesville to Appomattox. Forty years had
passed since the Irishman trudged the dusty roads of Virginia,
Maryland, and Pennsylvania and dodged rebel lead on most of those
fields. Blurred were the days and nights of boredom and chill, the
meddlesome Washington bureaucrats, and the maiming and killing.
It had, in his memory, come down to sunlighted charges and glory,
after all. The poem concluded:

> And they look back with pride to the days when they fought,
> That the work of the "Fathers" should not be for nought.
> And he should be excused, who in boasting has said,
> "I was one of the men of the Iron Brigade."[19]

And thus some six decades of life were coming to a close. The
effects of war wounds and advancing age seemed to press more
heavily upon Mickey each day. Neighbors, even some years before,
attested that the old soldier was troubled with a bad back, walked
in a stooped manner, and was occasionally completely debilitated
by pain. He was receiving a $14 monthly disability payment from
the Federal government.[20]

James P. Sullivan, who had seen more than most men of his age,
marked his 65th birthday on June 21, 1906. While his life's work
perhaps did not measure to his youthful visions, and while some
painful circumstances of postwar life might best be expunged from
memory, the world had generally treated him with favor. He had, if
little else, served as one of the stewards of the legacy of the 6th

Wisconsin and the Iron Brigade. Sullivan's legacy of writings would await a later generation to correct oversights and fill omissions.

That done, James Patrick Sullivan, immigrant, back-rank private, and wounded war veteran, husband and father, died October 22, 1906. His death certificate stated the cause as catarrh, or inflammation of the stomach, resulting in ulceration. Also contributing to his demise was a piece of metal lodged near the base of his skull for 40 years—a rebel shell fragment that had caught him at Weldon Railroad on August 21, 1864. The Irishman was buried on a Sunday, with but a few stooped and shrunken old men in faded blue coats and reunion badges in attendance, in the hillside Ontario Cemetery near the brooding eminence of Wildcat Mountain. George Sullivan, his first-born son, would join him there in years to come.

His final mention in the October 31, 1906, edition of the *Vernon County Censer* was brief:

Veteran James P. Sulivan

A long time resident of Vernon county, died at his Ontario home on the 22d, after a long and painful illness. He was sixty-six years old. He had been a practicing attorney at Ontario, in the eastern section of the county. Mr. Sullivan was a brave Veteran Captain of Co. K, 6th Wisconsin Infantry, and fought in many hard battles for the Union in the "Iron Brigade". He was wounded five times. His remains were buried by the G.A.R. on the 24th at Ontario.[21]

Within a year later, the Kickapoo River, Brush Creek, and Moore's Creek, fed by heavy rains, sent surging muddy water onto the streets of Ontario. The two-story frame building housing Sullivan's old law office and home was inundated and most of his war correspondence, diaries, notes, and other writings were swept away or destroyed. Few items were salvaged. Among them were a typed copy of Sullivan's story of Company K's mule, a Grand Army of the Republic badge, and the small metal cross struck for the 1885 Madison reunion of the Iron Brigade Association.[22]

His widow and second family soon moved away. Sullivan's grave was marked only with the simple stone the government provided for Civil War veterans. Sometime later another, more prominent, marker was added, probably by his son George. It listed the dates of birth and death, and identified the veteran as he would have wished:

James P. Sullivan
Sergt., Co. K
6th Wis. Vet. Vol. Inf.

NOTES

1. *Philippi Art Souvenir of La Crosse, Wisconsin* (La Crosse, Wisc., 1904); *History of La Crosse County, Wisconsin* (Chicago, 1881); Publius V. Lawson, *History of Winnebago County, Wisconsin* (Chicago, 1908); *Bunn & Philippi's La Crosse City Directory, 1888–89* (La Crosse, Wisc., 1888); *Wisconsin, A Guide to the Badger State* (New York, 1941), p. 205.

2. Bragg, despite his Democratic Party loyalty, was a respected Wisconsin politician. A three-term U.S. Congressman, the Fond du Lac lawyer had eschewed a fourth term in 1882. But he would run again in 1884, and serve two more years. The president of the Iron Brigade Association was John Gibbon, the old brigade's commander of 1861–62. But he still remained in the regular army, serving in the West. Because he was unable to attend many of the annual gatherings, Gibbon was but titular head. Bragg, as first vice president, was de facto leader; he usually selected sites for the reunions, and often, as in the case of Sullivan, secured speakers. Bragg may have regularly been re-elected to his post in the association, but there was perennial bickering and political wrangling for positions of power and prestige. Former 2nd Wisconsin comander and ex-Wisconsin governor Lucius Fairchild was an unrepentant Republican and a frequent mutterer. La Crosse was apparently selected as the 1883 site because a Democratic Party colleague, Gilbert M. Woodward, a veteran of the 2nd Wisconsin, was 7th District Congressman from the La Crosse area. *Dictionary of Wisconsin Biography*, p. 46; *Dictionary of American Biography*, Vol. II, pp. 587–88; Warner, *Generals in Blue*, pp. 41–42.

3. *Dictionary of Wisconsin Biography* (Madison, 1960), p. 201.

4. *La Crosse Republican and Leader*, September 15, 1883 and September 22, 1883; *La Crosse Chronicle*, September 13, 1883; *Milwaukee Sunday Telegraph*, September 30, 1883.

5. Sullivan was referring to Edwin B. Quiner's *The Military History of Wisconsin*, published in 1866. *Milwaukee Sunday Telegraph*, September 30, 1883.

6. When the 1880 Federal Census was taken in June, Sullivan claimed to have been Wisconsin-born. This may have resulted from earlier difficulties in proving that his father was a naturalized citizen, apparently a requirement for land purchase. U.S. Census, Wisconsin, 1880.

7. *History of Vernon County* (Springfield, Ill., 1884), p. 508; *Blue Book of the State of Wisconsin* (Madison, 1895), p. 258.

8. *Milwaukee Sunday Telegraph*, December 28, 1884.

9. *Milwaukee Sunday Telegraph*, May 18, 1884.

10. Dawes, *Service*, p. 47.

11. Possibly Eban B. Dunlap, who enlisted June 12, 1861, in the Lodi Guard, Company A of the 7th Wisconsin Infantry. He served with Battery B, 4th U.S. Artillery, veteranized, and finished the war in the Veteran Reserve Corps. *Roster of Wisconsin Volunteers*, Vol. I, p. 541.

12. Possibly Thomas B. Marsden of Friendship, who was a captain with Company K, 38th Wisconsin Infantry. He served from September 1864 to June 1865. *Roster of Wisconsin Volunteers*, Vol. II, p. 653.

13. James P. Sullivan, *Milwaukee Sunday Telegraph*, March 22, 1885.

14. The deaths of Anna and James can only be inferred by evidence

available: both children were enumerated in the U.S. Census of 1880, aged 8 and 2, respectively. For inexplicable reasons, the Sullivan family was not listed in the Wisconsin State Census of 1885, presumably because they may have been relocating at the time. As the U.S. Census of 1890 was destroyed, a gap in the record exists. But the Wisconsin State Census of 1895 enumerated only one female in the Sullivan household; wife Angeline. Finally, the U.S. Census of 1900 lists only George and John as offspring, as does the U.S. Pension Office Certificate of January 15, 1898. Anna and James were buried in the Ontario cemetery.

15. "Certificate of Examination," State of Wisconsin, September 1, 1897, *Vernon County Censor*, February 9, 1898.

16. James Fitz Sullivan had an extensive military career of his own. He wrote this brief biography: "I was born in Ontario, Wisconsin, March 24, 1901, and father died in October, 1906, which didn't give us much of an opportunity of becoming acquainted. Shortly thereafter, a 10-foot flood inundated the town and in the process destroyed my father's law office as well as the family home, and as you can imagine most family records disappeared. Mother left Ontario soon after to find work that she might support the family, and after a brief sojourn in Galena, Ill., I spent most of my boy hood in Fort Dodge, Iowa, working as grocery delivery boy (horse and wagon) messenger boy, Western Union, also Postal Telegraph, delivered *Fort Dodge Messenger*, was first kid ever to sell that paper on the streets of Fort Dodge, worked in Gypsum mills at various tasks, including coring of gypsum building blocks.

"Lied about age at last World War I draft, was inducted for very short period, couldn't find work in Omaha, Nebraska, so re-enlisted in army, was sent to 19th Infantry (then a 'crack' outfit, recently returned from Boxer Rebellion). Learned to make adobe bricks, use an old Enfield rifle and just made private first class (quite an honor in that outfit) and was transferred to the 96th Bombardment Squadron, then patrolling the Mexican Border with field at Douglas. Outfit then went to Kelly Field, Texas. I was sent to Sergeant Major's school at Kelly #1, became 96th company clerk, then went to Bombardment Group Supply. Sent to Kelly #1 to take charge of Salvage Division.

"This was during the time that General Billy Mitchell was arguing with the Navy and Congress that his bombers could sink the most heavily armored cruiser or battleship float, and it was our outfit, the 2nd Bomb Group, that was sent to Langley Field, Va., where we did prove him right, though he was later court-martialed and lost all his hard won honors. (Several years after his death, by act of Congress, they were restored). Was in charge of Bombardment Group Supply at Langley, then placed in charge of the Cost Accounting System. During this time did pass my examinations and was made a 2nd Lieut. Air Force Reserve. Discharged as a Technical Sergeant.

"Returned to Omaha, passed required test and became Piggly Wiggly grocery clerk, and do I remember those famous "fruit windows." Knew of vacancy at Nebraska Power Co. supply department, applied and was accepted. Later transferred to sub station department, served 3 1/2 year apprenticeship and became sub station wireman . . . .

"Pearl Harbor came along and as I couldn't get my previous Air Force rating restored, enlisted in Navy—held in Omaha with many others who were either AFL or CIO craftsmen until recruiter finally told us he had orders to ship us to Norfolk Operating Base to join just organized Navy Construction Battalions. Went to New Hebrides as member of THE FIRST NAVAL CONSTRUCTION BATTALION, (Seabees). Rated as electrician, and never strung wire as they found out I had army supply experience and I was placed in charge of Utility Bldg., at Malapoa Point. Injured spine while working, spent some time in French Hospital at Efate, then back to duty. New commander wanted to establish battalion newspaper to boost morale and held competition from which I was chose to edit the "Boondock" Bulletin, which later became the "Pioneer," copies of which are in Navy museums. Returned to states after two years. Could not pass the overseas exam, finally sent to fleet hospital and medically discharged. . . ." James F. Sullivan, letter to Lance Herdegen, May 28, 1990.

17. James P. Sullivan, "To Company 'K's' Reunion 1900," Andrew Gallup Papers, State Historical Society of Wisconsin.

18. James P. Sullivan, "The Old Veteran's Request." Andrew Gallup Papers, State Historical Society of Wisconsin.

19. James P. Sullivan, "The Iron Brigade." Andrew Gallup Papers, State Historical Society of Wisconsin.

20. General Affidavits of Ellen S. Johnson, September 11, 1893, and John Delaney, February 5, 1894, James P. Sullivan file, U.S. Pension Office.

21. The obituary, of course, contains errors. Sullivan was probably 65 at death, although his birth year was inconsistently recorded. During the war years he reached only the rank of sergeant.

22. The *Cashton Record* in 1907 reported: "The village [Ontario] is practically in a basin, and exposed to devastating effects whenever such a terrific flood of rain as this descends from the ills around it. In this case the storm [of July 21, 1907] was a literal cloudburst, along in the afternoon, and nothing like it was ever know there before: says the *Sparta Herald*. From accounts the water must have been fifteen feet deep on the public square, and houses were filled above the second floors. People were rescued on improvised rafts from second story windows, and even roofs. Business buildings were flooded and the stock of goods destroyed. Stock was drowned by the hundred, and the buildings wrecked and carried away."

APPENDIX

To Company "K"'s reunion 1900
Greeting from "Mickey"

Hail company "K" old comrades of mine
Who meet in reunion today.
Who meet to greet each as best friends do greet,
And list to what each may say.
About those stirring times in dim misty past,
When the company fought bravely and well
That our country should live, be united and free,
And secession should hear its death knell.

To tell over once more the long list of the killed,
Tho names of the living ones too.
The marches you made, the hardships you bore,
And dangers that you have passed through.
How nobly you fought to deserve the great name,
Brave Generals said was your due.
THE IRON BRIGADE! the name will never fade,
While history states what is true.

I would like to see Mauston and talk of the times,
When we drilled on the school house square
With Ticknor and Dawes with Kellogg and Creane [Crane],
When other brave boys who were there.
When right face and left wheel and right about march,
Seemed like tricks of the magical art.
When to make the salute like old "Pap" Holden did,
Was the highest aim of my heart.

Old comrades, I cannot be with you today,
It grieves me much for to write.
For things are not always within our control,
and business we sometimes can't slight.

Just think that Mickey would like to be there,
But not as in bye gone days.
Planning how to play some confounded fool trick,
Or suffering for his green ways.

And I hope that next year and for many more years,
You may meet as you met in the past.
And humbly I hope through the mercy of God,
We'll all meet in Heaven at last.
Old comrades of mine through the fast passing years,
That leads to mortality's goal.
With a heart filled with love and respect for each one,
I hold your name fast in my soul.

—*James P. Sullivan,*
Sergt., Co. K, 6th Wisconsin Vet. Vols.

THE IRON BRIGADE

—By James P. Sullivan
Mickey of Company "K"
6th Wisconsin Volunteers

There was a brigade of men which came from the west,
That in the Great Army was classed with the best.
In Camp, march or battle, or on grand parade,
There was none did excel the old "Iron Brigade."

Amongst the first to enlist 'till the war it was done,
Wisconsin's 2nd, 6th, 7th, Indiana's 19th, and Battery "B" for a
    son.
And re-enlisted as Veterans, for to each other they said,
"We have came to see it out," the old "Iron Brigade."

In camp none more peaceful, and by strict discipline ruled,
And in "Drill," "March," or "Manual," none better were schooled.
In the wild storm of battle it was never dismayed,
Nor gave to the enemy, the old "Iron Brigade."

In the battle of "Gainesville," that rude baptism of blood,
Th'o greatly outnumbered at close quarters it stood.
And fought two Divisions with very slight aid,
The famous "Stonewall," and "Ewell's," the old "Iron Brigade."

"Twas fierce, close, and bloody," Stonewall Jackson did say,
"And with Obstinate bravery" them Yanks stood at bay.
And when finally ordered to fall back Gibbon said,
"We'll give three times three for the "Iron Brigade."

At "Bull Run," it stood calmly, in that terrible hail,
Of shot, shell and shrapnel, and not once did quail.
When the foe was victorious, and could not be stayed,
"Gibbon will cover the rear" with the "Iron Brigade."

'Twas after "South Mountain," in the march through the glen,
That the veteran General Sumner said to his men,
"These men took that pass and great valor displayed,
Hats off while they pass by," the "Old Iron Brigade."

At "Antietam," that bloody field where twice in one day,
Though mostly badly cut up, it went into the fray.

And the gallant McClellan, to our Governor he said,
"They equal the best troops in the world, that "Iron Brigade.""

Just after Antietam, we got a new man.
The brave Colonel Morrow, with his 24th Michigan.
We liked not to share the good name we had made,
But "Fitz-Hughs" proved them worthy of the "Iron Brigade."

"Mine Run," "Fredericksburgh," and the "Stick in the mud,"
Those campaigns, where many losses did us no good.
"Chancellorsville," and "Fitz-Hughs," where the rebs were
     dismayed,
When it charged over the River, the old "Iron Brigade."

"Gettysburg," ah, "Gettysburg," we dream of yet.
When it beat back four times that old rebel Heth.
And tho' almost annihilated a grand charge it made,
Took General colors and all, did the "Iron Brigade."

"Wilderness," and "Cold Harbor," in that dreadful wood,
At "Spotsylvania" in the "angle of death" there it stood.
"North Anna," where Warren said the army was saved,
By the hardest of fighting, done by the "Iron Brigade."

"Tolopotomy," "Bethesa," where battery "B" made a charge,
Like a squadron of cavalry and the army at large.
Saw it destroy a "reb" battery, and skill it displayed,
Was "Typical" of the work of the old "Iron Brigade."

"Petersburg," "Weldon Rail Road," 1st and 2nd "Hatcher's Run,"
"Weldon Raid," where the Apple Jack made lots of fun.
Then the brave 19th left us, which would gladly have stayed,
With its friends and companions, of the "Iron Brigade."

"Five Forks," "Gravelly Run," "Burkesville Road," but where was it
     not,
When "Little Phil's" cavalry or the rebs fired a shot.
At "Appomattox," when the final surrender was made,
It was in the front line, the old "Iron Brigade."

When rebellion was crushed, and its work there did end,
And to homes, families and firesides its members did trend,
By honest industry and good conduct they made,
The best of good citizens that old "Iron Brigade."

And they look back with pride to the days when they fought,
That the work of the "Fathers" should not be for nought.
And he should be excused, who in boasting has said,
"I was one of the men of the Iron Brigade."

Ontario, Wis., March 17, 1902

The Old Veteran's Request

I saw the strong man meet his fate, I have seen the stripling die,
When the charging footmen met, or the sabre flashed on high.
When the bravest foes of North and South, met in battle's fiercest
  strife,
And when the screaming minnie balls, were seeking for a life.

Amidst the cannons deafening roar, amongs't the bursting shell,
And from the bayonets deadly thrust, where rose the rebels yell.
On the clouded mountain's top, beneath the sunny southern sky,
In the dusky mist of evening's glow, in the rivers muddy dye.

I have helped to hold the works all day, worked in the trench all
  night,
Have slept in mud in rain and snow, eat salt horse with delight.
Have marched when sick and sore and lame, done with little or no
  food,
Gone without sleep to fight greybacks, all for my country's good.

God bless my Country right or wrong, was my daily prayer,
Oh, God do slavery not prolong, let the black man freedom share.
Grant victory to the Union side, this war bring soon to end,
Let Thy wisdom all our leaders guide, and to us all be a friend.

I have felt the patriots fervid thrill, when my country called to
  arm,
And my best blood did freely flow to keep it from all harm.
I have sang the paeans of victory, when freedom gained the field,
I have felt the pangs of sore defeat, when right was forced to yield.

For four long years I marched and fought, and twas all my wish
  and care,
The Union should victorious be, and free from slaver's snare.
Ah, then I marched with springing step, and gay and careless
  mien,
Youthful heart beating so high, to reap my country's laurels.

But five and thirty years are past, I am old and feeble too,
I ask my country to recall what I then tried to do.
When on war's chance its life was staked, I gave it full and free,
I ask it now its strong and great, to be kind and just to me.

—By J. P. Sullivan, Sergt, Co. K, 6th Wis. Vet. Vol.

BIBLIOGRAPHY

BOOKS

1. Primary Sources

[Anderson, James S.] *The Papers of James S. Anderson* [edited by] Dennis R. Moore. [N.P.], 1989.

Annual Report of the Adjutant General of the State of Wisconsin. Madison: William J. Park & Co., 1866.

Bates, Samuel F. *The Battle of Gettysburg.* Philadelphia: T.H. Davis & Co., 1875.

Bryant, Edwin E. *History of the Third Regiment Wisconsin Veteran Volunteer Infantry, 1861–1865.* Published by the Veteran Association of the Regiment, Madison, 1891.

Chamberlain, Joshua L. *The Passing of the Armies.* New York: G. P. Putnam's Sons, 1915.

Chamberlain, Thomas. *History of the One Hundred and Fiftieth Regiment Pennsylvania Volunteers. . . .* Philadelphia: J. B. Lippincott Company, 1895.

Cheek, Philip, and Mair Pointon. *History of the Sauk County Riflemen, Known as Company "A" Sixth Wisconsin Veteran Volunteer Infantry, 1861–1865.* [N.P.], 1909.

Curtis, O[rson] B. *History of the Twenty-Fourth Michigan of the Iron Brigade.* Detroit: Winn & Hammond, 1891.

Dawes, Rufus R. *Service with the Sixth Wisconsin Volunteers.* Marietta, Ohio: E. R. Alderman & Sons, 1890.

Dudley, William W. *The Iron Brigade at Gettysburg, 1878: Official Report of the Part Borne by the 1st Brigade, 1st Division, 1st Army Corps.* Cincinnati: privately printed, 1879.

Fitch, Michael J. *Echoes of the Civil War as I Hear Them.* New York: R. S. Fenno and Co., 1905.

Gates, Theodore B. *The "Ulster Guard"* [20th N.Y. State Militia] *and the War of the Rebellion.* New York: Benj. H. Tyrrel, 1879.

Gibbon, John. *Personal Recollections of the Civil War.* New York: G. P. Putnam's Sons, 1928.

Humphreys, Andrew A. *The Virginia Campaigns of 1864 and 1865.* New York: Charles Scribner's Sons, 1883.

Johnson, Robert U. and Clarence C. Buel, eds. *Battles and Leaders of the Civil War.* (4 Vols.) New York: The Century Co., 1884–1887.

Kellogg, John A. *Capture and Escape: A Narrative of Army and Prison Life.* Madison: Wisconsin History Commission, 1908.

Kieffer, Harry M. *The Recollections of a Drummer Boy.* Boston: Ticknor and Company, 1889.

McClellan, George B. *McClellan's Own Story.* New York: Charles I. Webster & Co., 1887.

Nesbit, John W[oods], comp. *General History of Company D, 149th Pennsylvania Volunteers . . .* Revised Ed. Oakdale, Pa.: Oakdale Printing and Publishing Co., 1908.

Love, William D. *Wisconsin in the War of the Rebellion.* Chicago: Church & Goodman, 1866.

Otis, George H. *The Second Wisconsin Infantry.* Ed. by Alan D. Gaff. Dayton, Ohio: Morningside House, 1984.

Pollard, Edward Alfred. *Southern History of the War: The Last Year of the War.* New York: C. B. Richardson, 1866.

Powell, William H. *The Fifth Army Corps (Army of the Potomac).* New York: G. P. Putnam's Sons, 1896.

Quiner, E[dwin] B. *The Military History of Wisconsin.* Chicago: Clarke & Co., 1866.

Rauscher, Frank. *Music on the March, 1862–65, With the Army of the Potomac.* Philadelphia: Press of W. F. Fell & Co., 1892.

Rogers, Earl M., ed. *Memoirs of Vernon County.* Madison: Western Historical Association, 1907.

Stine, J. H. *History of the Army of the Potomac.* Philadelphia: J. B. Rogers Printing Co., 1892.

Stribling, Robert M. *Gettysburg Campaign, and the Campaigns of 1864 and 1865 in Virginia.* Petersburg, Va.: The Franklin Press, 1905.

Swinton, William. *Campaigns of the Army of the Potomac.* New York: Charles B. Richardson, 1866.

2. Secondary Sources

Biographical Dictionary of the United States Congress, 1775–1989. Washington, D.C.: U.S. Government Printing Office, 1989.

Byrne, Frank L., and Andrew T. Weaver, eds. *Haskell of Gettysburg: His Life and Civil War Papers.* Madison: State Historical Society of Wisconsin, 1970.

Carruth, Gordon, ed. *The Encyclopedia of American Facts and Dates.* New York: Thomas Y. Crowell, 1979.

Coddington, Edwin B. *The Gettysburg Campaign: A Study in Command.* New York: Charles Scribner's Sons, 1968.

Daiches, David, ed. *The Penguin Companion to English Literature.* New York: McGraw-Hill Book Company, 1971.

Davis, William C. *Death in the Trenches: Grant at Petersburg. (The Civil War).* Alexandria, Va.: Time-Life Books, 1986.

Dictionary of American Biography. (16 Vols.) New York: Charles Scribner's Sons, 1946.

Dictionary of Wisconsin Biography. Madison: State Historical Society of Wisconsin, 1961.

Faust, Patricia L., ed. *Historical Times Illustrated Encyclopedia of the Civil War.* New York: Harper & Row, 1986.

Gaff, Alan D. *Brave Men's Tears: The Iron Brigade at Brawner Farm.* Dayton, Ohio: Morningside House, 1985.

———. *If This Is War.* Dayton, Ohio: Morningside House, 1991.

Goldhurst, Richard. *Many Are the Hearts: The Agony and the Triumph of Ulysses S. Grant.* New York: Reader's Digest Press, 1975.

Griffith, Paddy. *Battle Tactics of the Civil War.* New Haven, Conn.: Yale University Press, 1989.

Herdegen, Lance J., and William J. K. Beaudot. *In the Bloody Railroad Cut at Gettysburg.* Dayton, Ohio: Morningside House, 1990.

Herzberg, Max J. *The Reader's Encyclopedia of American Literature.* New York: Thomas Crowell Company, 1962.

Hunt, Roger D., and Jack R. Brown. *Brevet Brigadier Generals in Blue.* Gaithersburg, Md.: Old Soldier Books, 1990.

Jaynes, Gregory. *The Killing Ground: Wilderness to Cold Harbor (The Civil War).* Alexandria, Va.: Time-Life Books, 1986.

Jimerson, Randall C. *The Private Civil War: Popular Thought During the Sectional Conflict.* Baton Rouge, La.: Louisiana State University Press, 1988.

Klement, Frank L. *Wisconsin and the Civil War.* Madison: State Historical Society of Wisconsin, 1963. Originally published in the *Blue Book of the State of Wisconsin,* 1961.

Korn, Jerry. *Pursuit to Appomattox: The Last Battles (The Civil War).* Alexandria, Va.: Time-Life Books, 1987.

Linderman, Gerald F. *Embattled Courage: The Experience of Combat in the American Civil War.* New York: Free Press, 1987.

Long, E. B., and Barbara Long. *The Civil War Day by Day: An Almanac, 1861–1865.* Garden City, N.Y.: Doubleday, 1971.

Martin, Jay. *Harvest of Change: American Literature 1865–1914*. Englewood Cliffs, N.J., 1967.

Mathews, Mitford, ed. *A Dictionary of Americanisms on Historical Principles*. Chicago: University of Chicago Press, 1951.

Mattern, Carolyn J. *Soldiers When They Go: The Story of Camp Randall, 1861–1865*. Madison: State Historical Society of Wisconsin, 1981.

McDonald, Grace. *History of the Irish in Wisconsin in the Nineteenth Century*. New York: Arno Press, 1976. [Reprint of the author's doctoral thesis, Catholic University, 1954.]

McDonald, G[race]. *Irish Immigration into Wisconsin, 1840–1860*. Master's dissertation, Catholic University, 1949.

Nolan, Alan T. *The Iron Brigade*. New York: Macmillan, 1961.

Oliver, John W. "History of Civil War Military Pensions, 1861–1885." *Bulletin of the University of Wisconsin History*, Series 844. Madison, 1917.

Ropp, Theodore. *War in the Modern World*. Durham, N.C.: Duke University Press, 1959.

Schaff, Morris. *The Battle of the Wilderness*. Boston: Houghton Mifflin Company, 1910.

Schlereth, Thomas J. *Victorian America: Transformations in Everyday Life, 1876–1918*. New York: HarperCollins Publishers, 1991.

Scott, Robert Garth. *Into the Wilderness with the Army of the Potomac*. Bloomington: Indiana University Press, 1985.

Sears, Stephen W. *George B. McClellan, The Young Napoleon*. New York: Ticknor & Fields, 1988.

Stewart, George R. *Pickett's Charge*. Boston: Houghton Mifflin, 1959.

Sutherland, Daniel E. *The Expansion of Everyday Life, 1860–1876*. New York: Harper & Row Publishers, 1989.

[Thomson, Orville]. *From Philippi to Appomattox: Narrative of the Service of the Seventh Indiana Infantry. . . .* Published by the author [1904?].

Trudeau, Noah Andre. *Bloody Roads South: The Wilderness to Cold Harbor, May–June, 1864*. Boston: Little, Brown and Company, 1989.

———. *The Last Citadel: Petersburg, Virginia, June, 1864–April, 1865*. Boston: Little, Brown and Company, 1991.

Tucker, Glenn. *Hancock the Superb*. Indianapolis: Bobbs-Merrill Co., 1960.

Warner, Ezra J. *Generals in Blue: Lives of Union Commanders*. Baton Rouge: Louisiana State University Press, 1964.

Welcher, Frank J. *The Union Army, 1861–1865: Organization and Operations: The Eastern Theater.* Bloomington: Indiana University Press, 1989.

Wiley, Bell Irwin. *The Life of Billy Yank: The Common Soldier of the Union.* Indianapolis: Bobbs-Merrill Co., 1952.

Zierdt, William Henry. *Narrative History of the 109th Field Artillery, Pennsylvania National Guard, 1775–1930.* Wilkes-Barre, Pa.: E. B. Yordy Co., 1932.

3. Area Histories and Guides

Blue Book for the State of Wisconsin. Madison: State Printer, 1880.

Blue Book of the State of Wisconsin. Madison: Democrat Printing Co., 1885, 1895, 1900, 1905.

Bunn & Philippi's *La Crosse City Directory,* 1888–1889. La Crosse, Wisc., Spicer & Buschman, 1888.

Current, Richard N. *The History of Wisconsin . . . The Civil War Era, 1848–1873.* Madison: State Historical Society of Wisconsin, 1976.

[Flower, Frank A.]. *History of Milwaukee, Wisconsin.* Chicago: Western Historical Co., 1881.

Haskins, Helen. *History of Juneau County.* Unpublished manuscript, 1930.

History of La Crosse County, Wisconsin . . . . Chicago: Western Historical Company, 1881.

History of Northern Wisconsin. Chicago: Western Historical Company, 1881.

History of Vernon County, Wisconsin. Springfield, Ill: Union Publishing Co., 1884.

Hood, Edwin C. *Plat Book of Vernon County, Wisconsin.* Minneapolis: C. M. Foote & Co., 1896.

Juneau County, the First 100 years. Friendship, Wisc.: New Past Press, Inc., 1988.

Kingston, John T. "Early Exploration and Settlement of Juneau County." *Collections of the State Historical Society of Wisconsin,* Vol. VIII. Madison: the society, 1879, pp. 370–410.

Koss, Rud[olph] A. *Milwaukee.* Milwaukee: The Milwaukee Herald, 1871.

Lawson, Publius V. *History of Winnebago County, Wisconsin.* Chicago C. F. Cooper and Company, 1908.

The Legislative Manual of the State of Wisconsin. Madison: Atwood & Rublee State Printers, 1863.

Marchetti, Louis. *History of Marathon County and Representative Citizens*. Chicago: Richmond-Arnold Publishing Company, 1913.

Martin, Lawrence. *The Physical Geography of Wisconsin*. Madison: University of Wisconsin Press, 1965.

Nesbit, Robert C. *The History of Wisconsin . . . Urbanization and Industrialization, 1873–1893*. Madison: State Historical Society of Wisconsin, 1985.

Philippi Art Souvenir of La Crosse, Wisconsin. La Crosse, Wisc.: L. P. Philippi Company, 1904.

Sanford, Albert H., and H. J. Hirschheimer. *A History of La Crosse, Wisconsin, 1841–1900*. La Crosse, Wisc.; La Crosse County Historical Society, 1951.

Still, Bayrd. *Milwaukee, The History of a City*. Madison: State Historical Society of Wisconsin, 1948.

Washington, City and Capital. Washington, D.C.: U.S. Government Printing Office, 1937.

Writers' Program, U.S. Works Progress Administration. *Wisconsin, a Guide to the Badger State*. New York: Duell, Sloan and Pearce, 1941.

CENSUS & NUMERICAL RECORDS

Alphabetical List of Soldiers and Sailors of the Late War Residing in the State of Wisconsin, June 20, 1885. Madison: Secretary of State, 1886.

Beaudot, William J. K., comp. "Sixth Wisconsin Database" [based upon the *Roster of Wisconsin Volunteers* and Other Sources]. Unpublished database, 1989.

Dyer, F. H. *A Compendium of the War of the Rebellion*. Des Moines, Iowa, 1908; New York; Thomas Yoseloff, 1953.

Fox, William F. *Regimental Losses in the American Civil War*. Albany, N.Y.: Albany Publishing Co., 1889.

Roster of Wisconsin Volunteers, War of the Rebellion, 1861–1865 (2 Vols.). Madison, 1886.

U.S. Census, Wisconsin, 1850, 1860, 1870, 1880, 1900.

Wisconsin Census Enumeration, 1895: Names of Ex-Soldiers and Sailors Residing in Wisconsin, June 20, 1895. . . . Madison: Democrat Printing Co., 1896.

Wisconsin Census Enumeration, 1905: Names of Ex-Soldiers and

Sailors Residing in Wisconsin, June 1, 1905. Madison: Democrat Printing Co., 1896.
Wisconsin State Census, 1855, 1865, 1875, 1885, 1895, 1905.

MANUSCRIPTS & RECORDS

Andrew Gallup Papers, State Historical Society of Wisconsin.
Rufus R. Dawes Papers, State Historical Society of Wisconsin.
Descriptive Book, 6th Wisconsin Infantry. U.S. National Archives & Records Service.
Morning Reports, 6th Wisconsin Infantry. U.S. National Archives and Records Service.
National Guard, Adjutant General's Office, Regimental Descriptive Rolls, 6th Infantry. State Historical Society of Wisconsin.
Order Book, 1st Brigade, 1st Division, 1st Army Corps. U.S. National Archives and Records Service.
Order Book, 6th Wisconsin Infantry. U.S. National Archives and Records Service.
Jerome A. Watrous Papers. State Historical Society of Wisconsin.
State Militia, Adjutant General's Office, Regimental Muster and Descriptive Rolls, 6th Infantry. State Historical Society of Wisconsin.
U.S. Pension Office. James P. Sullivan file. U.S. National Archives and Record Service.
War of the Rebellion, Official Records of the Union and Confederate Armies. Washington, D.C.: U.S. Government Printing Office, 1889–1900.

NEWSPAPERS & PERIODICALS

The Blackhat, Occasional Newsletter of the 6th Wisconsin Volunteers, Milwaukee.
Blue and Gray Magazine, Columbus.
Cashton Record, Cashton, Wisc.
Chetek Alert, Chetek, Wisc.
Gettysburg Magazine, Dayton, Ohio.
La Crosse Chronicle, La Crosse, Wisc.
La Crosse Republican and Leader, La Crosse, Wisc.
Mauston Star, Mauston, Wisc.
Milwaukee History.

Milwaukee Sentinel.
Milwaukee Sunday Telegraph/Milwaukee Telegraph.
The National Tribune, Washington, D.C.
Sparta Herald, Sparta, Wisc.
Vernon County Censor, Viroqua, Wisc.
Virginia Country Civil War, Leesburg, Va.
Wisconsin Magazine of History, Madison.

INDEX